China's Labor Market in the Transition

Chen Ying

China's Labor Market in the Transition

The Evolution From Segmentation to Integration

SSAP

palgrave
macmillan

Chen Ying
School of Economics
Yunnan University
Kunming, China

Translated by
Simin Tan
Singapore, Singapore

Yuanlin Wei
Global Tone Communication Tech Co., Ltd.
Beijing, China

ISBN 978-981-99-9162-4 ISBN 978-981-99-9160-0 (eBook)
https://doi.org/10.1007/978-981-99-9160-0

Jointly published with Social Sciences Academic Press
The print edition is not for sale in China Mainland. Customers from China Mainland please order the print book from Social Sciences Academic Press.

This work was supported by the Yunnan University Double First-Class Initiative.

This Palgrave Macmillan imprint is published by the registered company Springer Nature Singapore Pte Ltd.
The registered company address is: 152 Beach Road, #21-01/04 Gateway East, Singapore 189721, Singapore

About this Book

China's labor market was built upon the urban–rural duality and the planned economy, the two of which interacted with the market mechanism from the very beginning. Such interactions allowed the labor market to draw on the strengths of both the planned economy and the market system on the one hand, and caused its segmentation on the other. Proceeding from the two systems of ownership and household registration that play a vital role in China, this book attempts to explore the following questions:

- How has China's labor market evolved? Are there any patterns that can be discerned?
- Does the labor market show a shift from segmentation to integration? If yes, what is the rationale behind it? What are the implications for economists and policymakers?
- Where is China's labor market heading?

On the basis of a review of the past, a theoretical framework we have developed, and empirical evidences, we try to find answers to these questions.

First, we will look at how the two key systems, i.e., ownership and household registration, impacted the labor market in the pre-reform era when the planned economy still had a firm hold, and how they affected the wage determination mechanism and labor flow after 1978 when the reform and opening up policy was introduced. Due to the impact of the two systems, the transition to the market economy, and other factors, the labor market evolved from nearly complete segmentation before 1978 to multi-tiered segmentation afterward.

Second, we will define the concept of labor market integration, and classify the endogenous, exogenous, and induced factors that affect the labor market segmentation using the relevant concepts in classical economics, segmentation theory, and development economics. After an analysis of the three types of factors within a theoretical framework we have developed, we will come to the conclusion that multi-tiered segmentation is based on the double duality produced by the household registration and ownership systems, and compounded by endogenous segmentation, spatial segmentation, and the sorting effect. Double duality model based on the search-and-matching theory of Mortensen and Pissarides (1994, 1999) and Pissarides (2000) shows that the double duality leads to equilibrium in different senses in China's labor market, varying wage determination mechanisms and labor demand conditions, and higher labor mobility costs, corporate dismissal costs, and entry costs. A dynamic analysis shows, despite a growing trend toward integration, the double duality will continue to exist due to labor mobility barriers.

Finally, using the survey data of CHIPS (2002) and CGSS (2006), this book explores the segmentation of China's labor market and its changes from the perspective of labor mobility and pay levels. The use of a switching regression model proves the existence of the endogenous double duality which hinders the flow of labor across sectors. The extent of mobility barriers for different working populations is shown as follows:

1. Urban labor < rural labor;
2. Local non-rural labor < non-local non-rural labor < non-local rural labor < local rural labor;
3. Labor of provincial capital ≈ labor of municipality directly under the central government < labor of prefecture-level city < labor of county\county-level city < labor of town/township.

Segmentation indices of the labor market as a whole and by sub-sector were developed based on the OLS estimation and quantile regression with the Mincer equation, and the results for 2002 and 2006 show an increase in the wage gap caused by differences in the place of household registration and a decline in the wage gap attributed to ownership types. High segmentation tends to be attenuated in the lower conditional quantiles while low segmentation becomes more evident in the higher conditional quantiles, and pay levels tend to converge in the lower conditional quantiles and diverge in the higher conditional quantiles. Sectors with a higher concentration of "good" employers are less segmented than others. The difference between sectors in the segmentation index is significant, with the highest index score nearly three times that of the lowest. The results show that the law of one price does not hold in China's labor market and that there are still obstacles to labor mobility. However, changes in the constituents of segmentation indicate an endogenous force that drives the market evolution in the direction of integration.

Facilitating labor mobility between urban and rural areas, between public and private sectors, and between regions, promoting the equal distribution of labor resources and establishing an integrated labor market is essential in order to close urban–rural divide and achieve equal employment. Only in this way will the labor market become increasingly integrated and serve as an ever important driver of China's economic growth.

Contents

1 Introduction 1

1.1 Background 2

1.2 Research Question 10

1.3 Significance of the Study 12

1.4 Research Concepts and Summary 13

2 The Evolution of the Labor Market: A Review of Theoretical and Empirical Studies on Segmentation and Integration 17

2.1 Theories on the Evolution of Labor Markets Abroad: From Competition to Segmentation 18

2.2 Empirical Studies of the Evolution of Labor Markets Abroad: Tests for Segmentation 36

2.3 Understanding the Evolution of China's Labor Market: From Segmentation to Integration 38

2.4 A Review of Theoretical and Empirical Research on the Movement from Labor Market Segmentation to Integration 44

2.5 Basic Concepts 45

3 The Evolution of China's Labor Market from Segmentation to Integration: An Outline and the Reality 49
3.1 The "Complete Segmentation" of China's Labor Market Prior to the Marketization 50
3.2 The Early Years of Market-Oriented Reform (1978–1991): From "Complete Segmentation" to Gradual Easing 56
3.3 Stage I of Marketization (1990–2000): The Formation of Double Duality 71
3.4 The Labor Market in Stage II of Marketization (2001–Present): The Transition from Double Duality to Multi-Tiered Segmentation 87
3.5 The Evolutionary Characteristics of China's Labor Market 110

4 A Theoretical Analysis of the Evolution of China's Labor Market from Segmentation to Integration: An Expansion of the Classic MP Model 113
4.1 China's Labor Market Segmentation and the Theoretical Framework 113
4.2 The Evolution of China's Labor Market in the Context of "Double Duality": A Benchmark Model 126
4.3 Steady-State Equilibrium and Dynamic Analysis of the Double Duality of the Labor Market 143
4.4 Summary 159

5 An Empirical Study on the Evolution of China's Urban Labor Market Segmentation: Confirmation by Data from Various Sources 163
5.1 Sources of Data Validating the Evolution of China's Labor Market and the Empirical Approach 164
5.2 Validating the Evolution of China's Labor Market from Double Duality to Integration (I): Flow of Labor Between Segments 166
5.3 Validating the Evolution of China's Labor Market from Double Duality to Integration (II): Segmentation Measurement 196
5.4 Summary 211

6 Conclusions and Areas for Further Research 213
6.1 Summary and Conclusions 213
6.2 Major Innovations of This Study 218
6.3 Deficiency and Areas for Further Research 219

Appendices 221

References 225

List of Figures

Fig. 1.1	Marketization, institutions, and labor market integration	15
Fig. 3.1	The floating urban population and employment in China from 1981 to 1991	70
Fig. 3.2	Distribution structure of total wage income by registration type from 1978 to 2010 (*Source* 2014 China Statistical Yearbook)	74
Fig. 3.3	Average employee wages of different types of units in key years (*Source* 2011 China Statistical Yearbook)	75
Fig. 3.4	The evolution of China's labor market	111
Fig. 4.1	Factors affecting labor market segmentation and their effects	117
Fig. 4.2	Wage rate and market tightness at the equilibrium points of the labor market characterized by double duality (*Note* $y_I = y_O = 1, r = 0.025, \alpha = 0.5, \beta = 0.18, c = 0.35, b = 0.4, \eta = 0.675 \quad m(\theta_I) = 1.35 \times \theta_I^{-0.18}, m(\theta_O) = 1.35 \times \theta_O^{-0.5}, \varphi = 0.48, f = 4, k = 1.5, \lambda = 0.01, \gamma = 0.2, P = 1$)	145
Fig. 4.3	The Beveridge curve in the labor market characterized by double duality (*Note* $y_I = y_O = 1, r = 0.025, \alpha = 0.5, \beta = 0.18, c = 0.35, b = 0.4, \eta = 0.675 \quad m(\theta_I) = 1.35 \times \theta_I^{-0.18}, m(\theta_O) = 1.35 \times \theta_O^{-0.5}, \varphi = 0.48, f = 4, k = 1.5, \lambda = 0.01, \gamma = 0.2, P = 1$)	147

Fig. 4.4 Turnover costs in the context of equilibrium in the labor market characterized by double duality (*Note* $y_I = y_O = 1, r = 0.025, \alpha = 0.5, \beta = 0.18, c = 0.35, b = 0.4, \eta = 0.675$ $m(\theta_I) = 1.35 \times \theta_I^{-0.18}$, $m(\theta_O) = 1.35 \times \theta_O^{-0.5}$, $\varphi = 0.48, f = 4, k = 1.5, \lambda = 0.01, \gamma = 0.2, P = 1$) 148

Fig. 4.5 Graphical solutions for the θI and θO differential equations 155

Fig. 4.6 The dynamics of wages and wage differentials in the state and non-state sectors 157

Fig. 4.7 The labor market unemployment rate and mobility cost dynamics 158

Fig. 5.1 The QQ diagram of CHIPS (2002) and CGSS (2006) hourly log pay level 200

List of Tables

Table 3.1	Wage system reforms in China between 1978 and 1991	58
Table 3.2	Highlights of policies on labor mobility and employment in state-owned enterprises, 1978–1991	63
Table 3.3	Changes in the wage system between 1990 and 2000	73
Table 3.4	Key policies on labor mobility between 1990 and 2000	76
Table 3.5	Benefit provision and household registration system reform by urban type, 1990–2000	82
Table 3.6	Urban employment in agricultural households and non-agricultural households (2000 census)	83
Table 3.7	Rural–urban, urban–urban, rural–rural, and urban–rural migration (2000 census)	84
Table 3.8	Movement of labor by sector of ownership (January 1996–November 2001)	85
Table 3.9	Main wage systems after 2000	91
Table 3.10	Average wages by economic types since 2003 (Unit: yuan)	94
Table 3.11	Average wages by economic unit type and industry category in 2008 (Unit: yuan)	96
Table 3.12	Number and growth rate of rural migrant workers and urban workers between 2000 and 2010	98
Table 3.13	Distribution of migrant workforce by industry (percent)	98
Table 3.14	Changes in the employment of rural migrant workers in terms of industry across China, 2008–2014 (percent)	101
Table 3.15	Key policies and systems related to labor mobility introduced since 2000	103

Table 4.1	Job matching types within the dual structure	129
Table 4.2	Calibration parameters for the dual search-and-matching model	148
Table 4.3	Steady-state equilibrium in the dual market	152
Table 5.1	Descriptions of main variables tested by double duality	172
Table 5.2	Statistical descriptions of main variables of CHIPS (2002) data	173
Table 5.3	CGSS (2006) data main variables description	175
Table 5.4	The Spearman/Pearson correlation coefficient matrix between CHIPS (2002) and CGSS (2006) variables	177
Table 5.5	Estimated OLS and RSM results of CHIPS data (registered permanent residence, excluding the place of origin)	179
Table 5.6	Estimated OLS and RSM results of CHIPS data (registered permanent residence, including the place of origin)	181
Table 5.7	Estimated OLS and RSM results of CGSS (2006) data (registered permanent residence, regardless of administrative rank)	184
Table 5.8	Estimated OLS and RSM results of CGSS (2006) data (registered permanent residence, based on administrative rank)	186
Table 5.9	The endogenous coefficient of the dual structure in switching regression	195
Table 5.10	Estimated results of the Mincer equation of the dual structure	202
Table 5.11	Segmentation indexes calculated based on the estimated results of OLS and QRM	205
Table 5.12	Segmentation indexes calculated based on estimated results of OLS and quantile (CHIPS), with industry controlled	208
Table 5.13	Measurement of double duality indexes of five industries	209

CHAPTER 1

Introduction

> We should strive to foster an environment conducive to upward mobility in which every Chinese citizen is able to pursue a "Chinese Dream." That means whether they are the children of farmers in remote areas or of urban residents, they have equal opportunities for advancement and better life through their talents and hard work.
>
> —Su Hainan, Vice Chairman of the China Association for Labor Studies and Chairman of the Compensation Committee

Why has the number of senior high students quitting the college entrance examinations nationwide kept rising in recent years, with the figure increasing from 840,000 in 2009 to over a million in 2011? Why is the idea that deems schooling useless gaining ground again? Why do millions of college students each year prefer to sit for the civil service examinations or look for jobs at large state-owned enterprises (SOEs) instead of small and medium-sized private enterprises? Why are college students unwilling to start their own businesses? Why do college graduates have difficulty in obtaining employment, let alone high-paying jobs? Why are the coastal regions seeing a shortage of workers despite rising wages? Economists believe that individuals' economic behavior is the result of rational choice. If that is the case, what motivation on the micro level would produce macro-level outcomes as described above, and what kind of mechanism has changed the choices of rational economic actors

Y. Chen, *China's Labor Market in the Transition*, https://doi.org/10.1007/978-981-99-9160-0_1

and led to these outcomes? The above phenomena reflect the changing labor market over the past 30 years of China's market-oriented reforms as well as individuals' adjustment of their rational expectations of the labor market to align with reality. Such changes stem from what has occurred in the demand structure of the labor market, that is, changes in labor demand inside and outside the state system (*tizhi*) and between urban and rural areas, as well as changes in the distribution of wages and remuneration in various sectors of the economy. The barriers to obtaining "good jobs," which had been diminished in the early days of market-oriented reforms, are now on the rise. Behind all these phenomena, we see a **segmented labor market**, which has hindered the process of making the economy more market-oriented. Therefore, the solution to the above problems lies in how to minimize the segmentation and promote the integration of the labor market.

1.1 Background

In the course of the past half century, China experienced both slow progress during the centrally planned economy era and the subsequent rapid development and remarkable achievements brought about by the reform and opening up policy. While we are proud of the prosperity brought about by the "China model" and have rejoiced at the fact that according to various economic indicators, China has come out of the bottom of the global financial crisis earlier than other major countries in the world, we should also be aware that we cannot sit back and relax just yet. We are in some ways imperceptibly experiencing three kinds of setbacks: the waning role of the market relative to that of the government, the growing proportion of the public sector relative to the private sector (*guanjin mintui*), and the trading of efficiency for balance (Lu, 2010).

China is at a crossroads where the cyclical changes in the national economy brought about long-term effects, and in line with the periodic characteristics, the situation of workers in the labor market and the market structure have also changed. A study of the evolution of the labor market in the context of economic transformation is needed for us to better understand individual workers' economic behaviors (employment choices) within the existing labor market structure and their significance for the labor market in the long run.

1.1.1 Changes in Both Demographic and Economic Development Patterns Require Closer Attention to the Labor Market Evolution

i. Demographic changes caused a shift in the factor endowment structure, which in turn transforms the labor supply structure, and requires a change on the demand side accordingly.

China's demographic structure is undergoing changes in the following two aspects.

First, demographic transition.[1] When the economic development in China was at a low level, unconventional institutional arrangements and expected factors worked together to promote the rapid transformation of population reproduction, thus allowing the country to benefit at an earlier time from the age structure of its population. The first demographic dividend[2] and abundant labor resources have, to a certain extent, contributed to China's rapid growth for more than three decades. It is estimated that the first demographic dividend contributed about 15% to China's economic growth between 1982 and 2000 (Brandt & Rawski, 2008). The age structure of the population is expected to change in the following ways:

- There will be an increasingly aging population and the total dependency ratio is expected to rise, though the rate of increase is considerably slowing. It is estimated that the dependency ratio will peak in 2013 and then decline steadily, and by 2050, the expected dependency ratio will be only 85% of the 2013 level. According to the United Nations Population Division's *World Population Prospects* (2010 Revision), the year 2013 would see the peak of China's demographic dividend, when the dependency ratio would reach the trough value of 38.3 and rise thereafter. By definition, demographic dividend will continue for another 20 years until the dependency ratio exceeds 50% by the year 2030.

[1] Demographic transition is the shift from a situation where fertility and death rates are fairly high to a situation where both are very low.

[2] Mason and Lee (2006) have further expanded the concept of "demographic dividend" to the idea of two demographic dividends, with the first dividend brought about by the increase in the share of the productive age group due to demographic transition, and the second dividend a result of anticipated changes in the age structure of the population and the resultant adjustment of individual behavior and public policies accordingly.

- Dynamic changes have been observed in the proportion of the working-age population, especially the effective labor force (effective producers),[3] which first rises and then declines. The growth rate of the effective labor force peaked in the late 1980s and early 1990s. The proportion of the population aged 15–64 in the 2010 census was 74.53%, an increase of 3.36 percentage points compared to 2000. The average annual population growth rate from the fifth to the sixth census was 0.57%, which was 0.5 percentage points lower than the 1.07% seen between the fourth and fifth censuses. It is estimated that by 2020, the growth will cease and even turn negative. According to the UN Population Division's *World Population Prospects* (2010 Revision), assuming that the retirement age stays the same, China will lose 10 million potential workers by 2030 and 180 million by 2050 and join the likes of Japan and Western Europe.

Thus, the demographic transition implies a change in the relative abundance of production factors, and in the future, the role of the first demographic dividend that relies solely on the number of workers will steadily weaken. The full use of the "second demographic dividend" has become the primary choice for China. A transition from the first to the second demographic dividend is essentially a transition from an unlimited supply of labor resources to a shortage of labor resources, with economic growth purely driven by labor and capital investment losing momentum over time. Assuming that the employment demand for economic growth does not undergo major changes, structural unemployment will become the main problem in the labor market.

Second, urbanization. Today, China is in a stage of rapid urbanization which, in the next 20 years or so, will increase at an average annual rate of about one percent (Feng, 2009). Some scholars believe that China's urban population will exceed the rural population for the first time during the 12th Five-Year Plan period from 2011 to 2015, and China will therefore transform from a country with a majority of its population being rural residents to a country with an urban majority (Zhang, 2011). However, a noteworthy aspect to urbanization in China is that the process has been largely driven by migrant workers from rural areas,

[3] Brandt and Rawski (2009) argue that the effective labor force (effective producers) is the population weighted by age-specific labor productivity.

and granting them the status of city residents is a problem that urgently calls for resolution. On the one hand, urban non-agricultural industries are increasingly dependent on rural labor, pointing to a rigid demand for migrant workers and the economic importance of making them true urban residents. On the other hand, what China is experiencing now is not yet full-blown urbanization since the new entrants to cities are still being excluded from the urban public service and social security system, and have to move back and forth between urban and rural areas. Rural land thus becomes crucial, providing a safety net for them. How to ensure the transfer of rural labor to urban areas is an important issue for the rapid and steady development of China's economy and society in the future.

ii. The shift in economic development pattern urgently calls for a flexible and stable labor market

Since the implementation of the reform and opening up policy, especially after the global financial crisis, industrial transformation and upgrading, and institutional innovation have become the most important challenges for the Chinese economy following a period of resource-intensive growth.

First of all, the market demand structure has undergone changes. With rising labor costs and decreasing output of export-oriented products, there is an urgent need to change the way of economic growth that is driven by capital and labor resources at the lower end of the global value chain and to realize industrial transformation and upgrading. To do so, industries will have to tackle the problem that a large number of workers work in harsh environments and sacrifice their health and even lives for livelihoods in a market that lacks labor protection measures, capital, and social security. Efforts need to be made to prevent demographic dividends from benefiting a small number of investors exclusively.

Secondly, enterprise transformation is the main thrust in economic transformation or industrial transformation and upgrading, with enterprises playing a central part in this process. A bottleneck in the enterprise system has formed over the years as a result of the central planned economy. State-owned enterprises (SOEs) have experienced decentralization reforms since the 1980s as well as a wave of other reforms since the 1990s, and employment and wage distribution mechanisms at these enterprises have become increasingly market-oriented. However, the stability in employment and the corresponding social welfare benefits at these enterprises as well as the non-marketization of wage determination mechanisms, which are remnants of the planned economy period, have become obstacles to the rational flow of labor in the process of economic transformation. Just how to bring together efforts to realize SOE labor mobility with the implementation of non-state-owned enterprises under market economy conditions and how to utilize market rules to reform the existing separation between wage determination and employment selection mechanisms between state-owned and non-state sectors are other areas that also urgently need examination if we are to promote the construction of a flexible labor market. Moreover, over the years, the much misunderstood markets for production factors including labor, capital, and technology have lagged behind the commodity markets. The interaction between non-market factors and market factors in the process of transformation, and the invisible force for market segmentation have affected to a large extent the functioning of a unified market and the operations of the market system. Therefore, it is imperative in the process of economic transformation to bring together various labor market segments and make them an integral whole that is both flexible and stable, and in the meantime to encourage the labor force to move from the low-value-added sectors to the high-value-added sectors.

Both the demographic transition and the shift in the economic development pattern are momentous changes never seen in China before. What this also means is that structural employment and unemployment will be the primary problem in China's labor market in the future. Therefore, a question warranting our serious consideration is what kind of labor market will allow us to further reap the first demographic dividend, tap the potential of the second dividend, and overcome the constraints of demographic dividends during the transition period, and what kind of labor market can be both flexible and stable, and conducive to rapid urbanization.

1.1.2 The Coexistence of Economic Agglomeration and Regional Disparities Requires Us to Pay More Attention to Interregional Labor Market Segregation and Its Evolution Over Time

China is a unified big country. However, due to the differences between regions, we have to understand the Chinese economy as a combination of relatively independent smaller provincial economies. Thus, China's economic growth has been accompanied by profound changes in the geographic distribution of economic activities. The coexistence of regional economic agglomeration and dispersion and the persistent differences in economic growth between regions brought about a massive change in the economic landscape.

China's economic center of gravity is shifting heavily towards the coastal areas, with economic activities increasingly concentrated in a few developed regions. In this process, the coastal areas became a magnet for a large number of rural workers and high-quality professionals despite the constraints of the household registration system. While changes have occurred in the production factor endowment structure and even comparative advantages in economically developed regions, such changes, if any, have occurred in an insignificant way in underdeveloped regions. The growing outflow of labor and talent has correspondingly increased the economic dependence of the central and western regions on natural resource endowments, and this, coupled with policy influence, may have caused lingering distortions in the prices of production factors and even in the industrial structure, thus adversely affecting the efficiency of regional economies and especially industrial reconfiguration. As a result, changes in the regional industrial structure may not have necessarily met the needs of economic transformation and industrial structure upgrading.

In addition, China's administrative division system has accorded cities with varying status in the administrative hierarchy. This, together with the continuation of the redistribution system that had been set up before the advent of the reform and opening up policy, exacerbated the regional, institution-based barriers that make labor flow and integration across regions difficult, causing a labor demand-and-supply imbalance between regions. Although institutional barriers to labor mobility are gradually being removed, the existence of the household registration system and the urban–rural gap in social welfare make labor mobility inadequate, giving rise to a "spatial mismatch"[4] in the regional distribution of China's labor market. In this vein, another question warranting our attention is under

[4] The "spatial mismatch" referred to in this paper is different from what urban economists in the West speak of, i.e., limited to the spatial mismatch of the labor market within a single city. Here, what is emphasized is a broader definition of "spatial mismatch" in the labor market. As pointed out by Coulson et al. (2001) spatial mismatch in the labor market stems from an asymmetrical distribution in spatial terms of the demand and supply of labor skills.

what conditions can the problem of "spatial mismatch" be solved in a labor market that squares with the realities.

1.1.3 The Growing Prominence of Problems in the Social Structure Requires an Economic Approach to Social Problems and the Evolution of China's Labor Market

China's economic reforms are changing not only the income structure and living standards, but also the social fabric. The main factors affecting China's social structure, the college entrance examination, the household registration system, and work units,[5] have changed significantly since the implementation of the reforms. In particular, the post-1992 top-down economic transformation has, through the introduction of market mechanisms, the reform of state-owned enterprises, and the strategy of opening up the coastal areas, resulted in the reallocation of social and economic resources in many aspects and on various levels. Generally speaking, this has led to an increase in the concentration of wealth in society, a more reified class structure,[6] and the diversification and fragmentation[7] of social

[5] The "work unit" or *danwei* is an institutional innovation, a necessary organizational form in the transition from an agricultural society to an industrial society. It has existed not just in China but also several other countries experiencing similar periods of transition in history. The work unit provides employment and pays workers' wages, as well as guarantees lifetime employment, seniority ranking, and social security from cradle to grave. Some even run their own hospitals and kindergartens. Therefore, the work unit can achieve complete social control. Work units can be found at various levels: the provincial and ministerial level, prefectural level, county level, and township level. The work unit in China has two characteristics: lifelong employment and full social security. It brings together the workplace, one's place of residence, and the social welfare system. It pays workers their wages as well as provides housing, childcare services, education, medical care, and even funerals. In many cases, it also manages the worker's love life, marriage, divorce, and family planning choices. It is self-contained within its four walls and gates (mostly with guards). Ownership by the people is only an ideal, and the reality has been unit ownership. The unit in the eyes of the individuals is not so much an organization that provides products and services to society, but a self-sufficient community and welfare entity.

[6] The class structure reification referred to here is the phenomenon where economic stratification took shape following the introduction of reform and opening up and social mobility followed certain standards and became more regular. The main manifestations are: A gradual formation of boundaries between classes, a decline in the rate of upward mobility for the lower classes, the emergence of class characteristics in lifestyles, gradual formation of certain cultural patterns, and the strengthening of internal class identity.

[7] Li Qiang (2008) suggests that following the introduction of the reform and opening up policy, the "fragmentation of social group interests" means that interests within the

interests. There is an inextricable link between the social structure and the operation of the labor market. In recent years, the intertwined problems of inequality in income distribution and social inequality have drawn the attention of both economists and sociologists, who have studied these issues from the perspectives of wage differentials and social stratification, respectively, and have come to various conclusions and prescriptions for the problem of inequality. However, what China has to deal with is far more complex than the either–or dichotomy (Yao, 2010). When pursuing the goal of establishing a fair, just, flexible, and efficient market for the allocation of labor resources, we must not ignore the impact of the social structure on the way the labor market works, as the resulting institutional implications are far-reaching. A key entry point for studying the evolution process of China's labor market during the transition period is integrating a sociological study of social structure problems into the mainstream economic analysis framework.

1.1.4 Explaining the Phenomena of China's Labor Market Requires the Search for the Best Fit Between Widely Accepted Economic Theories and the Theory of Dualism

Compared with the markets for goods and for factors of production, the labor market is important in that labor is both a production factor in economic activities and consumers, and as such, the operations of the labor market are more closely related to human welfare. Making labor demand and supply truly market-driven is more complex than with other markets, not just because of the significant gaps between regions, between urban and rural areas, and between traditional sectors and emerging sectors, but also due to changes in the distribution of interests which, caused by changes in the social structure amidst market reform, have a direct impact on the marketization process. The particular development experience of China as a large country in transition[8] shows

group were more differentiated and individualized or the "integrated social aggregates" prior to the reform and opening up started to disintegrate.

[8] Lu Ming (2009) believes that the definition of development as a large country in transition to be as follows: "Transition" means China's transition from a planned economy to a market economy, "development" means the transition from the traditional dual economy to a modern, integrated economy, and "large country" means that there is bound to be large differences between regions as China's economy transforms and develops.

that in the transition from a planned economy to a market economy, the path dependency, stability, and adaptability of the system can make the labor marketization process even more complicated. This is especially true at a time when economic reforms are advancing ahead of other supporting reforms, old and new systems coexist alongside market-oriented mechanisms, making it more difficult to understand the labor market phenomena in China's transition period.

One of the main reasons for this problem is the lack of a consistent theoretical framework. While mainstream macroeconomics and labor economics are suitable for explaining labor market phenomena in neoclassical conditions, they are an inadequate explanation in situations where there is an unlimited supply of labor within a dual-sector economy. Although most Chinese scholars and policy researchers agree that the theory of the dual-sector economy developed by W. A. Lewis and other scholars can be used to explain the phenomenon of economic development where there is an unlimited supply of labor, it can only be used alone rather than being integrated with the basic hypotheses and analytical frameworks of mainstream economics (Cai, 2010). Thus, once the Chinese economy reaches the Lewis turning point, showing both the features of the dual-sector economy and neoclassical economy, the separate application of the aforementioned two theories will make it difficult to understand and explain labor market phenomena at specific stages of development (Cai, 2010). Therefore, with no ready-made paradigm for explaining the problems in China's labor market, we will have to examine the logic behind the market's evolution and then build a suitable theoretical framework for our analysis.

1.2 Research Question

The core question of the research is the evolution of the labor market from segmentation to integration, which is the ultimate goal of the labor marketization process. What China has experienced since the introduction of the reform and opening up policy provides a good opportunity for researchers to validate their hypothesis on the integration of a fully segmented labor market over time. The research question is the key to understanding the development of China's labor market. It can be further broken down into questions on three levels:

- How has China's labor market evolved? Are there any patterns that can be discerned?
- Does the labor market show a shift from segmentation to integration? If yes, what is the rationale behind it? What are the implications for economists and policymakers?
- Where is China's labor market heading? Is integration possible?

Level 1: How has China's labor market evolved? Are there any patterns that can be discerned?

Answering this question requires us to examine historical data for a closer look at the characteristics of wage determination mechanisms and labor mobility in the process of labor marketization in China, and to understand the degree of marketization and the way forward for China's labor market. Western economic theory has it that labor mobility reduces regional economic disparities, accelerates the equalization of factor rewards, and promotes the integration of the labor market. Since the implementation of market reforms, the state-owned and non-state-owned sectors of the economy have developed in tandem and become increasingly diversified, and market mechanisms have been given full play in the allocation of labor resources. Following layoffs due to the reform of SOEs, the employment allocation mechanism outside the planned economy kicked in and the labor market was formed quickly. The household registration system, which restricts labor mobility, has been reformed through trial and error, rural surplus labor has been released, and the degree of mobility has been greatly improved. Looking back at these achievements of reform and our successful experiences and lessons allows us to better discuss foreign theories and experiences from China's own perspective as well as create and explore solutions to new problems such as the employment plight of college graduates, the shortage of migrant workers, and issues concerning the new-generation migrant workers. Therefore, looking back at our experience regarding wage determination and changes in labor mobility in China's labor market is the central thrust of our study of the labor market.

Level 2: Does the labor market show a shift from segmentation to integration? If yes, what is the rationale behind it? What are the implications for economists and policymakers?

These questions are essentially about the characteristics of the evolution of China's labor market (that is, its distinct evolutionary model) understood through the establishment of a theoretical framework. China needs to address a series of problems in the course of its economic development, such as its approach to economic growth, its industrial structure, and urban–rural and interregional gaps. Here, labor resources play a critical role, and an ever-improving labor market is a key link that affects the transformation of the economic development model. Therefore, as mentioned above, only by establishing a theoretical framework that can explain the phenomena of China's labor market can we further examine this issue in the future and analyze implications of corresponding policies and institutions.

Level 3: Where is China's labor market heading?

The answer to this question indicates the evolutionary path of China's labor market integration in the future. More than 30 years of reform and opening up and a series of policy adjustments since the 2008 financial crisis demonstrate that China's development is at a crossroad as it continues to undergo complex structural adjustments. It is thus necessary that we take a closer look at the future direction of China's labor market which is crucial for structural adjustment and improvements in the factor markets.

1.3 Significance of the Study

Building and improving the factor markets that connect urban and rural areas is a basic task of China's socialist economic reform and development, and also the key to the fundamental adjustment of urban–rural relations. An important part of the task is for the labor market to move toward integration. Therefore, a study of the evolution of China's labor market in an attempt to answer the abovementioned questions has both theoretical and practical significance:

- In theoretical terms, the study serves to expand our understanding of China's ever-improving labor market, and free us from the old idea that deems labor market segmentation and integration as two polar opposites. By combining mainstream labor economics theories and dualism, and creating a new theoretical framework, it examines in a broader sense the pathway toward labor market integration and helps enrich the application of labor economics theory in China.
- On the practical level, based on the existing characteristics of labor market segmentation alongside the trend toward integration, the study looks at what inherently drove China's labor market to

evolve from segmentation to integration and its implications for the economy and welfare. It also proposes policies for the adjustment of changes in labor supply and demand and other relevant recommendations to promote such integration.

In this way, this study seeks to gain a more comprehensive and deeper understanding of the essence of labor market integration on both the theoretical and practical levels.

1.4 Research Concepts and Summary

1.4.1 Research Concepts

China's labor market developed amidst the interactions between the market-oriented reforms and traditional institutions[9] which were a legacy of the planned economy period. Figure 1.1 shows the role of market-oriented reforms and institutions in labor market integration. This process of "marketization" has allowed the market to move away from the traditional planned economy model where production factors are allocated according to planned instructions, and instead toward allocation based on the supply-and-demand relationships in the market. This has improved both factor mobility and allocation efficiency, which is conducive to labor market integration. So, how do institutions work in the labor market? This study is mainly focused on the institutional factors, such as how the ownership and household registration systems and market-oriented reforms interact to affect the development of the labor market, how ownership determines the pay level of workers, and how the household registration system has become a key factor in labor mobility and choices. Within the traditional system, wages are fixed and labor mobility is relatively low, which is not conducive to labor market integration. In the process of reform and opening up (with the process of marketization being the most representative), the role of market-oriented reforms in resource allocation in the labor market has penetrated the traditional system and interacted with the traditional system. The singular wage determination mechanism, which has benefited from the impact of

[9] The traditional institutions here refer to the household registration and ownership systems from the planned economy period.

marketization on the free allocation of resources, has tended toward diversification due to changes in the ownership structure, and labor mobility has increased due to the continued relaxation of the household registration system. Conversely, the path dependency of the system continues to work to maintain the stability of the system itself and reduce the degree of wage diversification and free movement amidst the impact of marketization. Thus, in this text, we will look at how the ownership and household registration systems work in China's labor market amidst the process of marketization, and whether the market will become more integrated or segmented in the future?

1.4.2 Chapter Summary

This book is divided into six chapters. Below is a summary of each chapter.

In this chapter, the introductory part, we start with a description of the current situation and the theoretical issues, put forward the research question, and discuss why this study is necessary in both theoretical and practical terms. The research concepts and chapter arrangements are also described.

Chapter 2 contains the literature review, which summarizes the theoretical and empirical works on the topic. First, we look at what has been discussed by overseas scholars, the methods they have used, and how they understand the change of the labor market from a state of integration to segmentation. Then, we examine domestic research, proposing that China is a "natural laboratory" for studying the evolution from labor market segmentation to integration. Finally, we analyze the concepts of integration (segmentation) and equilibrium, describe the relationship between them, and propose the pathway toward the goal of labor market integration.

Chapter 3, based on an analysis of historical data, explains how market and institutional factors have worked on market integration (segmentation) in the evolution process of China's labor market. The evolution process is divided into four stages: the almost "completely segmented" stage before marketization (1949–1978); the embryonic stage of the labor market in the early days of marketization (1989–1990); the stage of double duality (1990–2000); and the stage of multi-tiered segmentation based on double duality (2000–). Such an evolution occurred in response to a change in China's population structure, and is mainly attributed to the household registration and ownership systems which

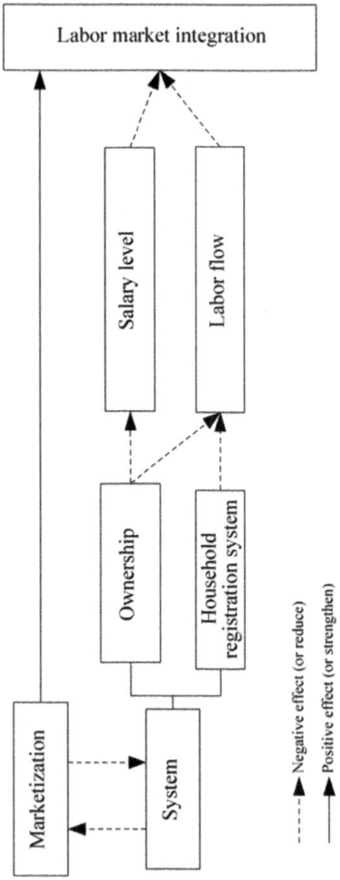

Fig. 1.1 Marketization, institutions, and labor market integration

caused the dichotomy and difference inside and outside *tizhi*. Due to the impact of the marketization process and a host of other factors, the almost completely segmented labor market has been replaced by one that exhibits the features of "multi-tiered segmentation" based on the household registration and ownership systems. It is also proposed that the double duality of China's labor market is expected to be reduced in the future and greater labor market integration will occur due to the market-driven allocation of labor resources.

In Chapter 4, a theoretical framework is proposed in order for us to construct an extended model of the classic MP model for China's dual labor market. Based on the history and evolutionary process of the labor market described in Chapter Three, it is then proposed that the existing segmentation of China's labor market is not only double duality as in traditional SLM theory but also a more complex form of segmentation. We classify the main factors affecting the integration of the labor market, analyze the functions of each, then in conjunction with China's realities we propose that the current segmentation of China's labor market is double duality based on the household registration system and the ownership, that multi-tiered segmentation has been formed by the superposition of endogenous segmentation, spatial segmentation, and the group effect, and that individual behavior and choices on the micro level can strengthen or weaken such segmentation. Then, based on the duality, we construct a search model that includes the heterogeneity of both workers and enterprises, and following the location of static equilibrium and dynamic analysis of the model, simulation is used to explore the trends of this duality and to cover the conditions that promoting labor market integration.

Chapter 5 is an empirical analysis of most data sources on the evolution from segmentation to integration in China's labor market. Here, we use the large survey datasets from Chips (2002) and CGSS (2006) to test for the existence and endogeneity of the duality using the switching regression model and also verify the barrier effect of the double duality in terms of labor mobility. Then, referring to the methods of constructing a segmentation index by Orr (1997) and Zhang Zhaoshi (2009a), we use OLS estimation and a quantile regression model to test for the degree of segmentation and changes of the double duality in China's labor market as a whole and by industry.

Chapter 6 contains the conclusions and directions for further study.

CHAPTER 2

The Evolution of the Labor Market: A Review of Theoretical and Empirical Studies on Segmentation and Integration

In physics, Newton's laws of motion presume no friction exists in nature. Likewise in classic economics, a perfectly competitive market exists where there is no transaction cost or friction. In the real world, however, transaction cost or friction is everywhere. It is precisely because of information asymmetry regarding job vacancies and needs for jobs that both the supply and demand sides in the labor market need to pay transaction costs in their search for suitable employees or jobs. This makes it difficult to find the ideal, perfectly competitive labor market in the real world. Western economics, which has a history of several hundred years, has sought to integrate perfectly competitive labor markets without friction into studies of macroeconomic cycles, which compromised the resultant policies or institutions designed to raise employment. Understanding the labor market and its pattern of changes based on the existence of transaction costs can shed light on the "black box" of the labor market operation. In this chapter, we will first look at important theories abroad relating to the labor market and its pattern of changes, the origin of the theories, and their implications for us. Then, we will review the main findings and clues concerning China's labor market, and areas for further research. Finally, we will analyze the concepts of equilibrium and integration in the labor market.

Y. Chen, *China's Labor Market in the Transition*,
https://doi.org/10.1007/978-981-99-9160-0_2

2.1 Theories on the Evolution of Labor Markets Abroad: From Competition to Segmentation

Whereas neoclassical economics, drawing upon the classical economic idea of "perfect competition" in the labor market, gives importance to non-market factors in explaining the non-competitiveness of the labor market, institutional economics, and development economics approach the non-competitiveness of the labor market using the dual sector model proposed by economists such as W. A. Lewis. On the subject of labor market segmentation, these two schools of thought also vary in terms of research methods and theories, and as such, the theoretical underpinning and analytical framework that incorporate the two will be the way forward for research in this area. Despite substantial differences in methodology and theoretical foundations, both schools deem the labor market a "black box." Opening this "black box" and introducing the behavior mechanism of enterprises and workers in the labor market stand as the link between them. The emergence of the theories of job vacancies and searches in the 1970s has made it possible to bridge the gap between them.

2.1.1 The Historical Context of Labor Market Evolution Studies Outside China

1. Neoclassical economics and competitive labor markets: Market clearing and wage differentials

Following the introduction of the idea of "competitive labor market" in 1776 by Adam Smith, economists such as Alfred Marshall (1890), John Bates Clark (1899), Schultz (1964), and Gray Becker (1962, 1964, 1966)—the latter two of whom formulated the human capital theory—helped to enrich the research in this area. When dealing with the topic of labor market, traditional neoclassical economics emphasizes the role of market mechanisms and market factors in determining pay levels and labor resource allocation. In a perfect market structure, the markets for goods and factors are in equilibrium, all products are cleared, and resources are allocated most efficiently.

In *An Inquiry into the Nature and Causes of the Wealth of Nations*,[1] Adam Smith wrote that in the real world, the common wages of labor depend on the contract between the employer and employees (Volume 1, p. 60) and in the general sense, "the money price of labour is necessarily regulated by two circumstances; the demand for labour, and the price of the necessaries and conveniences of life" (Volume 1, p. 79). Therefore, both employers and employees will have an impact on overall wages, but wages are ultimately determined by supply and demand in the labor market. At the same time, Smith also discussed the causes of wage gaps and focused on five factors that caused considerable imbalances in labor wages and capital profits: the agreeableness or disagreeableness of the employment; the level of difficulty and expense of learning the employment; the stability of employment; the level of responsibility associated with the employment; and the probability of success in them.

Thus, "the wages of labour vary with the ease or hardship, the cleanliness or dirtiness, the honourableness or dishonourableness of the employment". Thus in most places, take the year round, a journeyman taylor earns less than a journeyman weaver. His work is much easier. A journeyman weaver earns less than a journeyman smith. His work is not always easier, but it is much cleanlier. A journeyman blacksmith, though an artificer, seldom earns so much in twelve hours as a collier, who is only a labourer, does in eight. His work is not quite so dirty, is less dangerous, and is carried on in day-light, and above ground. Honour makes a great part of the reward of all honourable professions. In point of pecuniary gain, all things considered, they are generally under-recompensed, as I shall endeavour to show by and by.

Thus, wages vary according to the difficulty, cleanliness, and image of the business: They vary according to the difficulty of learning the business and the cost of learning; they vary according to the stability or certainty of the business; they vary according to the kind of responsibilities the employee is expected to bear; they vary according to the possibility of obtaining the needed qualifications; and they vary according to the probability or impossibility of success in each industry. (Book I, Chapter X) However, while the factors that create the wage gap only affect both sides of labor supply and demand, the decisive factor is the market itself. Subsequently, Alfred Marshall (1890) and John Bates Clark (1899) have

[1] Adam Smith. *An Inquiry into the Nature and Causes of the Wealth of Nations*, trans. Wang Ya'nan. Commercial Press, 1981.

used the concept of marginality that emerged at the end of the nineteenth century and the analytical paradigm of labor market clearing to propose that the equilibrium of supply and demand in the labor market is the employment and pay level formed by the interaction between the diminishing marginal demand of enterprise labor and the maximization of utility in individual labor supply. However, in addition to compensatory wage differentials arising from different working conditions in the labor market, wage differentials arise for a variety of other reasons.

Later on, classical economists such as Marshall studied competitive labor markets further within the framework of marginal analysis. They believed that the labor market is the gathering of buyers and sellers of labor, a place to exchange a certain amount of labor services at an agreed price between willing parties.[2] On the micro level, they analyzed the interactions between the utility-maximizing worker and the profit-maximizing firm in the labor market to form the pay level and employment volume cleared by the labor market. On the macro level, they assumed that: First, the labor market is a "spot market," and that the price of labor (the pay level) forms an equilibrium pay level in the open labor market through bargaining between the supply and demand sides; second, the price mechanism plays an important role in determining the pay level and the allocation of labor factors. The link between the markets is obvious. When the pay level in one market changes, the pay level in other markets is adjusted immediately to achieve equilibrium between markets.

In the 1960s, economists such as Schultz (1964), Gray Becker (1962, 1964, 1966), and Jacob Mincer (1974) abandoned the assumption of labor homogeneity and used the concept of human capital to explain the issue of non-competitive labor markets caused by non-homogeneous labor. The key idea behind the introduction of the concept of human capital into the analytical framework of perfect competition is that when individual utility is maximized, differences in human capital accumulation lead to differences in skill levels and labor productivity between individuals. In a situation of perfect competition both in the goods market and the labor market, different wages are paid according to the difference in marginal productivity between individual workers. Therefore, the difference of wages is explained by the heterogeneity of the labor force. The research here was focused on the role of public investment in general

[2] Derek Bosworth et al. (2003), *The Economics of the Labor Market*, China Economic Press.

training and private investment in specialized training (Becker, 1964), and as a result, human capital-centered explanations of wage inequality focus on worker heterogeneity as the main source of wage differentials, generally tending to include human capital (Mincer, 1974). In other words, one worker in the labor market earns more than another because he or she has had more education and is more skilled, and workers with certain skills in the same firm earn more than those with low or no skills because their skills result in higher marginal productivity. In addition, studies have found that jobs that pay high wages to workers have unattractive job characteristics, such as monopolies or higher accident rates, to compensate for those characteristics.

Such analyses follow a common theoretical framework: First, they emphasize the role of market mechanisms and market factors in determining pay levels and labor resource allocation, and take other influencing factors such as laws, institutions, and culture as pre-determined factors; second, the assumptions of human behavior patterns are the economic man, rational choice, and independent preferences; third, an assumption about the nature of the labor market is that the labor market is highly competitive and there are a large number of actors on both the supply and demand sides, and both parties have the right to choose freely and may freely enter and exit the market. The optimal allocation of resources can be achieved through the equilibrium of the labor market.

Thus, based on the idea of perfect competition, in the research from classical labor economics to neoclassical labor economics it is believed that the labor market is cleared, market forces determine labor prices and employment, and wage differentials in the labor market are compensatory wages given to different workers due to (1) differences in working conditions and job nature; and (2) payments to marginal labor productivity due to differences in individual human capital levels. Therefore, the labor market is perfectly competitive, and the causes of non-competitive labor markets stem from working conditions and individual characteristics. (3) As long as workers or firms can freely enter and exit different labor markets, a competitive economy will be characterized by a single wage. Therefore, from the perspective of classical labor economics, it is not difficult to see that the labor market is not only competitive but also a unified whole. In other words, the ideal labor market is a fully integrated market with such characteristics.

2. Sources of ideas on labor market segmentation: The concept of "non-competitive groups" and the introduction of early institutional concepts

John Stuart Mill was among the first who emphasized that institutions cause market segmentation. Unlike Adam Smith's neoclassical view, which emphasized competitive wage determination in the labor market, John Stuart Mill and John Cairnes were in favor of institutions as a substitute for market processes. Unlike Smith and other political economists, Mill analyzed the role of education and social class as determinants of "pre-market segmentation" caused by the characteristics or nature of workers before they enter the labor force. Mill believed Smith's idea of wage compensation to be wrong. Instead, he thought that the existence of non-competitive groups means that competition does not produce the same return on investment in different forms of human capital as Adam Smith and neoclassical economics believed.

Mill believed that social, occupational, and spatial transfer barriers make it very difficult, if not impossible, for workers to move between markets. In particular, low-skilled manual workers and their children can only struggle in low-income employment fields for a long time due to the lack of opportunities to improve their work skills. For those in the low-income bracket, the kind of jobs that they aspire to are always out of reach. He also believed that the comfort level of the working class would fall should wages fall, with a lasting and devastating impact on their living conditions.

Although A.C. Pigou, one of the representatives of the Cambridge school, also believed in Say's law, he also suggested the classic view of labor market segmentation in his book *Employment and Equilibrium*. He thought that the clearing of the labor market is rare and the situation of non-clearance is a lot more common, and that workers cannot always be in "perfectly competitive" jobs. He believed that the main reason for this was institutions, and suggested that these institutional factors include unions, access to unemployment compensation, and other major barriers affecting the labor market. He recognized that the labor market was segmented, not just in terms of factors of production that reflect the heterogeneity of labor, such as skills, experience, and competitiveness but more importantly, strict limits on labor mobility between industries. "Centers of production" existed in the labor market, and the observed stagnation of labor between these centers was the result of the local connections formed by workers with the centers of production.

As the pioneers of the labor market segmentation school, Mill and Pigou's basic ideas of institutional segmentation paved the way for later scholars to study wage differentials in the labor market from the perspective of segmentation.

3. Labor market segmentation from the perspective of the institutional school and the development economics: Duality and wage differentials
   i. The double duality of the labor market according to the institutional school

Since the 1970s, many economists have turned away from the dominant competitive analysis method and have instead emphasized the segmentation nature of the labor market and the important influence of institutional and social factors on labor remuneration and employment. They are known as the labor market segmentation (LMS) school. Kerr (1954) describes five sources of barriers: (1) Individual worker preferences; (2) Individual employer preferences; (3) Collective worker behavior; (4) Collective employer behavior; and (5) Government action. These barriers exist due to the segmentation of the labor market into smaller parts. Among them, institutional rules define the boundary between the internal and external composition of the labor market. The internal labor market is a unit of management, and the price and allocation of labor are determined by a series of management rules and procedures. In the external market, prices and allocations are determined by supply and demand. As a result, the labor market is no longer seen as a continuous, whole entity but divided into several distinct markets, each with different characteristics and allocation mechanisms. Peter B. Doeringer and Michael J. Piore (1971) have, based on this, proposed a labor market model with a dual structure, an idea which became a typical representative of early labor market segmentation theory. The duo hypothesized that an economy consists of two types of labor markets, the primary labor market and the secondary labor market: The primary market is characterized by high wages and benefit levels and stable employment, while the secondary market is characterized by low wages and benefit levels and unstable employment. The structure of a dual labor market and wage determination mechanisms differ markedly between the two parts. The primary market is a highly organized formal labor market that exists entirely within a given enterprise. Here, there are detailed rules and procedures to guide employment to regulate the relationship between supply and demand, mainly to do with recruitment, training, and output adjustment. Market forces basically do not play a role here. The secondary market is consistent with the labor market described by the neoclassical school—employers decide to hire labor based on the comparison of marginal labor contribution and marginal cost, and pay workers based on labor marginal contribution or market wages, which will tend to a fixed level based on supply and demand. The dual labor market segmentation theory emphasizes the role of the demand side of the market and institutional factors. Although the labor supply side can indeed play a certain role, its influence is far smaller than that of the labor demand side, and it is not as powerful as social and institutional factors in explaining such phenomena. Researchers at this stage emphasized the influence of labor union and company policies as well as social factors. They believed that institutional and social factors are the most important determinants of wages, thus revealing wage differentials and wage discrimination in the real economy and excluding the competitive factors emphasized by classical economics from the scope of labor market analysis.

ii. Urban–rural duality in development economics

Similar to the institutional school's idea of a dual labor market, but different in terms of the primary and secondary sectors is the idea put forward by Lewis (1954) and Kuznets (1955) based on the differences in the distribution of urban and rural labor resources and the economic characteristics of the two sectors. Both believed that the differences in the wages of workers resulted from differences in the economic sectors where they could find work. According to Lewis (1954), income in the traditional (basic survival) sector sets a floor for wages in the modern sector. However, in practice, wages must be higher than this floor, usually with a wage gap of at least 30% or more in the two sectors. Kuznets (1955) further expanded on the dual-structure theory and the variation of wage differentials across sectors with his proposal of the famous Kuznets curve, and subsequent scholars emphasized the existence of dualism based on the human capital theory of Schultz (1961, 1962), Becker (1962, 1964), and Mincer (1962, 1974), and have also analyzed comparable workers to understand the reasons why different sectors pay different pay levels with controls for population heterogeneity. As a result, numerous empirical studies have been performed based on this to discuss the different levels of wage payments received by the same kind of workers.

iii. New developments of the idea of dual structure

In recent years, some scholars have further expanded on the theory of the dual structure and have come to new understandings based on segmentation theory and Lewis' view of the dual structure. One of them is Gray Fields, who brought together all of these ideas. Fields (2009) discusses the differences and interrelationships between wage determination mechanisms in the formal and informal workforce within a dual structure. First, in the formal labor market, wage and employment levels are determined in four different ways: models of market clearing, wage determination above market-clearing levels (including minimum wages, labor unions, public sector payment policies, multinational corporations, and labor security systems) caused by institutional reasons (Fields, 1999; Fields & Wan, 1989), wage determination above market-clearing levels due to efficiency wages (Akerlof & Yellen, 1986; Leibenstein, 1957), and wage determination above market-clearing levels due to changes in supply behavior (Bardhan & Rudra, 1981; Drèze & Mukherjee, 1989; Osmani, 1991; Solow, 1990). Second, Field provides three basic ideas about wages and employment in the informal sector: the labor market in the informal sector is seen as the ultimate choice for free entry, preferring the formal sector; the informal sector is a more desirable sector for workers compared to the formal sector; and the informal sector itself is inherently dualistic, so it is possible to combine the first two characteristics. Fields (2009) has also proposed that there are three modes of interconnection between the formal sector and the informal sector: an integrated labor market with market clearing (i.e., an integrated labor market with equal wages and no unemployment); a model with wage duality but no unemployment; and the Harris–Todaro model, which expands on an earlier model and which addresses both wage duality and unemployment duality. Gary Fields (2009) argues that a model that integrates the formal and informal sectors and their interconnections can be extended to n sectors to analyze their wage differentials with an examination of the differences in wages and employment decisions in the formal and informal sectors and their interrelationships, and that based on the construction of this model, it can be extended to 36 different labor market models.

4. New developments in classical economics and the segmentation of the labor market: Transaction friction and wage differentials

According to the paradigm of perfect competition held by classical economists, there is no unemployment in the labor market, and employment information is completely sufficient. According to those of the institutional school and the development economics, however, unemployment in the labor market is caused by institutional barriers in sectors or barriers put up between urban and rural areas. With both the perfectly competitive market in classical economics and the idea of dual market segmentation put forward by the institutional school and the idea of an urban–rural dual structure in development economics, it is implied that the employment information of the labor market is completely sufficient. However, the difference lies in whether institutional factors should be used to discuss labor market segmentation. That is, the functioning of the labor market has always been treated as a "black box." Will opening up this "black box" lead to a clearer understanding of the functioning of the labor market? Can institutional factors be integrated into the framework of the perfectly competitive market paradigm? The key to opening this "black box" is Mortensen's (1984) job search-and-matching framework. Unlike other theories that analyze market segmentation for wage differentials and mobility constraints, job search theory assumes that workers search for their best opportunities among different employers, which in turn leads to wage differentials in the labor market. After nearly 30 years of development, the classic Mortensen–Pissarides search-and-matching model (1994) has been fully applied to issues such as wage differentials in the labor market, balancing unemployment, and the evaluation of labor market policies and institutions. A look at foreign literature shows that research has been primarily carried out along three pathways: the first is to apply search matching to the problem of the dual or multi-tiered segmentation of the labor market; the second is the application of job search-and-matching theory to labor market segmentation problems owing to spatial mismatch; and the third is the discussion of labor market segmentation caused by differences in the social structure, with reference to the concept of social capital.

i. The applications of search-and-matching theory to the problem of dual or multi-tiered segmentation of the labor market

Smith and Zenou (1997) argue that the labor market is "endogenous" and that this is closely linked to mass unemployment in the labor market. In search-and-matching theory, the dual-structure theory is approached from two aspects: First, based on the hypothesis of the dual structure, the reason for the emergence of the dual structure and its result are expounded by using the search-and-matching theory; and second, based on the labor mobility caused by the Harris–Todaro expected income mobility difference between urban and rural areas, a job search model is introduced to analyze the rationality and existence conditions of Todaro's paradox.

The first area of research happens on two levels: The first is the division of the formal and informal sectors in developing countries, which provides scholars with more opportunities and interest in studying the informal sector.

(1) Rauch (1991) and Loayza (1996) were interested in how the informal sector emerges. They argued that enterprises and workers enter the informal sector in order to avoid taxes or to circumvent formal sector regulation from the government (Dessy & Pallange, 2003; Fugazza & Jacques, 2004). (2) Since efficiency wages in the primary labor market are higher than the market-clearing level, there will be persistent voluntary unemployment when the economy is stable. When there are aggregate demand shocks in the economy, unemployment rises and the secondary labor market emerges. Thus, the division of the labor market is not an exogenous phenomenon caused by factors such as the system, but is determined solely by economic factors. The fact that a large number of the jobs created by the economic recession are from the secondary labor market in reality also proves the endogenous theory of this dual labor market. (3) Yves Zenou (2009) focused on the informal sector of the labor market and indicated that the emergence of the informal sector was largely due to job search friction in the formal sector. The literature related to this pertains mainly to the theory of rural–urban migration proposed by Harris and Todaro. The main argument here is that urban job creation increases

rather than reduces urban unemployment, as this has a negative effect on rural migration, and outweighs the positive effect of job creation.

The second is based on the standard job search-and-matching model, and examines the segmentation of the labor market at equilibrium while considering the heterogeneity of workers and or of enterprises, or both at the same time; alternatively, the existing state of labor market segmentation is used to theoretically discuss fluctuations in unemployment in a segmented labor market. The former approach has been carried out using the following ideas: (i) The labor market is segmented when workers or enterprises are heterogeneous, with the two distinguished by skill bias. It is proposed that whether the labor is fully or partially segmented in the simulation with random matching is determined by parameter values, and this determination then becomes persistent due to certain parameter values (Albrecht & Vroman, 2002). Acemoglu (1999) analyzed steady-state equilibrium in the case of a free entry of jobs and random matching (non-directional matching) when the type of work created by the enterprise matched the type of workers available, and believed that there is both a pooling equilibrium and separating equilibrium in the labor market, and used this multiplicity to study changes in unemployment levels. (ii) When both workers and enterprises are heterogeneous at the same time, the segmentation of the labor market depends on the search strategy adopted by workers. When the search is random and there is more than one vacancy, the equilibrium is partially segmented; when workers undertake directed searches, the equilibrium state of the labor market is one that is completely segmented (Merlino, 2009). Taking the heterogeneity of jobs and external shocks as the starting point, Costain J. et al. (2011) discussed the changes in unemployment in a dual labor market caused by the existence of two types of contractual structures (long-term and short-term), the overall shock to productivity, and in a dual labor market in experiencing special shocks.

The second aspect primarily comes from Wahba and Zenou (2005) who examined the Todaro paradox in the framework of efficient wages and the search-and-matching model. Zenou's application of the Todaro paradox in their thesis was different from that of classical literature: wages and employment in cities are endogenous, and so, if exogenous policy factors lead to an increase in the equalization of urban employment and unemployment, the Todaro paradox exists. With a focus on urban unemployment insurance, Zenou argued that the environment in developing countries can be interpreted as family or institutional support in the urban sector. In the efficiency wage model, we find that there is no Todaro paradox, and in the search-and-matching model, this is not always the case, as a reduction in urban unemployment insurance would lower urban employment and unemployment levels. In fact, even in both models, unemployment insurance policies have a direct impact on migration decisions, as it directly affects the expected utility of unemployment lifecycle after moving to the city.

ii. The applications of search-and-matching theory to the spatial segmentation of the labor market: A new interpretation of the spatial mismatch hypothesis

The application of job search theory to spatial differences in the labor market stems from the spatial mismatch hypothesis (SMH) proposed by Kain (1968) with regard to urban labor markets. This hypothesis was based on the spatial separation between the concentration of unemployed workers in metropolitan centers in the United States and the concentration of low-skilled jobs in the suburbs. It was proposed that the spatial mismatch of the labor market was caused by what was an asymmetric distribution of labor skill demand and supply in space.

Coulson et al. (2001) have argued that there are three key features to spatial mismatch in the labor market: (1) The unemployment rate of low-skilled residents in urban centers exceeds that of suburban residents; (2) Job vacancies in suburban enterprises are higher than in urban centers; and (3) The wages of low-skilled workers in suburban enterprises are higher than in urban centers. The common methods used for verifying the above are measurements of labor market outcomes based on micro or macro data or using the distance between residence and employment center as an indicator measure, and SMH has been demonstrated in articles by Holzer (1991), Ihlanfeldt (1992), and Zax and Kain (1996) using the various approaches described above.

In summary, the main question of this hypothesis is: Why is it that unemployed workers in one location cannot easily and freely fill vacant positions in another? The result is a different labor market outcome for different individuals due to the difference in their place of residence. Early on, urban economists focused on explaining this problem from a spatial perspective, and considered racial discrimination (Turner et al., 1991) and commuting cost differences as possible reasons for this problem, though these were not the most important reasons for the problem. As labor economists became even more interested in the issue, a third explanation emerged: the difficulty faced by workers in cities in gathering information on employment. Some research evidence suggests that this cost may be the root cause of the problem (Wilson, 1996). Although this problem has been validated through various phenomena and empirical research in the United States, the theoretical basis for the problem remains unclear. This is a puzzle that called urgently for the attention of labor economists. Arnott (1998) constructed a model that contains commuting cost and housing discrimination. The equilibrium outcome is to have low-skilled black workers commuting to the suburbs from the city for work, though differences in unemployment and vacancy rates across regions were not examined. Brueckner and Martin (1997) presented two spatial mismatch models, highlighting housing discrimination and transportation costs. However, with these models they did not discuss the difference in unemployment and vacancy rates between the suburbs and city centers.

The rise of search-and-matching theory provides the theoretical basis for solving this puzzle. Coulson et al. (2001) followed the approach of Diamond (1982), Mortensen (1982), and Pissarides (1985) to model search-and-matching behavior related to work information as a process in which individuals bear the costs and spend time looking for work. A search equilibrium model of two sectors under spatial segmentation was constructed. The difference between the cost of a worker's search and the cost of an enterprise's entry is sufficient to produce all the characteristic facts of a spatial mismatch. In addition, Wasmer and Zenou (2002) used a job search model to discuss how commuting distance prevented Blacks from accessing work information, thereby keeping them from work centers. In fact, very little information reached where black people live, which reduced their search efficiency and their chances of finding a job. The policy implication of the two models is that governments should develop policies to reduce inadequacies in job information to reduce search costs in cities.

In recent years, the analysis of labor market segmentation based on the spatial mismatch hypothesis has introduced factors such as land rent and housing choice, linking the labor market and real estate market and discussing the interactions of the three decision-making processes of labor mobility, employment, and housing. Wasmer and Zenou (2002, 2006) and Smith and Zenou (2003) have introduced land markets into the standard search-and-searching model, assuming that cities were single centers, i.e., that all jobs were located in the same location. The relationship between the land market and the labor market is achieved through search density. In fact, in these models, the commuting distance affects search density as it is impossible for more distant workers to obtain better job information. Since the overall variable influences the choice of a worker's place of employment, the result is that land market equilibrium depends on the overall variable (e.g., wages and labor market tightness). On the other hand, since the efficiency of the overall job match depends on the average position of the unemployed, the equilibrium of the labor market essentially depends on the equilibrium formation of the land market. Sato (2004) expands on this framework based on worker heterogeneity introduced according to the cost of training. The results are similar to those of the above model, assuming that all workers are trained after the fact and are homogeneous in terms of productivity. Yves Zenou (2009) introduced the land market into the Mortensen–Pissarides model and endogenized the job destruction rate in their discussion of post-ante worker heterogeneity. It was found that in the cities, workers with high productivity and high wages lived closer to work centers, had lower transportation costs but paid higher rents, and workers who were homogeneous *ex ante* were heterogeneous afterward in terms of production and were able to obtain the corresponding wage distribution. During the bargaining process, wages are set with a spatial element because the enterprise needed to compensate the workers for the cost of space. Unemployment rates and minimum productivity were low compared to non-spatial models, and job creation rates were high in non-spatial models as new friction arose in the labor market through transport costs and land rental in urban spaces.

iii. Applications of the search-and-matching theory in relation to social stratification in the labor market: An interpretation of the embedded nature of social networks

Research that applies job search theory to the labor market in connection with social networks seeks to explain the economic outcomes of micro-level behavior. Caliendo et al. (2010) analyzed the relationship between social networks and the job search behaviors of unemployed individuals. Individuals with larger networks experienced higher productivity in informal searches because of the useful information conveyed by networks in the course of their job searches. As a result, job search theory suggests that informal search channels are more commonly used by individuals with a larger network, and that informal searches can be more easily replaced by formal channels. Holzer (1988) expands on the standard job search model to consider multiple search methods in his analysis of why job seekers choose to look for jobs via their friends and relatives. He found that connecting with friends and relatives creates a high probability of job opportunities. Rees (1966) and Peter Doeringer and Michael Piore (1971) report that workers tend to recommend someone similar to themselves. Assuming that the labor market is based on reverse selection, employers seek referrals from highly competent employees. In contrast, Hall and Wanous (1981) argued that what job applicants receive from these referrals are realistic job trials. Wauthy and Zenou (2010) have attempted to combine job search and matching, social networks, and the dual structure of developing countries in their exploration of pay levels and unemployment. Therefore, the study of this issue is still in its infancy.

2.1.2 *The Objectives of Labor Market Evolution: Competitiveness and Integration*

Academic understanding of both labor market integration and segmentation can be said to have happened at the same time across the West. This was true especially in the Western developed countries that had experienced the construction and development of the market system during the Industrial Revolution—their segmented labor markets were gradually integrated over time, and the existing market economy systems already had labor markets that allocated labor resources using the price mechanism, and the free flow of labor was a natural phenomenon. With the increase of the rate of free labor flow, the result of the force of supply and demand between the markets—the degree of labor market integration remained at a high level, and therefore, early investigations of the integration of the labor market within a country occurred between the mid-nineteenth century to the early twentieth century, and subsequent research on the integration of modern labor markets paid particular attention to the integration of the labor market in the process of the integration of the United States, Mexico, and the European Union.

1. The integration of the labor market during the Industrial Revolution in the developed Western nations

Western countries such as Britain and France have historically undergone a transition from segmentation to integration. From the seventeenth to the eighteenth century in Europe, the labor market in the era of the industrial economy was segmented. Postel-Vinay (1994) has argued that the picture of the evolution of the French labor market in the nineteenth century does not support a narrative of a linear shift toward full integration, but rather, a narrative of one labor market replacing the other, each with its own specific integration and segmentation models. First, partly integrated labor markets have been embedded for centuries in complex cross-sectoral arrangements that successfully address seasonal variations in agricultural labor demand by allowing seasonal worker migration. Seasonality is an intrinsic attribute of agriculture in general and of farming in particular. It is also a major problem for farmers and is also relevant to many industries, especially those located in border regions. As the commercialization and specialization of agriculture intensified between 1750 and 1870, the formal competition between industry and agriculture for available workers during harvest season became increasingly intense. This competition produced a fairly high level of spatial and cross-sectoral integration within a short period of time. However, the integration of the seasonal labor market was disrupted by the subsequent agricultural depression and increased full-time employment of workers in industry and mining. As a result, the sectoral segmentation of the labor market became even more severe than before.

Hunt's empirical studies of market integration in the 1980s (1973, 1986) show that the wage gap between the urban and rural labor markets in England and Wales declined markedly in the second half of the nineteenth century, while George R. Boyer and Timothy J. Hatton (1994) found that the issue of market integration was more complex than what Hunt's analysis suggested. George R. Boyer's statistical analysis of wage differentials between agricultural workers and carpenters shows that regional wage differentials for carpenters declined in the second half of the nineteenth century, while regional wage differentials for agricultural workers increased. Meanwhile, Boyer divided England and Wales into six regions and tested the degree of market integration in each region by using a simple error correction model. The results of these tests indicate that some regions were more integrated than others. In particular, the agricultural labor market in the southwestern and eastern regions was less integrated than in other regions. Overall, Britain's labor market in 1914 was far from fully integrated.

In addition, using wage and price data for 23 occupations in 12 major cities, David and Rosenbloom (1990) examined the degree of geographic integration in the US labor market between 1870 and 1898. In contrast to the intensification of nationalization in other markets during the same period, the labor market was characterized by large and persistent differences in real wages within and between regions, and there is no doubt that labor markets were far from fully integrated in the late nineteenth century. Stanley Lebergott (1964) and Richard Easterlin (1960) found a long-term convergence of wage and income levels in the United States beginning in the middle of the nineteenth century, and a large body of literature suggests that labor market integration levels are also increasing in the pre-war period. On the other hand, the existence of a large north–south wage gap for most of the twentieth century was explained by the lack of labor market integration in those regions.

The research on labor market integration during this period focused on the comparison of wage differentials between agriculture and industry. The main features are: First, extensive use was made of historical data to observe changes in wage series between different regions as a way of judging the degree of integration; second, the analysis method of time series such as error correction methods was introduced to observe whether the wage gap had converged from the characteristics of time-series data, thereby evaluating the degree of integration of the labor market.

2. Research on labor market integration in modern developed countries in the West

On one hand, the formation of an industrialized economy promotes the progress of agricultural technology and frees up more agricultural labor for industrial production; on the other hand, given that the speed of technological progress is faster than that of human capital accumulation, more workers become unemployed due to the effect of capital substitution. The emergence of the tertiary sector has led to the movement of labor from the primary and secondary sectors to the tertiary sector, thus accelerating the degree of labor integration in these countries. After

World War II, the high-welfare policies of the European nations led to a high unemployment rate, and research in these countries focused more on policies and institutional analysis to address unemployment and social integration issues arising from immigration; at the same time, the United States maintained a low unemployment rate for a long time due to its flexible employment policy, and because of the geographical connectivity of the United States and Mexico, research on labor market integration focused on the degree of integration of the US and Mexico labor markets as a result of the North American Free Trade Agreement (NAFTA). Cortez and Islas-Camargo (2004) used the Hodrick–Prescott filter to estimate the cyclical composition of manufacturing employment in California and Texas and four cities on the US–Mexico border to study labor market dependencies between the two countries. The estimates from this study indicate greater labor market integration between northern Mexico and the southern United States after 1994. Raymond and Robertson (2000) created a three-region model with migration and transaction cost characteristics by taking the impact of domestic wage changes on neighboring countries and the changes in wages between the two places given assigned error as their evaluation criteria. Using a time series of total labor supply and demand and households, they showed that with NAFTA, the US and Mexican labor markets had become integrated and that wage shocks in the United States had the greatest impact on Mexico in the border cities, where wages converged toward US pay levels faster than in inland cities. For Mexico, cities with relatively concentrated foreign capital and labor mobility were more vulnerable to wage shocks and converged more quickly toward US pay levels. What Raymond and Robertson (2000) inferred from this is that among the forces driving labor market integration, such as commodity flows, capital flows, and labor mobility, labor flows were the main mechanisms.

Using time-series data on wages, the researchers mentioned above used the convergence of wage differentials to test for labor market integration in Western countries in the early and mid-to-late twentieth century. Foreign scholars in Europe, the United States, Mexico, Argentina, and other countries focused on the competitive labor market to discuss the subject of integration without linking integration and segmentation, indicating that wage determination mechanisms in the labor market are consistent.

2.2 Empirical Studies of the Evolution of Labor Markets Abroad: Tests for Segmentation

In addition to the aforementioned tests for labor market integration using time-series wage data, there has been even more research focusing on testing the segmentation of the labor market. The point-of-segmentation test is actually another way of testing for labor market integration. Leontaridi (1998) has systematically summarized the tests for labor market segmentation. They described three central components to segmentation theory, which form a series of tests that confirm or reject the segmentation hypothesis (Psacharopoulos, 1978; Ryan, 1984): First, there were less clearly identifiable segmentation in the labor market, and there was no clear and established statistical method in the existing discussion; second, lack of mobility impeded labor mobility between segments, which meant that the labor market was not cleared; and third, different employment and wage-setting mechanisms were in place in each segment, and neoclassical theories of human capital were less or less evident in the lower segments of the labor market.

Thus, the question of interest in empirical research is not whether the labor market is segmented, but how the segmentation occurs. Leontaridi (1998) has suggested that two methodological issues are important when conducting empirical tests for labor market segmentation: the first and foremost issue is how to define and describe segmentation in the labor market, and the second question is how to test the validity of a range of statistical and econometric techniques so as to test some or all of the above three hypotheses.

1. The definition of labor market segmentation

In the earliest studies, it was assumed that the labor market was divided into two sectors, the primary and the secondary sectors (Doeringer & Piore, 1971). This is a view that has been accepted in most cases even today. However, it was not clear from empirical tests what the boundaries of demarcation were, and to what degree segmentation had occurred. Early researchers tested for the dual nature of income distribution to find evidence of such duality, and unfortunately, there has been no evidence to prove that there was a dual structure concerning income distribution (Reich, 1984). Hence, since the 1970s, many researchers have adopted a large number of different criteria to define segmentation, primarily: First, defining segmentation by job characteristics. Differences in job characteristics, such as wages, job benefits, general and professional training, and job security, in the primary or secondary sectors have been used (Flatau & Lewis, 1993; Rosenberg & Rosenstein, 1980); secondly, segmentation has been defined by industry characteristics. Factors such as technology, organizational structure, nature of product demand, and labor union strength with the adoption of a dual-structure approach of central-versus-peripheral industrial sectors (McNabb, 1987; Reich et al., 1973) have been used to measure the segmentation between primary and secondary labor markets; Osterman (1975) has used subjective measure to arbitrarily divide jobs into secondary sectors and primary sectors with a two-tier structure based on the theory of a dual labor market structure. Robert Blauner (1964): Separating production and the final product in the sense of property rights, must not have an influence on general management policies, employment conditions, and indirect work processes. Third, occupational rating scales have been used to define segmentation. Psacharopoulos and Tinbergen (1978) and McNabb and Psacharopoulos (1981) have used occupational rating scales to assign individuals to either the primary or secondary labor market. Occupations were classified as "occupational hierarchy units" depending on the nature of the work and the employment status. This measures the degree of segmentation of the labor market.

2. Methods used to test for segmentation

Statistical and econometric tests proved two of the most important assumptions about labor market segmentation: (1) There is no reward for education, experience, or even experience in some cases for a significantly low-wage labor market, and workers have no on-the-job training; and (2) There are no economic barriers that prevent the movement of labor between sectors. The latter hypothesis is crucial to the theory of segmentation, as the existence of intersectoral mobility implies wage equalization between sectors, i.e., any differences will be the result only of competition between enterprises and workers. The following methods were used to study the abovementioned hypotheses: the SLM model with human capital factors included, the factor analysis method, the cluster analysis method, and the switching regression method.

2.3 Understanding the Evolution of China's Labor Market: From Segmentation to Integration

If we are to say that overseas scholars have gradually constructed a theory of labor market segmentation from their understanding of labor markets tending toward segmentation, then, the natural laboratory created by the application and practice of China's labor market theory since the advent of the policy reform and opening up is the showcase for the most complex kind of labor market segmentation and also serves as a realistic basis for the further development of labor market segmentation theory. The development of China's labor market is different from that of Western market economies, and has its own unique characteristics and mechanisms. It cannot be studied simply by applying the West's labor market segmentation theories.

After 1949, especially after 1958, the influence of the dual institutional factors of the planned economy system and the household registration system created a nearly "perfectly segmented" labor market in China before the introduction of the reform and opening up policy in 1978. Since then, economic transformation, the gradual relaxation of the household registration system, and the migration of a large number of rural laborers have gradually weakened the barriers that had led to complete segmentation of China's labor market. Due to these practical characteristics, most scholars have recognized the applicability of Lewis' practical and highly concise dual-structure theory within development economics (1954) to China, and accordingly, domestic scholars put forward the view that urban–rural division is the greatest division in China's labor market.

In China, the research on China's labor market has focused on the segmentation of the labor market, with the most representative views including: First, institutional segmentation is the most important feature of China's labor market segmentation. From 1949 on, China implemented a series of systems (especially the household registration system) which led to the division of China's labor market along the urban–rural line (Lai, 1996). Zhang Li and Yuan Lunqu (2007) have divided the labor market into two categories: The first is a labor market that is dominated by the government sector, which is characterized by a relatively average wage rate controlled by the government, in which the rate of return of human capital is neither considered nor underestimated. In essence, it is a non-market-oriented wage determination mechanism, which does not or rarely consider the supply of the labor market and the differences in employees' productivity. The other type is the market-oriented labor market, where labor resource allocation and wage determination are consistent with the labor market described by neoclassical economics. Enterprises increase or decrease their level of labor hiring according to the comparison of workers' marginal contribution with marginal cost, and pay according to their workers' marginal contribution or market wages. Guo Congbin (2004) has used the occupational socioeconomic status index (SEI) to divide the labor market into primary and secondary labor markets with reference to overseas work on dual labor market segmentation and sorted out their job characteristics and calculated their Mincer income function respectively. The study results showed that dual-system labor market segmentation existed in China, and that the higher the level of economic development in a region, the weaker the degree of labor market segmentation. Second, segmentation and non-uniformity and the multiple levels at play created a complex picture of segmentation of China's labor market, including:

1. A labor market in the state sector and the labor market in the non-state sector; the labor market in the state sector is further divided into the quasi-labor market for contract workers and the labor market for temporary and migrant workers; and the labor market in the non-state sector is divided into the urban labor market and the rural labor market (Li & Liu, 1999).
2. It was believed that in addition to the double duality between urban and rural areas, the urban labor market also had a dual nature, and the urban labor market was defined as consisting of two types of markets: the typical state-owned enterprises and new sectors. The former represented the traditional labor market, and the latter the type "produced in response to the logical process of market-oriented economic reforms (Cai, 1998)."
3. China's labor market had multiple, intersecting divisions, namely urban–rural segregation, regional segregation, sectoral segregation, the division between the formal labor market and subsidiary labor markets (Li 2002), and it was clearly divided into the rural employment sector, the urban informal employment sector and the urban formal employment sector (Xu, 2002).
4. China's labor market has also been divided into three segments: a perfectly competitive rural labor market, a perfectly competitive urban labor market, and an incompletely competitive urban labor

market. Then, on this basis, a two-stage rural–urban labor migration model was constructed, meaning that labor migrated from a perfectly competitive rural labor market to a perfectly competitive urban labor market, and from these two labor markets to an imperfectly competitive urban labor market (Zhu, 1999).

5. China's labor market has also been divided into four segments that correspond to the following four economic sectors: agriculture, the rural non-agricultural industries, urban formal industry, and urban informal industry. It was also believed that the rural non-agricultural industry only has an impact on the local rural labor, and with the deepening of the reform of state-owned enterprises and the streamlining of government institutionalization, the ability of the urban formal industry to absorb labor has continued to decline. At the same time, urban informal sector's role in absorbing labor has continued to grow (Zhu,, 2001).
6. China's labor market has the typical characteristics of duality, that is, the urban labor market has "internal–external duality" and "urban–rural duality," and there is a "nesting" relationship between the two types of duality with the "urban–rural duality" is embodied in the secondary part of the "internal and external duality (Zhang, 2009a)."
7. China has also been theorized to have a "three-tier dual" labor market, with the dualism on the first tier being agricultural and non-agricultural sectors in rural areas, between which labor flows are relatively free; on the second tier is the separation between the rural sector and the urban sector; and on the third tier is the separation between labor registered under the rural household registration system and labor registered under the urban household registration system within the urban sector.

Apart from discussing various types of market segmentation, in China, scholars have also divided the development of segmentation in China's labor market into four typical stages since 1978. The first stage was in the first few years of reform and opening up since 1978, where China's labor market was divided into the urban formal sector and the rural labor sector, and the urban formal sector was actually also divided. In the second stage, which occurred almost between 1985 and 1991, China's labor market was divided into an imperfectly competitive urban labor market, a perfectly competitive urban labor market, and a perfectly competitive rural labor market. In the third stage, which occurred almost between 1992 and 1997, China's labor market was similarly divided into an imperfectly competitive urban labor market, a perfectly competitive urban labor market, and a perfectly competitive rural sector. However, certain new features appeared in the imperfectly competitive labor market. In the fourth stage, after 1998, China's labor market has been divided into a perfectly competitive labor market in the cities and a perfectly competitive sector in the countryside (Cheng & Ma, 2003).

In China, empirical testing for labor market segmentation began in the 1990s, and has gone from discussing the household registration system, the ownership structure, and industry segmentation with the dual structure as a starting point to integrating all three. **First, early research focused on the divisions produced by the household registration system.** Xin Meng (2001) used Brown's decomposition method to break down data relating to the income gap and occupational division between rural migrant labor and urban residents and found that there were significant differences in occupational access and pay levels between the two groups, and that these differences could not be explained by differences in labor productivity but because rural migrant labor was discriminated. Yao Yang (2004), building on Roy's (1951) income maximization model, used cross-sectoral joint employment to estimate the structural industrial labor supply function, imposing various structural constraints on competitive markets, entry rationing, and time rationing using 1994 survey data from Yin County. As a result, they found that the competitive market model was significantly rejected. The entry of workers from the rural population into local industrial enterprises was constrained by entry and time rationing, and rapid industrial development did not bring about the integration of the local labor market in this region. Wang Meiyan (2005) has used the wage decomposition method to examine the relationship between the difference in employment opportunities and income in the urban labor market, and noted that the difference in household registration arrangements was the main reason for the difference. Zhang Yuan and Wang Hao (2011) used 2005 survey data of 1% population sample in Shanghai to divide the urban labor force into local workers, local rural residents, non-local workers, and non-local rural residents in order to study the regional and household registration discrimination against migrant workers and migrant rural residents in the urban labor market. It was found that compared to the local workers, non-local rural residents were discriminated against by 56.5%, and after this proportion was further broken down, 26% came from regional discrimination, 30.5% was a result of the household registration system, meaning that discrimination as a result of the household system was the main component.

Second, subsequent to the reform of state-owned enterprises, empirical research has focused on ownership structures where segmentation occurred. Dong et al. (2002) have looked at whether differences in ownership structure would lead to segmentation of the labor market in the process of China's economic transition, and whether market-oriented reforms reduced gender discrimination and discrimination due to the household registration system by using the OLS regression analysis of enterprise survey data collected in Dalian and Xiamen in 1998. It was found that among four different ownership structures (the state-owned enterprise, the township enterprises, the Sino-foreign joint venture, and the wholly foreign-owned enterprise), there was no difference in the returns to workers' education, and the returns were very high. Heckman 2SLS was also used to analyze the determinants of workers opting to work at foreign-funded enterprises and non-foreign-funded enterprises, and it was found that the wage factor did not play a significant role in these choices.

Third, industry segmentation has replaced ownership segmentation as the main kind of segmentation. Nie Sheng (2004) has proposed that there has been a coexistence of both segmentation by ownership and segmentation by industry in China's labor market, and data has shown that ownership segmentation gradually evolved into industry segmentation from the mid-1990s. Subsequently in 2004, Nie (2004) conducted a comprehensive analysis of the labor market segmentation on the part of employers since the advent of the policy of reform and opening up in China. He believed that there had been segmentation by both ownership and industry in China, and that in the mid-1990s, ownership segmentation in the labor market evolved to industry segmentation. This evolution is a unique phenomenon in the process of economic transition and also a process of growing market power. **Fourth, the convergence of industrial monopolies and ownership segregation has been the main trend of research in the past two years**. Sylvie Démurger et al. (2009) have analyzed the segmentation effect of China's urban labor market on the employee income gap between different sectors between 1995 and 2002 by using urban occupational income data in these years and the Oaxaca–Blinder decomposition method. The results of the analysis confirm that not only was there a segmentation effect in the determination of employee income between different sectors, and it was also still increasing. This was mainly reflected in a marked trend toward a widening wage gap between the monopoly sectors and the competitive sectors, as well as an increasing share of the intersectoral wage gap in the interpretation of market segregation factors. Ye Linxiang, Li Shi, and Luo Chuliang (2011) analyzed data from the first national economic census and found that industry monopoly and ownership were important factors that affected the enterprise wage gap, though the influence of ownership was greater than that of industry monopoly. The results show that industry monopoly is a prerequisite for wage gaps to occur and that ownership is a necessary condition for wage gaps, and the combination of the two would lead to growing enterprise wage gaps.

There has been relatively little research on labor market integration in China. Whether China's labor market can move from segmentation to integration with the goal of urban and rural labor market integration has been a key research focus for domestic researchers. Du Yang and Cai Fang (2004) have used data on China's industrial structure to prove that China's labor market has been moving toward integration since the introduction of the policy of reform and opening up. Gan Chunhua and Zhang Bingshen (2007) believed that the urban–rural labor market integration has been manifested in the integration of urban and rural labor markets and the integration of the intra-urban rural migrant workers and non-rural migrant workers' markets.

What the abovementioned studies tell us is that: First, Chinese scholars do not have a common standard for the division of the labor force, and lack a solid theoretical basis; further, the type of division is the method of analysis or ideas proposed for the phenomenon. Second, our understanding of empirical tests for labor market segmentation has improved over time with the changes in reality, but it is not difficult to see that all the main ideas discussed take the household registration system, ownership, and industry monopolies as the starting point. Apart from the literature in the past two years that combined the latter two factors, other studies more or less simply focused on a single factor. Third, research on labor market integration needs to be deepened both theoretically and empirically.

2.4 A Review of Theoretical and Empirical Research on the Movement from Labor Market Segmentation to Integration

The research on labor market segmentation in the Western nations has been ongoing for decades. However, market segmentation in these instances has been the product of perfectly competitive markets and has been primarily manifested in the division of primary and secondary labor markets due to production characteristics, or employment discrimination due to personal characteristics like ethnicity and gender. Outside of China, research on labor market segmentation and integration has often been a matter of divide-and-conquer. The theory of labor market segmentation based on a dual structure is centered on the influence of institutional and social factors on wage differentials between different sectors, and there have been attempts in recent research to link the dual structure to the framework of competitive equilibrium. The classical economic theory based on the competitive equilibrium describes wage differentials caused by varying individual characteristics, industry, and working conditions. In the past 30 years of research, as represented by the search-and-matching theory, the equilibrium framework of classical economics has been organically combined with the idea of market transaction to provide a theoretical basis for the integration of the classical and labor market segmentation theories as well as lay the theoretical foundation for the study of labor market moving from segmentation to integration with the equilibrium framework as the starting point. At the same time, on the empirical front, there have been breakthroughs in both statistics and econometrics, and empirically based research on labor market integration has focused on whether a region or an economy can be considered as integrated based on the convergence of wage time series.

The fragmentation of China's labor market, which is markedly different from what has happened in the Western countries, has arisen in the course of the transformation from a planned system to market mechanisms, and takes the form of institutional segmentation. This, and the fact that China is a major developing country, has made China's labor market more complex than those of other developing and even developed countries around the world. In China, research on labor market segmentation also emerged after the 1990s, and the analysis of this issue has been primarily based on the experience and theoretical framework of the Western countries, and there is a gap with reality in China. Therefore, thought on segmentation in China's labor market has been highly varied. In addition, lack of data is also a major constraint to the research on this issue. Empirical research has been gradually carried out from point to point, and our understanding of whether the segmentation of the labor market can be transformed into integration has also been limited. Therefore, the study of this issue should be combined with China's reality, and pay close attention to the gap between reality and theory.

2.5 Basic Concepts

It is necessary that we analyze the concepts of integration (segmentation) and equilibrium in the evolution of the labor market. Understanding the connotation and denotation of integration, a concept that is the opposite of segmentation, is as important as analyzing the connotation and denotation of segmentation.

2.5.1 Distinction Between the Concepts of Market Integration and Equilibrium

Market integration is the opposite of market segmentation. The idea of market integration, which stands as the opposite of segmentation, has often been defined as one market being influenced by another through the Walrasian shift of excess demand. The analysis of commodity market integration holds that against the background of macroeconomic opening, the "law of one price" (LOP) can be used to describe the degree of market integration and whether the market is fully integrated or whether the expectations of the law of one price have been realized. The law of one price aiming at competitive equilibrium is the result of competition in the spatial market with the condition of perfect competition, where there is no arbitrage between markets. Taking this as a criterion for market integration indicates the ideal trend of trade or flow of goods and services between markets, though this law cannot reflect actual trade or flow behavior (Baumol & Gomory, 1992). The "tradability" of goods or services is reflected in the transfer of Walrasian excess demand from one market to another. When markets are integrated, supply and demand in one market can affect prices and/or volumes in another, and positive trade flows where tradability is available are sufficient to justify spatial market integration, though this does not necessarily require equal prices across markets.

Therefore, while market integration is closely related to "tradability" or "competitiveness," which reflects the behavior of commodity trading, the concept does not equal equilibrium, because equilibrium means no-arbitrage behavior between markets. Barrett (2002) has argued that the two markets i and j are competitively balanced over a long term, which means that the margin benefit of internal market arbitrage is 0. When $p_{it} \leq \tau(p_{it}, p_{jt}, C_{jt}) + p_{jt}$, p_{it} is the price in i at t time, τ is the transaction cost of spatial arbitrage. This is a function of the price and transportation cost C_{jt} between the two locations. The equilibrium conditions in which trade takes place is when, in the abovementioned formula, the left side is equal to the right side. When the two markets are integrated and competitively balanced in the long run, they can be considered "fully integrated," a special case that is the subject of much attention in existing literature. The LOP test is a test of the fully integrated hypothesis, not a test of integration (possibly incomplete) or perfect competition (possibly segmented). Therefore, most of the literature on the integration of spatial markets is not focused on conceptual analysis but on competition equilibrium and Pareto efficiency. Markets are integrated when they are perfectly competitive or when trade barriers are ineffective, regardless of whether there is physical logistics between markets or whether prices in one market respond to shocks in another.

Therefore, when there is no arbitrage between markets, the market is in equilibrium; the market integration emphasizes the interaction of markets due to Walrasian transitions in the presence of excess demand; and the usual law of one price is used to test complete integration, and the integration of commodity markets emphasizes spatial integration more. We can argue that the intermarket tradability of commodities is a sufficient condition for market integration, and that a competitive equilibrium is a necessary rather than a sufficient condition for full market integration.

2.5.2 Distinction Between the Concepts of Labor Market Integration and Equilibrium

In our opinion, the biggest difference between the labor market and the commodity market is whether, in the price formation mechanism, the bargaining actor with the enterprise is separate from the traded good itself. In the labor market, workers are both bargaining actors who bargain with enterprises and carriers of labor price, namely, wage. They two are inseparable; however, in the commodity market, they two are separate. The "tradable goods" in the labor market are inseparable from the transaction actors on the supply side, and thus have the following characteristics: (1) The spatial mobility of "tradable goods" in the labor market is lower than that in the commodity market; (2) The price of "tradable goods" in the labor market—the pay level of labor is inelastic; and (3) Unlike the asociality of commodities, the sociality of workers in the labor market makes their mobility subject to the constraints of the social structure. Thus, labor market integration analysis is much more complicated than commodity market integration analysis.

Pissarides (2000) considers trade in the labor market as a decentralized economic activity. It is uncoordinated, time-consuming, and has high sunk and bargaining costs for both enterprises and workers. Enterprises and workers must consume considerable resources prior to job creation, goods production, and job rent payments, which are not characteristic of the Walrasian labor market. The concept of labor market integration must therefore be defined with the heterogeneity, sociality, and mobility of workers taken into account. Given that the labor supply is rigid and inelastic, drawing on the analytical thinking of market integration, we can suppose that labor market integration is the realization of the transfer of excess labor demand and excess supply willingness between different markets with the condition of search friction (i.e., transaction costs) in the labor market. When markets are integrated, supply and demand in one market can affect prices and/or labor mobility in another market. The law of one price in competitive equilibrium, that is, the convergence of pay levels is a necessary condition for labor market integration, while the free flow of labor between different markets is a sufficient condition for integration. We believe that the labor market is fully integrated when the two conditions are met at the same time. Otherwise, as long as there is the possibility of arbitrage, there will be no complete integration, and the labor market will always be segmented.

CHAPTER 3

The Evolution of China's Labor Market from Segmentation to Integration: An Outline and the Reality

In contrast to the development of the labor market in the Western countries, which consider the existence of segmentation under unified and competitive conditions, in China the allocation of labor resources has gone from the planned economy mode to market conditions. The construction of the labor market started from the highly unified arrangement of labor resource allocation and wage determination during the planned economy period. Therefore, many scholars believe that there had been no labor market in China since the founding of the People's Republic of China, especially the implementation of the household registration system in 1958, till the implementation of the reform and opening up. To sort out and examine the evolution of China's labor market, this paper holds that China's labor market prior to the introduction of the policy of reform and opening up was an almost completely segmented labor market due to the influence of the system. In the more than 60 years since the founding of the People's Republic of China, China's labor market has undergone changes from complete segmentation to multi-tiered segmentation and gradually, toward integration in the future.

Y. Chen, *China's Labor Market in the Transition*,
https://doi.org/10.1007/978-981-99-9160-0_3

3.1 The "Complete Segmentation" of China's Labor Market Prior to the Marketization

At present, the prevailing view in Chinese academia is that there was no labor market in China before the introduction of the policy of reform and opening up. The reason is that the planned economy fundamentally excluded the market. For the convenience of analysis and the need to examine the changes in the time series of labor resource allocation, this paper considers the labor market before reform and opening up to be an extreme labor market pattern that lacked the market competition mechanism. It is believed that, in terms of the allocation of labor resources—in terms of the volume of employment and the mechanism of wage formation—it is the functioning of the system that precludes the complete segmentation of the labor market by market mechanisms. The planned economy and the household registration system were the most important institutional factors in the segmentation of the labor market before China's reform and opening up. The effect of the former was to ensure the full employment of the urban labor force while lowering the pay level, to smooth out the rate of return for the human capital and the effort level of the heterogeneous labor force, and to fix the pay level between different industries or occupations as undifferentiated wages; the effect of the latter was to keep rural residents in the countryside and on the land, as well as to minimize labor mobility between different industries, occupations, regions, and urban and rural areas (with essentially zero mobility) while efforts to accelerate early and primary industrialization were underway.

3.1.1 Labor Prices in a Planned Economy

China's traditional economic system began with the strategy of prioritizing the development of heavy industry as its logical starting point. At a time when capital was scarce, the implementation of the strategy to prioritize capital-intensive heavy industry required government actions to artificially reduce the prices of various production resources, factors of production, and goods in order to reduce production costs, and allocate resources through highly centralized planning. Within this planned economic system, labor force employment was an important element of the long-term, medium-term, and even short-term plans for national economic development. For example, in the typical planning process, emphasis is placed on the integration and balance of the national economy, and the balance of human power, material, and financial resources which are broken down into five areas: finance, credit, foreign exchange, materials, and labor.

Before 1956, China's labor market came into being from scratch. The state-run economy and its various economic components coexisted under state leadership. There was no complete wage system, though the original wage system did coexist with the supply system in the early days of the founding of the People's Republic of China. In other words, the state economy was a supply-in-kind economy while in the private economy the old wage system continued to exist. At the first National Wage Conference in 1950, it was made clear that "wage points" were to be the yardstick for the calculation for wages across the country. The "Measures for a Standard Unit of Calculation for wages Across China (Draft)" formulated in 1951 specified the types and quantities of physical goods to be paid out at each wage point that could then be converted to monetary wages for employees. Special allowances were also granted to workers in designated "special" areas. It was on this basis that wage reform was carried out between 1951 and 1953, and a wage grade system for workers in state-owned enterprises was established. In the same period, when efforts were underway to promote wage reform in state-owned enterprises while retaining the original wage system of the private economy, a series of measures were introduced to promote the establishment of labor-management consultation conferences in private enterprises to realize the transformation of private ownership into public ownership.

The year 1956 was a watershed year in which the wage grade system was created. The "Decision on Wage Reforms"[1] promulgated by the State

[1] The 1956 "Decision on Wage Reforms" has three distinct features: (1) The system of "wage points" and price allowances was abolished, and wages are directly set in monetary terms. The country was divided into 16 wage zones and monetary wage standards by industry. For areas with high price levels, additional allowances were put in place. (2) Improvements were made to the graded wage system for workers. Various wage grades were established according to the characteristics of the production technology of workers in different industries. (3) Improvements were made to the graded wage system for enterprise staff and agency staff with job grades and wage standards determined by what posts they held. The country was divided into 11 zones in terms wage standards, and separate standards were used for technical personnel and administrative personnel. A job

Council put in place a standard for the various types of wages existing at the time and laid the foundation for the wage system in the planned economy period. The system of "wage points" and special allowances was abolished, and a uniform wage standard, which was directly set in monetary terms, was fully implemented. The labor market was virtually eliminated. During the Cultural Revolution that occurred between 1966 and 1976, many collectively owned enterprises, which were basically cooperatives, were established by various neighborhoods and commune and became more like local state-owned enterprises in terms of their characteristics. Therefore, until 1978, the wages of Chinese enterprises were determined by the state-directed plan, and a singular, direct division of labor was implemented throughout society. All wage distribution plans are drawn up by the central authorities, and the local authorities, enterprises, and departments were only the executors of the central authorities' plans. The wage management model in enterprises was based on the annual wage plan, and the macro-control model of total wages was directly approved by the competent government organs.

On one hand, the wage grade system adopted by the state facilitated direct intervention in individual wage income to help realize an overall adjustment of total wages and to prevent the accumulation of wages from crowding out and undermining the planned goals. However, the implementation of this wage system also made the distribution relationship between the state and enterprises a one-size-fits-all one. State-owned enterprises lacked the autonomy in production and operations, and were required to turn over all profits to the state. With the egalitarian "big pot of rice" in place, motivation for individual workers was lacking, and the phenomenon of "skiving" and "time-wasting" workers was a common one. This, together with the lack of an institutionalized wage growth mechanism, caused pay levels to be more or less frozen during the Cultural Revolution period.

Altogether, the egalitarian wage grade system prior to 1978 had three notable characteristics as it ensured that there was no difference in labor income levels: **First, there was no direct and significant relationship**

rank system was also implemented. For example, administrative personnel were divided into 30 grades; technical personnel in state organs were divided into 18 grades; and a 13-grade wage system was implemented for scientific research personnel and university teaching personnel.

between the price of labor and labor supply and demand. The classical theory of labor economics considers equilibrium in the labor market as the "offsetting" of the conflicting desires of workers and enterprises, and this is how the level of wages and employment observed in the labor market are determined. However, during the planned economy period, although there were a certain number of "informally employed groups," the recruitment process also required the preparation of plans. With the government's many regulations on employment and labor remuneration, a legal labor market did not exist, and employment and wages were fixed by the government with no direct and significant connection with the market. **Second, there was no direct and significant relationship between the price of labor and human capital investment within the framework of the planned economy**. Human capital theory emphasizes the role of education and training, which have a decisive effect when it comes to income. The level of wages in the workforce is considered to be the result of the return on investment in the worker's human capital. Despite the fact that educational attainment is stipulated by the wage system to obtain corresponding pay level, there was no direct and significant correlation between workers' remuneration and individual investment in human capital, since workers' wages were fixed. **Third, labor prices in a planned economy are not directly and significantly linked to labor productivity**. The wage-efficiency theory points out that the higher the worker's effort in the production process, the higher the productivity, and the higher the level of remuneration. wages during the planned economy period were fixed, meaning that the incentive function of wages was inhibited, and state-owned enterprises lacked vitality and efficiency.

3.1.2 Labor Mobility Within the Household Registration System

The household registration system[2] has long been in existence, and as a secondary social system, it has had a major impact on social relations, especially urban–rural relations. The initial forms of the urban and rural

[2] The Chinese household registration system is established based on household registration and management. It includes the routine population registration and reporting system, the resident household registration or identity registration and management system, and the social and economic management system related to household registration in terms of employment, education, security, and migration (Lu 2002).

household registration and management systems and the corresponding methods came into being between 1953 and 1957. Then, in 1958, the Standing Committee of the National People's Congress passed the "Regulations of the People's Republic of China on Household Registration," which specified that the household registration management system was to be implemented nationwide. The movement of urban and rural populations was restricted through national law, regulations, and various systems, marking the formal formation of the unified household registration system in urban and rural areas across the country.

Strictly speaking, the 1958 ordinance was only at the first level, and its impact may have been largely indirect rather than direct. According to the government document, the main goal of household registration management was "to prove citizenship and facilitate citizens to exercise their rights and perform their obligations; to provide population data for the construction of the national economy, culture, and national defense; and to help identify and prevent counter-revolutionary and various criminal activities." As such, early on, the household registration system did not strictly control citizens' free movement. To a large extent, the people still enjoyed the freedom to make changes to their household registration location, relocate, and transfer their household registration, and the system was more or less based on the principle of individual willingness. Only article 10 of the Regulations stipulated that, in order to move from rural areas to cities, residents must have a school admission certificate, an employment certificate issued by the municipal labor department, or a certificate of admission issued by the municipal household registration authority. Thus, the purpose of household registration was to systematically control the number of "legal" urban households. However, the official launch of the industrialization process with heavy industry as the main development goal would inevitably lead to greater demand for labor. Between 1949 and 1957, 70 to 80 percent of the total increase in the urban population was made up of rural–urban migration, similar to the general situation in developing countries. However, as the urban population grew and the cost of labor increased, the government had to take administrative and economic measures to control as much as possible the flow of rural residents to the cities. Since the implementation of the household registration system in 1958, migration had been severely restricted. In particular, since 1961, the government called for a reduction in the number of workers in cities, and planned to reduce the urban population by more than 20 million within three years. In 1961, more than 10 million workers were repatriated. In 1962, the rural–urban net migration rate was −11.58 percent, and between 1961 and 1965, the urban population declined by an average of 4.41 percent per annum. At the same time, the government also made a number of additions to the household registration system. For example, in 1960, the control of daily necessities and consumer goods was strengthened, and the urban grain ration supply system and the daily commodity stamp-based supply system were strictly implemented. In 1966, in order to more effectively prevent rural residents from entering the city, the state began to adopt new measures to strictly control the recruitment of new workers by the collectively owned enterprises and institutions in the cities. The centralized labor allocation system was implemented in urban areas to limit the growth of legal household registrations in these areas.

During this period, the household registration system restricted the movement of labor between urban and rural areas via two channels. **The first channel: The centralized labor allocation system**. Through this measure, the normal channels for rural residents to enter the cities were controlled, as they would not be legally registered in the city if they do not enter the city as a state employee. **The second channel: The control system for the allocation of urban day-to-day living resources corresponding to household registration**. Unauthorized entrants to cities would struggle to survive in towns as various day-to-day living resources, such as food stamps, oil stamps, and cloth stamps were distributed through ticket systems that could only be accessed by legal residents. These two channels, together with the system of travel permits and accommodation registration, were the key measures in what were strict controls on relocation or movement without endorsement by the authorities. Therefore, it was very difficult for individuals to stay and live in the cities, let alone seek work in cities, unless it was for collective business or acceptable personal reasons. Between 1961 and 1976, the urban and rural structures of Chinese society were basically separated, and the process of urbanization was more or less stagnant.

3.1.3 Summary

Between 1949 and 1978, under the dual influence of the planned economy and the household registration system, the pay level was completely separated from labor supply and demand, the return on investment in human capital, and the labor productivity of workers; the employment system worked hand in hand with the household registration system and controls over the allocation of day-to-day living resources, resulted in no or low mobility of labor between urban and rural areas, regions, and sectors. In such circumstances, the supply and demand of the labor market and its pricing were completely regulated by the government in a highly centralized manner, and there was no labor market in the classical economics sense. Within the planned economic system, what was reflected in this period includes: First, labor mobility between cities and sectors was low; second, the price of labor (pay levels) reflected neither supply and demand in the labor market nor the return on investment in human capital; and third, given the egalitarian income distribution model, there was essentially zero difference except for the difference between grades. These three typical characteristics show that the almost complete restriction on urban and rural labor mobility in China before the marketization stage was close to a complete division of the labor market. However, the convergence of pay levels within the planned economy was different from the segmentation characteristics of the labor market, so it is difficult to use the evaluation standard of mainstream economics for labor market segmentation. Combining the viewpoints of development economics and institutional economics, this paper holds that the segmentation of China's labor market within the planned economy was one of nearly "complete segmentation," and it is precisely because of this that the near stagnation of labor mobility and the near indifference of income levels make the starting point of labor market construction in China different from other countries. Therefore, what is shown is the development process of the labor market with Chinese characteristics.

3.2 The Early Years of Market-Oriented Reform (1978–1991): From "Complete Segmentation" to Gradual Easing

The issues caused by the traditional planned economy, such as low wages, high accumulation, and low consumption, finally came to the fore. In 1978, at the Third Plenary Session of the 11th Central Committee of the Communist Party of China, the idea of focusing on the planned economy and attaching importance to market regulation as an auxiliary role was put forward. This was a departure from the traditional system where the economy was completely controlled by government programs. The initial stage of reform and opening up was a stage in which labor market policies were gradually relaxed from complete control to diversification. In this stage, the household registration system began to become less stringent, and the wage pricing mechanism began to become more flexible. These indicators reflect the gradual relaxation of the state of complete division of labor planning allocation to the stage of market allocation.

3.2.1 Wage Determination Mechanisms for the Transition from a Traditional Planned Economy to a Market Economy

At the beginning of reform and opening up, the urban economic system did not change much compared to the planned economic period. With the rural contract responsibility system being the starting point for reform, work began to promote the reform of the urban resource allocation method. However, urban enterprises have not yet become substantially independent operating units, and state-owned enterprises were the main vehicles of wage reform. In 1978, the reform measure of "delegating power and transferring profits" was adopted for state-owned enterprises, and the wage distribution system was reformed accordingly. Table 3.1 shows the main course of the reform of the wage system in the early stage of reform and opening up. The landmark event at this stage was the release of the 1985 "Notice on the Reform of State-Owned Enterprises." According to this notice, state-owned enterprises were to implement the method of linking wages to productivity. The significance of the reform lies in the introduction of a market mechanism in the determination of total wages and the establishment of a mutual promotion-and-restriction relationship between total enterprise wages and the results of production and operation, thus breaking the principle of equal distribution and widening the wage gap between different enterprises due to varying benefits.

Wage reform in the early stages of reform and opening up can be divided into two periods: In the first period (1978–1984), the principle of distribution according to work done was restored, and it was also the initial period for the reform of the wage distribution system. During this period, the state increased the wages of employees working in enterprises, organs, and public institutions on five occasions, after a long period of stagnation on the wages of employees; the bonus and piece-rate wage systems were restored for enterprises; and enterprises with approval

Table 3.1 Wage system reforms in China between 1978 and 1991

Year	*Wage system*
1978	State-owned enterprises trial incentive and piece-rate wage system
1982	"Regulations on Rewards and Punishments for Enterprise Employees," funding program management, all regions and departments barred from exceeding the total direct bonus control level without the prior consent of the Ministry of Labor and Personnel and the State Planning Commission
1983	The "two-step reform of profits and taxes" would clarify the economic responsibilities of enterprises to the state through the statutory form of taxation. In the first step, the state gave up control over the total amount of corporate bonuses, though caps were still retained for companies with better benefits and more incentive funds; in the second step, caps were abolished in the reform of profits and taxes such that bonuses were completely linked to the economic gains of enterprises and enterprises gained considerable autonomy in how they would use their funds internally
1984	At the Third Plenary Session of the 12th Central Committee, the "Decision on the Reform of the Economic System" was adopted. The Decision stipulates that reforms that "better link the wages of enterprise employees with the improvement of enterprise economic benefits" should be undertaken and that bonuses were to be linked to the economic benefits of enterprises, with "no cap on the top, and the levying of a bonus tax"
1985	According to the "Notice on the Reform of State-Owned Enterprises' wages," the total wages of employees of state-owned enterprises were to be linked to the economic gains of enterprises. The basic philosophy of this reform was to separate enterprise wages from the pay levels of administrative bodies (including public institutions). The total amount of the enterprise's wages was to be linked to the taxes and profits handed over to the state, and the internal wage distribution was to be handled by the enterprise itself as it deemed fit. On the other hand, administrative organs and public institutions would continue to apply the wage system prescribed by the state. In particular, the administrative organs used the system of "structural wages," which included basic wages, job responsibility wages, length-of-service wages, and bonuses
1986	Clear statement that the enterprise can decide the distribution form and method by itself within the scope of the total wages and policies stipulated by the state; "The 'Four Interim Provisions' on the Reform of the Labor System"[3]
1988	Introduction of the piece-rate and flat-rate wage systems

Sources Cai Fang (2008) and Hu Fangwen (2005)

[3] The "Four Interim Provisions" on the reform of the labor system were: The "Interim Provisions on the Implementation of Labor Contracts at State-Owned Enterprises," the "Interim Provisions on the Recruitment of Workers by State-Owned Enterprises," the "Interim Provisions on the Dismissal of Workers Found to Have Breached Discipline at State-owned Enterprises," and the "Interim Provisions on Unemployment Insurance for State-Owned Enterprises."

were allowed to simplify and consolidate their wage standards. In a few enterprises, new measures such as floating (i.e., non-fixed) wages and self-funded floating raises were tried out. In the second period (1985–1991), the hammer was taken to two "big pots of rice"[4] as adjustments were made to distribution relationships. With the reform of the planned economy system, state-owned enterprises generally adopted the responsibility system for contract management, and introduced major reforms in wage distribution in conjunction with the second tax for profit reform. The main ones are as follows: First, the method of linking the total wages of enterprises to economic gains was implemented nationwide, and efforts were made to explore the use of regional and industry wage standards to control the total wages of enterprises, to decouple from the wage distribution of government agencies and public institutions, and to implement a classified and graded system of wage management. Second, the state issued the reference wage standard for state-owned enterprises to break up the ossified eight-level wage system. Many enterprises experimented with a number of new basic wage systems such as the floating wage system, the structural wage system, and the job responsibility wage system, and internally various new forms of distribution proliferated. Third, state organs and public institutions undertook reforms of the existing duty grade wage system and introduced a system of structural wages based mainly on job responsibility wages. Fourth, measures to adjust redistribution were also introduced. Payroll adjustment taxes, bonus taxes, and personal income adjustment taxes were included. However, from the start, these measures failed to produce their intended results.

The key idea for reform at this stage was to try to change the system of distribution to more clearly reflect the productivity of workers, and in 1985, the "work-efficiency linkage system" became the turning point in the history of the income distribution mechanism. It allowed enterprises greater autonomy in distribution, and in addition to the direct control of the total wages of enterprises by the state, as long as they are within the scope of the approved total wages, enterprises could more or less formulate wages according to the market mechanism.

[4] The two "big pots of rice" referred to how workers could rely on the enterprise for their livelihood, and how enterprises could rely on the state for their continued existence. ("Enterprise" here primarily refers to state-owned enterprise.).

However, there were two main problems at this stage of reform. First, the use of the traditional prescriptive wage scheme exposed certain negative effects, which are the "leaking" of wages and the fact that enterprises tended to "report only profits and not losses."[5] As a result, contradictions and frictions between the old and new mechanisms occurred shortly after the implementation of the work-efficiency linkage system, leading to a serious disconnect between enterprise wage plans and the realities of the region, industry, and enterprise. Zhong Jiyin (1990), who looked at data on China's labor wages taken from a sample survey of 403 state-owned enterprises between 1978 and 1987, found that the degree of correlation between the total wages at these enterprises and the economic gains of these enterprises was the highest in 1985 and then rapidly declined.

Secondly, wage reform in this period was designed to enable enterprises to allocate wages according to their benefits and to open up differences in wages between different enterprises with varying benefits. In practice, however, the wage reform of 1985 did not improve the internal allocation mechanism of enterprises, and the wage gaps between all categories of workers in the state sectors were not widened but instead narrowed. According to Zhang Minglong (2000), at that time, the proportion of employees' basic wages, job responsibility wages, and length-of-service wages in their total wages was on the decline, while the proportion of various bonuses and allowances was growing. By 1988, income from bonuses and allowances accounted for about 40 percent of the total wages of employees in the state sectors. Allowances for each employee (who received the same amounts across the board) included cleaning allowances, book allowances, transportation allowances, non-staple food subsidies, and price subsidies; as for bonuses, in state organs and public

[5] According to Cai Fang (2008), linking employees' wage to company performance had two major drawbacks. First, it encourages off-the-books compensations. When their total expenditure toward wage is subject to a rigid ceiling imposed by the government, companies have an incentive to breach such constraint. They may, by capitalizing on their de facto operational right, strengthen "insider control" and hand out cash or in-kind payments to employees off the books, resulting in wage inflation that is effectively concealed. Second, it encourages companies to link employees' wages to corporate performance selectively, i.e., only if the company made profits but not if they suffered losses. Profitable enterprises complied with such linkage and saw their overall wage grow, but enterprises that suffered losses tended to resist the linkage. But since their total expenditure toward wage is set by the government, these companies would haggle with the authorities in order to make sure their employees' wages would grow despite revenue losses.

institutions they were basically evenly distributed, as in 50 percent to 70 percent of enterprises. Moreover, in terms of labor force participation, the four transitional provisions on labor force participation in 1986 produced little change. Qi Liangshu's study (2005) shows that the reform of the labor and employment system in 1986 also did not achieve significant results.

As such, the top-down wage determination mechanism reform in the early stage of the reform had the following characteristics: First, the government-led labor system had a profound effect on the wage determination mechanism across the country. In particular, the "work-efficiency linkage system" still exists in large and mid-sized state-owned enterprises. Second, the way the market allocates labor resources was beginning to be considered in the distribution system, and the pay level of state-owned enterprises was beginning to be linked to the productivity of workers. However, the graded wage system under the leadership of the government still played a role, and the relationship between pay level and labor supply and demand and human capital investment level was not obvious. Third, the non-public economic component had yet to enter policy considerations.

3.2.2 *Labor Mobility as the Household Registration System was Relaxed: From Strict Control to Mobility with Permission*

This stage of labor mobility can also be divided into two periods: The first was the period of strict control (1978–1983), during which the household registration system and the employment system of urban and rural separation did not fundamentally change at the beginning of reform, and labor mobility was still strictly controlled. The second was the period of orderly guidance (1984–1991). During this period, the household registration system was relaxed, and a considerable amount of rural surplus labor began to transfer to non-agricultural industries, small towns, and even large and mid-sized cities. Labor became more mobile.

On the policy level, between 1978 and 1984, the household contract responsibility system led to the rapid development of agricultural production. The surplus rural labor became increasingly obvious, and with the national economy in the recovery period, the employment of a large number of individuals in the urban labor force was an issue that had to be tackled as well. Strict restrictive policies remained in place. As shown in Table 3.2, the free movement of rural labor between urban and rural areas was severely restricted during this period, and the urban–rural divide was very clear. Correspondingly, the employment system was clearly showing the characteristics of urban–rural division. At the same time, the employment of residents with urban household registration was completely arranged by the state, and most of them were employed in state-owned and collectively owned enterprises and public institutions. The wages and security benefits at the state-owned enterprises and public institutions were better than those of collectively owned enterprises, and segmentation could also be seen within the urban labor market. Between 1981 and 1991, a series of incentive policies and measures were introduced to allow rural labor to flow into urban non-agricultural employment (as shown in Table 3.2). For example, migrant workers who worked, engaged in business, and provided services were allowed to take care of their own rations and settle in towns. Rural collectives and individual rural residents were permitted to engage in long-distance goods transportation and trading for what was known as the "Three Types of Agricultural and Sideline Products" as well as other agricultural and sideline products that were allowed to trade. These developments marked the official relaxation of the urban–rural system of strict division.

As we can see from Fig. 3.1, which contains data on the floating urban population in China and their employment status between 1981 and 1991, in 1985, rural–urban labor mobility grew significantly and then continued to rapidly grow in the succeeding four years. Then, it maintained a steady growth after a slight decline in 1989. As we look at the timing of policy adjustments shown in Table 3.2, it is clear that the increases or decreases in labor mobility between 1981 and 1991 were closely related to whether policy was being relaxed or tightened. On the other hand, a large movement of labor can be observed in terms of the number of changes in the agricultural labor force. Between 1978 and 1988, the share of agricultural labor in the non-state labor force dropped rapidly from 70.5 percent to 59.3 percent, with an average annual decline of 1.72 percentage points, compared to an average decline of only 0.65 percent in the preceding 26 years.

Due to the gradual phasing out of the day-to-day living resource allocation system related to household registration in the early stage of reform and opening up, as well as the massive release of rural surplus labor, labor mobility at this stage had the following characteristics: First, the employment channel of "unified contract and distribution" was still the choice when it came to urban employment. Intra-urban labor mobility was

Table 3.2 Highlights of policies on labor mobility and employment in state-owned enterprises, 1978–1991

Year	*Issuing authority*	*Document name*	*Key policy thrusts*
1980	CPC Central Committee, the State Council	"Opinions on Further Work in the Area of Urban Labor and Employment"	The role of labor service companies was fully recognized as an important measure for the tackling of the employment issue The "three-in-one" employment policy was proposed. According to the policy, it would be necessary to actively create conditions for employment and to work on promoting employment through labor department recommendations, privately organized employment initiatives, and individual job-seeking all at the same time within the ambit of overall planning and guidance by the state Surplus agricultural labor should be absorbed through the development of commune and brigade-run enterprises and joint-venture enterprises in urban and rural areas, and new small towns should be built gradually. Efforts were to be made to control the inflow of rural residents into large and mid-sized cities and to control the increase in food consumption. Rural workers who fell outside planned headcounts were to be reduced in number and sent back. When recruiting from the countryside was truly necessary, strict control was to be exercised, and approval was to be obtained from the people's government of the province (or municipality or autonomous region)

(continued)

Table 3.2 (continued)

Year	*Issuing authority*	*Document name*	*Key policy thrusts*
October 1981	CPC Central Committee, the State Council	"Provisions on Opening Up New Pathways, Revitalizing the Economy, and Solving the Employment Problem in Urban Areas"	Through the development of a greater array of business operations and the establishment of commune and brigade-run enterprises, the surplus rural labor would be properly arranged locally and prevented from flooding into the towns and cities. Migration of the rural population and labor force into the towns and cities was to be strictly controlled in accordance with existing policies. Rural residents seeking to move into the towns and cities were to be required to abide by the relevant review and approval procedures, and the departments of public security, food, and labor were to perform the corresponding tasks and cooperate with each other in a concerted manner. The use of rural labor was to be strictly controlled, and efforts should be made to continue to withdraw unplanned rural labor

Year	*Issuing authority*	*Document name*	*Key policy thrusts*
December 1981	The State Council	"Circular on the Strict Control of Rural Labor Entering Urban Areas and the Conversion of the Agricultural Population into a Non-Agricultural Population"	(1) Strict controls on recruitment from the countryside; (2) Serious efforts to "clean up" the rural labor used by enterprises and public institutions; efforts to strengthen the household registration and food management systems
1983	Ministry of Labor and Human Resources	"Notice on the Trial Implementation of the Labor Contract System"	Trial implementation of the labor contract system with newly recruited workers, the "new system for new employees, the old system for the existing employees" in what would be a period of transition
January 1984	CPC Central Committee	"Notice on Rural Work on in 1984"	To allow rural residents engaged in labor, business, and services to take care of their own rations and settle in towns

(continued)

Table 3.2 (continued)

Year	*Issuing authority*	*Document name*	*Key policy thrusts*
October 13, 1984	State Council	"Notice on the Entry into Towns and Settlements of Rural Residents"	Rural residents entering towns for labor, business, and services play an important role in promoting the development of towns and boosting the economy of urban and rural areas, and efforts should be made to support them Public security agencies were to grant permanent residence registration to rural residents and their family members who apply to work or engage in business or services in the town, who have a fixed residence in the town and have the ability to operate or who have worked in a township enterprise or institution for a long period of time, complete the household registration procedures in a timely manner, and issue to these residents the "Household Registration Book for Self-Managed Rations." These residents were to be counted as part of the non-agricultural population Food agencies were to ensure the supply of various grains and oil, and were permitted to issue the "Permit for the Supply of Grain and Oil at Increased Prices." Local governments were to make the building, buying, and renting of houses easier

Year	*Issuing authority*	*Document name*	*Key policy thrusts*
January 1, 1985	CPC Central Committee, the State Council	"Ten Policies for the Further Activation of the Rural Economy"	Economic exchanges between the urban and rural areas were to be expanded… Rural residents were to be allowed to enter the cities to open shops and workshops, set up service businesses, and provide various services, and cities were required to provide convenience in the use of land and service facilities
July 1986	The State Council	"Interim Provisions on the Recruitment of Workers by State-owned Enterprises"	Enterprises recruiting workers were to run simple, clear-cut recruitment procedures, which were to be open to all urban industrial workers who met the conditions specified as well as persons permitted by the state to be recruited from the countryside

(continued)

Table 3.2 (continued)

Year	*Issuing authority*	*Document name*	*Key policy thrusts*
July 1988	Ministry of Labor, the State Council Leading Group for the Economic Development of Poverty-stricken Areas	"Notice on Strengthening the Development of Labor Resources in Poverty-Stricken Areas"	Vigorous efforts would be made to organize the export of labor services as the focus of labor resource development in poor areas Efforts would be made to organize the labor movement between regions in accordance with the principles of "East–West Union, Urban–Rural Union, Targeted Poverty Alleviation, Long-Term Cooperation" Economically developed areas along the coast, especially large and mid-sized cities
April 1989	Ministry of Civil Affairs, Ministry of Public Security	"Notice on Further Efforts to Control the Outflow of Migrant Workers"	To make effective arrangements for the surplus rural labor; to repatriate and resettle migrant workers who had "gone out" in the proper manner

Year	*Issuing authority*	*Document name*	*Key policy thrusts*
January 1991	Ministry of Labor, Ministry of Agriculture, Development Research Center of the State Council	"Notice on the Establishment and Implementation of the Pilot Project for the Development and Employment of China's rural labor"	To select several provinces and counties as pilots to carry out various experiments to promote rural employment, summarize the successful experiences and best practices found in various places and promote these nationwide, and to study and formulate guidelines, policies, and regulations for rural employment as the means to promote the development of rural employment

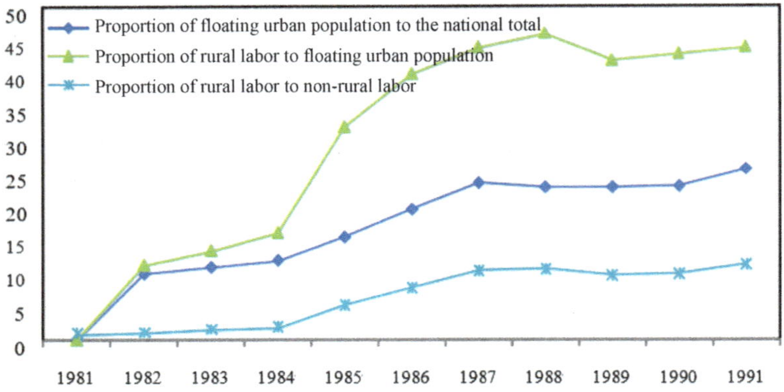

Fig. 3.1 The floating urban population and employment in China from 1981 to 1991

limited to small-scale adjustments under the unified employment system, and the mobility rate was relatively low. Therefore, rural migrant labor could only choose employment in cities and towns outside the coverage of this employment channel. Second, the elimination of the day-to-day living resource system linked to household registration became a catalyst for the flow of rural surplus labor. Third, labor mobility from rural to urban areas was highly sensitive to institutional and policy adjustments. When policies are relaxed or tightened, labor mobility also significantly changes.

3.2.3 Summary

The initial stage of marketization saw the emergence of the labor market, and policy adjustments had the typical characteristics of "crossing the river by feeling the stones." While the redistribution system from the planned economy period remained, market factors began to penetrate into the planned system. While the main body of the wage determination mechanism was still a strict and standardized wage system, some enterprises began to link the pay level to the level of their economic gains. On the other hand, while the restrictions on rural–urban labor mobility had been relaxed to an appropriate degree, but the policy on mobility was still very restrictive. At the same time, there was essentially no free movement of labor with state-owned enterprises in the urban areas.

3.3 Stage I of Marketization (1990–2000): The Formation of Double Duality

Several of the most important events in this period shaped the direction of labor market reforms: (1) With the reform of state-owned enterprises, layoffs at a considerable number of state-owned enterprises impacted the labor market and created the new characteristic of labor mobility; (2) The rural labor began to flood into the cities, and the "rural migrant workers" began to become one of the main forces in the urban labor market; and (3) Further opening up of the coastal regions and the vigorous development of the non-state-owned economy called for the establishment of a modern enterprise system, thus affecting the wage determination mechanism at enterprises.

3.3.1 The Wage Determination Mechanism in Stage I of Marketization (1990–2000)

Between 1990 and 2000, the central government determined that China was to adhere to the principle of distribution according to work as the "main body" with multiple forms of distribution in place. Production factors such as capital and technology were to be allowed and encouraged to participate in benefit distribution, and efforts were to be made to explore the establishment of a system of income distribution in line with the modern enterprise system. Table 3.3 contains a list of the changes in the wage system that occurred between 1990 and 2000. A variety of new distribution methods were introduced in the public sector and state-owned enterprises on top of the existing method of planned distribution, and the market mechanism became the wage determination method because of the rapid development of the non-public sectors of the economy. As a result: (1) The reform goal of enterprises' wage distribution system, which was to be "determined by market mechanisms, with independent distribution by enterprises, democratic participation of employees, and supervision and guidance by the government," was established. (2) There were further reforms to the internal wage distribution system at enterprises, especially state-owned enterprises, with wage system relating to job skills implemented and explorations into distribution methods based on production factors. (3) There were also reforms to the way in which total wages were being managed and improvements to the method of linking total wages to economic benefits, and some enterprises also carried out pilot projects for collective wage negotiation. (4) There were further reforms to the wage system at state organs and public institutions: state organs implemented a wage system of job grades, and public institutions implemented wage systems that met their very specific needs in their respective industries. (5) There was greater use of legal and economic means to adjust the distribution of wages and incomes, establish the minimum wage system, wage guidelines, labor market wage guidelines, and other systems, as well as to further improve the personal income tax system.

In tandem with the adjustments made to the aforementioned wage policies and systems, adjustments were also to be made to the corresponding wage determination mechanisms as changes occurred in ownership structures over the process of transitioning to a market economy. On one hand, as market reforms went underway and adjustments were being made to the wage system, the total amount of wages rose rapidly, from 295.11 billion yuan in 1990 to 1095.47 billion yuan in 2000, with a real growth rate (after deducting the price index) of 10 percent. As a result of the many adjustments in the wage system and the rapid expansion of the non-state sector, the total wage bill has grown rapidly. At the same time, significant changes and adjustments in the wage structure can be observed around 1990. As can be seen from Fig. 3.2, the total wage bill in the state sector fell from 78.7 percent in 1990 to 70.6 percent in 2000, in the collective sector from 19.7 percent in 1990 to 8.68 percent in 2000, and in the non-state sector from 15.6 percent in 1990 to 20.62 percent in 2000.

Pay levels became more diverse as total wages increased. As we can see from the illustration, changes in the registration structure type are a reflection of different types of wage decisions, and the wage system that has adapted to the marketization process does not lead to a narrowing income gap between different workers but instead one that is beginning to widen. In Fig. 3.3, we see the differences in employee pay levels between different types of units and the national average pay level since the introduction of the policy of reform and opening up. The marketization process began in 1993, and following the reform of state-owned enterprises in 1998, the gap between the pay levels of different types of units and the national pay level began to widen in 2000. As shown in Fig. 3.3, it is more obvious that between 1993 and 2000, wages at joint

Table 3.3 Changes in the wage system between 1990 and 2000

Year	*Wage system*
1992	Establishment of an intra-enterprise distribution system centered on the "wage system relating to job skills."
1992	At the 14th CPC National Congress, it was proposed that a socialist market economy system be established so that the market would be able to play a fundamental role in the allocation of resources, including labor resources
1993	The "Decision of the Central Committee of the Communist Party of China on Several Issues Concerning the Establishment of the Social and Economic System" was adopted at the Third Plenary Session of the 14th CPC Central Committee, meaning that the concept of the "labor market" was formally adopted and that the labor market was regarded as a factor market that was to be fostered and developed
1993	"Notice on the Printing and Distribution of the Opinions on Strengthening the Implementation of Macro Control of Enterprise Total wages" issued by the Ministry of Labor
1994	"Notice on the Printing and Distribution of the Regulations on the Administration of Labor Wages of Joint-Stock Limited Companies" issued by the Ministry of Labor
1994	"Notice on the Implementation of the Minimum Wage Guarantee System," issued by the Ministry of Labor
1994	Labor Law of the People's Republic of China, the State Council
1995	The Ministry of Labor's "Notice on Improving and Perfecting the Measures for the Flexible Labor Wage Plan" stipulated that the regulatory scope of the regional flexible labor wage plan covered enterprises of various types, including local and central state-owned enterprises, urban collectively owned enterprises and other enterprises (including township enterprises) in the area of coverage
1995	"Notice on the Printing and Distribution of the 'Measures for the Reform of the Labor Wage and Social Insurance System in Pilot Enterprises in the Modern Enterprise System,'" Ministry of Labor and the State Economic and Trade Commission
1996	Establishment of a macro guidance system for corporate wages and incomes: To establish wage guidelines, a labor market price guidance system, and an enterprise labor cost forecast and early warning system
1999	The "Decision on Several Major Issues Concerning the Reform and Development of State-Owned Enterprises" was adopted at the Fourth Plenary Session of the 15th CPC Central Committee

stock companies, joint ventures, foreign-invested companies, and companies with investment from Hong Kong, Macao, and Taiwan were higher than the national average, while wages at SOEs matched the national average. However, wages at urban collectively owned units and other economic units were lower than the national average. As can be seen

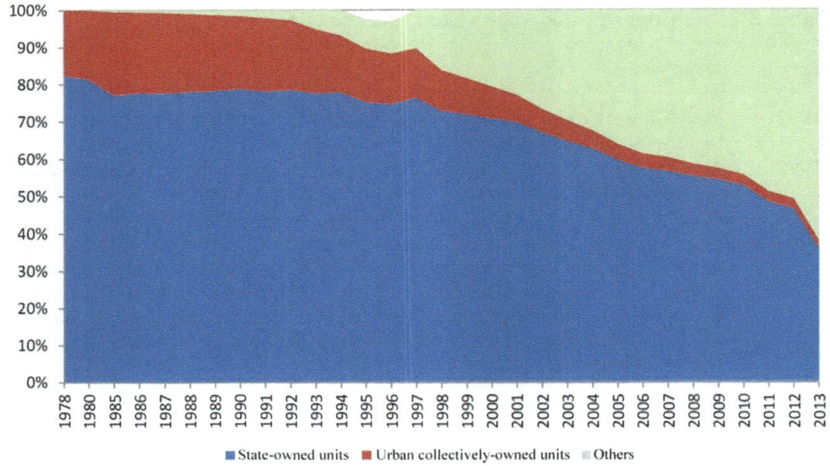

Fig. 3.2 Distribution structure of total wage income by registration type from 1978 to 2010 (*Source* 2014 China Statistical Yearbook)

from the figure, between 1990 and 2000, the wage gap between different economic types began to widen, and the "trumpet" was beginning to widen.

3.3.2 *Labor Mobility in Stage I of Marketization (1990–2000): An Orderly Flow*

In the initial stage of reform and opening up between 1978 and 1990, after the state adopted a restrictive policy in response to the substantial labor flows from rural areas that had begun to appear, the "floating population" began to significantly rise again in 1990 in the majority of cities, forming a large-scale wave of "migrant workers." The impact of the Asian financial crisis and SOE reforms also added to the reserve of labor that had to be "digested" by the cities. Labor mobility during this period was divided into two parts, the first being rural–urban mobility originating from the rural labor and the other being labor mobility following intra-urban labor market shocks. Guiding the effective movement of labor through market-based allocation became the main form of policy adjustment during this period in response to this change.

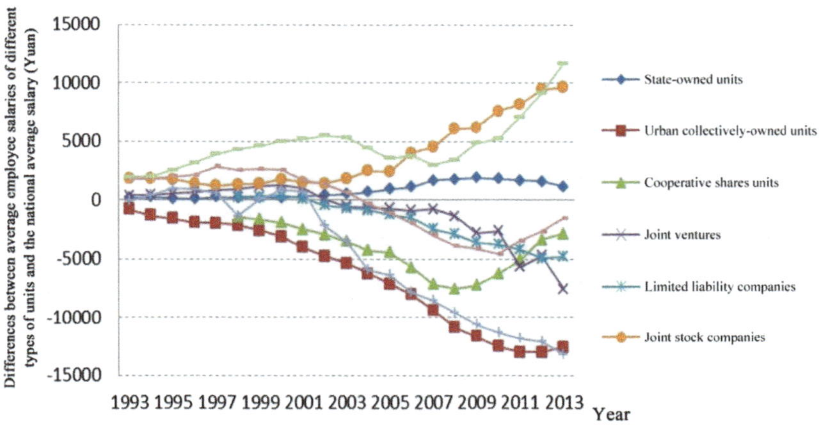

Fig. 3.3 Average employee wages of different types of units in key years (*Source* 2011 China Statistical Yearbook)

First, in terms of changes in labor mobility policies (Table 3.4), an employment system with the labor contract system as its core came into being through a series of adjustments in systems and policies such as the Labor Law, the labor contract system, and this system changed the relationship between enterprises and employees. Labor mobility became inevitable and the basic institutional system of the labor market gradually took shop alongside the labor market.

In terms of the size and speed of rural labor flows, this period coincides with the phase of large-scale rural labor mobility. The opening up of coastal areas to the outside world and the creation of non-agricultural employment opportunities through foreign direct investment drew the rural labor out of the agricultural sector. In 1993, 62 million rural workers were employed, four times as many as in 1989. Since then, the number of rural labor flows increased year by year. However, labor flow was slowed down in the mid-to-late 1990s by the Asian financial crisis and a decrease in employment opportunities in the non-public sector of the economy, as the number of laid-off and unemployed persons in the towns and cities increased sharply, creating more competition. Labor migration in this period dropped to an average of about 3.6 million per year. However, in general, the number of rural migrant workers was still increasing as a whole.

Table 3.4 Key policies on labor mobility between 1990 and 2000

Date	*Issuing authority*	*Document name*	*Key policy thrusts*
1990	The State Council	Regulations on the Administration of Employment Service Enterprises	Provides a third-party mechanism for the allocation of labor resources to the market
October 1992	Ministry of Labor	Circular on the Expansion of the Trial Implementation of the Labor Contract System	All provinces, autonomous regions, and municipalities directly under the central government were to trial the labor contract system for all employees in cities and counties, with the trial to include enterprise cadres, permanent workers, labor contract workers, and other workers
1993	The State Council	General Conception of the Reform of the Labor System Over the Course of Establishing a Socialist Market Economy	For the first time, the concept of the "labor market" was explicitly introduced; a timetable for the full implementation of the labor contract system was also clearly set out
1994	Ministry of Labor	Labor Law of the People's Republic of China	A legal basis for the labor and employment practices of urban and rural residents and enterprise recruitment and employment

Date	*Issuing authority*	*Document name*	*Key policy thrusts*
1994	Ministry of Labor	Interim Provisions on the Administration of Cross-Provincial Movement and Employment of the rural labor	Provisions on the cross-provincial recruitment of the rural labor and cross-provincial movement and employment of the rural labor as well as the procedures to go through; provisions on the cross-provincial employment services for rural labor, the responsibilities of organization/management agencies and sources of management fees. The main methods were: stringent management by means of permits, controlling the scale of labor flows, ensuring social security, and implementation at various administrative and departmental levels

(continued)

Table 3.4 (continued)

Date	*Issuing authority*	*Document name*	*Key policy thrusts*
1997	Ministry of Public Security	Pilot Program for the Reform of the Household Registration Management System in Small Towns	Persons with rural household registration who had legal and stable non-agricultural occupations or stable sources of income in small towns, and who had lived for two years in his own legal and fixed domicile, would be eligible to apply for permanent urban household registration: (1) Those who had worked in small towns or who had established businesses in the secondary and tertiary industries; (2) Management personnel and professional and technical personnel employed by state organs, social groups, enterprises, and public institutions in small towns; and (3) Residents who had purchased commercial housing in small towns or had legally built their own housing. The registration of the immediate family members of the aforementioned persons living together may also have their permanent residence in the towns
July 1998	Ministry of Public Security, approved by the State Council	Opinions on Resolving Some Highlighted Problems in Current Household Registration Management Work	Anyone who had legal and permanent housing, a legal and stable occupation or sources of income in the city, and who had lived for a certain number of years and met the relevant regulations of the local government would be allowed to settle in the city

Date	*Issuing authority*	*Document name*	*Key policy thrusts*
July 2000	State Council	Opinion on the Promotion of the Healthy Development of Small Towns	Stipulates that the household registration management system in small towns should be reformed. All rural residents who had a legal and permanent residence, a legal and stable occupation or sources of income, and who had lived for a certain number of years in county-level urban areas, county towns, and small towns below the county level were eligible for registration as urban residents and enjoyed the same treatment as urban residents in terms of their children's schooling, eligibility for joining the army, and employment., with discriminatory practices expressly forbidden. For rural residents who had settled down in small towns, agencies were not allowed to charge any fees for increasing the capacity of the towns or any other similar fees. Rural residents who had settled in the towns may, at their own will, continue to have the land contract management right and were also allowed to transfer it for profit in accordance with the law

The main policy and institutional option in this period was to guide the rural and urban labor flows. In Table 3.4, we see a list of the key supporting policies that were implemented during this period. To sum up, the labor flow policies in this decade were mainly focused on the following aspects: (1) Guiding the flow of rural labor in a standardized and orderly manner and carrying out pilot work on rural labor development and employment, such as the development of township enterprises to attract the rural surplus labor force; (2) The discussion of various measures for the orderly mobility of rural labor, such as the implementation of the labor contract system and the implementation and improvement of temporary residence permit while actively working to guide rural labor flows and regulating labor flows through rural labor mobility training and service improvements; and (3) Efforts to promote the study on the reform of the household registration system (Table 3.4).

Although the three aspects of labor market policies or institutions were interlinked to guide labor flows in an orderly manner, the reality remains that the free movement of rural labor was more or less restricted.

On one hand, the reform of the household registration system, which was still in the exploratory stage, was still the main force that restricted labor mobility. This was true especially in the mid-sized and large cities, where household registration remained an insurmountable barrier for rural labor mobility. Cai Fang (2008) believed that the reform of the household registration system and its progress in various cities across the country can be summarized into three modes, as shown in Table 3.5, with the reform intensity from the strongest to the weakest. He also summarized the relationships between urban welfare, mode of public service financing, and the reform of the household registration system, and divided these into three levels. On the first level, the city's welfare commitments and the quantity supplied were linked to one's household registration status and closely related to how the city's public services were financed. On the second level, urban welfare commitments and the mode of public service financing determined how much "weight" household registration had, and on the third level, the "weight" of household registration determined the motivation and progress of the local government's reform of the household registration system on the one hand and also the attractiveness of different types of cities to migrants on the other. In Table 3.5, we can see that the household registration system in small towns became less restrictive during this decade but also less attractive to the mobile labor force at the same time, and not vice versa.

Therefore, the exploration of the reform of the household registration system between 1990 and 2000 did not reduce the entry barriers for labor mobility. The household registration barriers of different urban categories varied according to the degree of economic openness and the size of the urban population. The household registration system still plays a role in protecting the employment of urban workers and excluding rural migrants from equal access to urban social benefits.

On the other hand, there were limited employment opportunities for the migrant labor force in the urban areas. According to the 2000 census data (Table 3.6), migrants tended toward manufacturing (40.3 percent) and retail and wholesale (28.8 percent), and the most likely jobs they took up after moving to the cities were business and service worker (36.4 percent) and production and transport worker (51 percent). In contrast, local residents were relatively a lot better distributed in terms of jobs and industries, and they tended to go for jobs with state organs, party and mass organizations, enterprises, public institutions and technical occupations, and occupations and industries with high barrier of entry such as in finance, education, and healthcare.

Secondly, labor mobility between cities began to emerge especially within the urban labor market after the impact of SOE reforms. Although labor mobility continued to exist between urban areas in the era of the planned economy, levels were low and controlled by the state, and therefore has received less attention compared to rural labor mobility. However, from the 1990s on, the rapid development of the coastal areas has driven labor mobility between cities outside the system. The 2000 census data shown in Table 3.7 shows that the scale of labor mobility between cities has become second only to rural–urban labor mobility. Therefore, labor mobility between cities is a reflection of the fact that the ability to allocate resources between cities has greatly improved.

The power of the market-based allocation of resources is examined in terms of labor mobility between the state and non-state sectors within towns. Looking at the results of China's urban labor force survey, Giles et al. (2006) found that between 1996 and 2001, only 26 percent of males and 26 percent of females had left their jobs voluntarily, meaning that significant barriers to labor mobility between jobs remained. Table 3.8 is the transformation matrix of China's labor market survey. Among the 944 people who left state-owned enterprises, 64.5 percent were still unemployed, only 16.7 percent found jobs in the state sector (including state-owned enterprises, state-controlled enterprises,

Table 3.5 Benefit provision and household registration system reform by urban type, 1990–2000

City type	*Level of urban welfare commitments and provision*	*Mode of public service financing*	*"Weight" of household registration and degree of reform*	*Attractiveness to migrant populations*
Small towns	Few promises, provision according to commercial model	Self-financing	"Low weight"; motivation for reform and be among the first	Very small
Common coastal cities	Provision of the necessary social and public services	Self-financing and redistribution, with the former being increasingly important	Gradually decreasing "weight"; the motivation for reform is gradually increasing and progress is made relatively fast	Larger
Common cities in mainland China	Fewer commitments as time goes by, some public services are under-supplied	Weak redistribution channels, weak self-financing capacity	Gradually decreasing "weight"; the motivation for reform is gradually decreasing; and certain degree of progress made	General
Beijing, Shanghai, and other special cities	Relatively high level of commitments and provision	Self-financing channels are available, but redistribution channels remain important	"Weight" remains high; the motivation for reform is insufficient and progress is slower	Massive

Note Quoted from Cai Fang (ed.), *Thirty Years of China's Labor and Social Security System Reforms*, Economic Management Press, 2008, p. 206

and collectively owned enterprises), and 14.1 percent of workers found a new job in the private sector. The labor mobility at state-controlled enterprises and collectively owned enterprises had a similar transformation to that of state-owned enterprises. Among those at foreign-invested enterprises, private enterprises, and the self-employed, a relatively high proportion of workers who left went on to jobs in similar sectors while

Table 3.6 Urban employment in agricultural households and non-agricultural households (2000 census)

	Local inhabitants (percent)	*Migrants (percent)*
Occupation		
Government administrators	6.0	2.7
Skilled worker	19.8	4.8
Clerical worker	13.0	5.0
Business and service worker	24.5	36.4
Production and transport worker	36.7	51.0
Other	0.1	0.1
Industry		
Mining	2.2	1.0
Manufacturing	31.9	40.3
Public utilities	2.5	0.4
Infrastructure development	5.6	10.7
Geological survey and water management	0.5	0.1
Transport, postal services, telecommunications, warehousing	7.8	4.2
Retail and wholesale business	17.8	28.8
Finance and insurance	2.6	0.5
Real estate	1.3	0.8
Social services	7.2	8.5
Healthcare, sports, social welfare	3.6	1.0
Education, culture, arts	7.1	1.8
Scientific research and technical services	1.3	0.3
Government, non-governmental organizations	7.8	1.2
Other	0.9	0.3

Source Based on data from the fifth national census, 2000

very, very few went on to jobs in Party and government agencies, state-owned enterprises, and state-controlled enterprises. Barriers to entry into state-owned entities and the high proportion of entry into the non-public sector meant that market mechanisms were one of the main ways in which labor resources were being allocated, which also implied that the system of exclusive employment under the planned economic system was still functioning to a certain extent.

In addition, the shocks following the reform of state-owned enterprises and the financial crisis in the late 1990s brought to the fore the

Table 3.7 Rural–urban, urban–urban, rural–rural, and urban–rural migration (2000 census)

	Rural–urban	*Urban–urban*	*Rural–rural*	*Urban–rural*
Migrants with no local registration (percent)	49.14	31.12	16.32	3.41
Migrants with local registration (percent)	25.34	48.19	21.93	4.53
Total migrants (percent)	40.84	37.07	18.28	3.81

Note "Migrants" are those who have moved to their current place of residence since 1995 and who have resided in these areas for more than six months in the previous year

Source Brandt and Rawski, ed., Rawski, ed., *China's Great Economic Transformation*, Ge Zhi Publishing House and Shanghai People's Publishing House, p. 161

problem of labor mobility within urban labor markets. By the mid-to-late 1990s, SOEs were overwhelmed by the decades-long employment policies of "unified contract and distribution" and "high employment and low income," and SOE losses were widespread. SOEs in many places became bankrupt, merged with other enterprises, or divested their back-office operations as a result. In 1997, at the 15th National Congress of the Communist Party of China, it was noted that with the deepening of enterprise reform, technological progress, and the restructuring of the economy, the movement of people and worker layoffs were inevitable. Beginning in 1998, employees at state-owned enterprises were laid off on a large scale, and this formed the second major employment shock following the implementation of the policy of reform and opening up. The most massive waves of layoffs occurred from 1998 to 2000, and the impact lasted until 2005. The large number of laid-off state-owned enterprise employees became a difficult and major problem in employment at the time. According to the estimates of the government agencies then, about two-thirds of laid-off workers were re-employed, with a significant proportion of them taking up jobs in different industries and employer ownership types. According to the results of a survey of five cities conducted in 2001 by the Institute of Population and Labor Economics of the Chinese Academy of Social Sciences,[6] 42.1 percent of those laid off had jobs in manufacturing before their job changed,

[6] The cities surveyed are Shanghai, Shenyang, Zhengzhou, Xi'an and Fuzhou.

Table 3.8 Movement of labor by sector of ownership (January 1996–November 2001)

		New sector (percentage deviation from previous sector)								
		Number of workers who left their jobs (percent of sector employment)	*Party and government organs*	*State-owned enterprises*	*State-controlled companies*	*Collectively owned enterprises*	*Foreign-invested enterprises*	*Private enterprises or self-employment*	*Other*	*percent of the population still unemployed in November 2001*
Previous sector	Party and government organs	68 (30)	26.5	44	4.4	10.3	2.9	8.8	1.5	41.2
	State-owned enterprises	944 (50)	1.8	8.5	1.2	7.0	1.8	14.1	1.2	64.5
	State-controlled companies	247 (51)	0.8	2.0	11.7	6.9	2.4	14.2	0.4	61.5
	Collectively owned enterprises	673 (45)	1.3	1.2	0.4	14.7	1.3	16.9	1.8	62.3
	Foreign-invested enterprises	66 (71)	0.0	4.5	0.0	6.1	33.3	16.7	0.0	39.4
	Private enterprises or self-employment	427 (72)	0.9	3.5	0.9	4.7	1	41.2	0.9	45.9
	Other	45 (34)	0.0	0.0	4.4	4.4	0.0	17.8	20.0	53.3
	Total	2470 (50)	2.0	4.6	2.1	8.7	2.6	19.6	1.5	58.9

Source Giles et al. (2006)

and only 14.4 percent remained in manufacturing by the time they were in their second or third job. While only 13.1 percent of workers were originally in wholesale, retail, and trade and catering jobs before, the proportion rose to 25.9 percent by the second or third job; the situation with social services is similar, with the proportion rising from 8.4 percent pre-layoffs to 18.9 percent of all post-layoff second or third jobs. Correspondingly, there has also been a significant change in terms of their employer ownership type. 33.1 percent of these workers pre-layoffs were employed by state-owned enterprises, and 22.7 percent were employed by private enterprises. Post-layoffs, the proportion of state-owned enterprises decreased to 11.2 percent, and the proportion of private enterprises increased to 47.6 percent.

This tells us that as market reforms continued between 1990 and 2000, the barriers to the labor flow between urban and rural areas, sectors, and regions continued to lower. However, the bottom-up incremental reform method followed by the labor market fueled the market-based method of labor resource allocation, and the outside-in stock shock caused to the labor market made labor market segmentation even more complex as policies kicked in to protect the state sector.

3.3.3 Summary

Between 1990 and 2000 when the market-oriented reform was promoted and achieved some initial results, the labor market developed in tandem with the rapid rise of the economy. However, the reform of the labor market was not perfect. The main characteristics of China's labor market at this stage are as follows: First, the string of incremental reforms and radical stock adjustments implemented ensured the rapid formation of the labor market and the establishment of a basic labor market. Second, the market allocation of labor resources was formally established, and the wage determination mechanism of labor supply and demand began to affect wage distribution mechanisms and became an important part of such mechanisms, enlarging the role of human capital and labor productivity on wage determination. Correspondingly, the trend of free movement of rural–urban and urban–urban labor and labor within cities gradually increased, and the free movement of rural labor in geographical areas coexisted with barriers to mobility within urban sectors. Third, wage determination mechanism reforms in the non-state sector coexisted at the same time as the institutional wage determination mechanism in the state sector, and thus, the economy as a whole had a "dual-track" structure in terms of wage determination mechanisms, and the coexistence of multiple economic types within the non-state sector caused greater differentiation in pay levels. Fourth, exploratory attempts at reform of the household registration system at various levels increased the flow of labor, though the difference in the "weight" of household registration in large, mid-sized, and small cities (towns) indicates that the entry barriers for labor in the megacities were being raised. Taken as a whole, the decade since 1990 has been the stage of the establishment and development of the labor market, and also the stage of the formation of double duality of the labor market in China due to the combined effect of the household registration system and the ownership type.

3.4 The Labor Market in Stage II of Marketization (2001–Present): The Transition from Double Duality to Multi-Tiered Segmentation

In the twenty-first century, China, in accordance with the direction of market reforms, has relaxed restrictions on labor flows when necessary and with factor price determination gradually diversifying. Labor mobility and wage determination mechanisms that are compatible with the market economy are more or less established in the labor factor market.

3.4.1 Wage Determination Mechanisms in Stage II of Marketization (2001–)

In this stage, further reforms have been undertaken with regard to China's wage distribution system by building on the achievements of Stage I. Human capital and labor productivity have become important factors in determining labor remuneration. However, the trend of the diversification and individualization of wage determination mechanisms has become increasingly obvious. To this end, the central government has put forward the principle that production factors should be allocated based on contribution and participation, and required that allocation should be based on both work and production factors.

During this period, the economic structure became even more complex. The rapid development of the non-public economy led to the emergence of a stream of new economic entities and the total wage structure of various economic types changed dramatically. Figure 3.2 shows that the state sector's share of total wages decreased from 70.6 percent of total wages in 2000 to only 35.85 percent in 2013, a decrease of 34.85 percentage points. Correspondingly, the non-state sector's share doubled from 20.6 percent in 2000 to 60.7 percent in 2013. The overall increase in total wages is a reflection of the proportions of various sectors in national income and the diversification of the economy in recent years. This point is also illustrated in Fig. 3.3. Therefore, it is necessary for us to conduct further analysis of the diversified wage system. In this paper, we analyze the wage determination processes of the state sector, or the internal sector, and the non-state sector, or the non-state sector.

First, let us analyze the process of wage determination in the state-owned or internal sector. Wage determination in the internal sector comprises primarily the wage policy of administrative and public institutions and state-owned enterprises. Following several rounds of wage reforms, administrative institutions began to differentiate in terms of their wage determination mechanisms in 2006. A unified wage system was implemented with administrative units across the country through the Civil Servant Law while public institutions remained still the focus of reform. Based on a simplified wage structure, the implemented wage reform foregrounded incentive functions relating to job positions and performance and brought about great changes in wage determination mechanisms. However, the wage determination of these two types of agencies followed the administrative wage system linked to the traditional system, and pay levels were essentially kept on the average level. Public institutions began to consider wage determination models that were closer to the enterprise models. After many wage reforms, SOEs have established a basic wage system with position wage as the mainstay, which is linked to the economic gains of the enterprise. While a variety of distribution methods have also been adopted by the enterprise based on its specific needs with some autonomy and flexibility, the market mechanism in the wage determination process, such as the enterprise collective consultation and negotiation system, has yet to be fully established as the necessary conditions have been lacking. Thus, despite the diversification of wage distribution, the wage determination process remains to a considerable extent the same as the old wage system associated with the planned economy, and because of industry competitiveness and monopoly, wage differentials within the state-owned enterprise sector are relatively large.

Second, let us analyze the process of wage determination in the non-state sector. From Table 3.3, we can clearly see that the non-state sector has been gradually established from scratch and grown with the development of the market economy. Therefore, since its emergence in China's labor market, it has naturally had a wage determination mechanism in which prices are determined by supply and demand. In general, apart from wages and basic social insurance, in the non-state sector, other forms of social welfare are not provided, and there are also fewer income-sharing mechanisms. The role of labor productivity and human capital in determining wages is fully reflected in the non-state sector. However, it is also not difficult to see that the non-state sector is composed of multiple economic types. While pay levels are determined based on supply and demand, different economic types have different pay levels due to differences in labor supply and demand structure, labor productivity, and industry differences (as shown in Fig. 3.3). This means that in the non-state sector there are still differences in the wage determination process due to differences in the bargaining power of workers and the market power of the firm. In addition, since migrant workers have become a very important part of the labor force, it is necessary to examine the issue of migrant workers' wages. According to the results of a survey of migrant workers by the National Bureau of Statistics over the years, the average growth rate of migrant workers' wages from 2001 to 2007 was 7.9 percent, and the average growth rate of migrant workers' wages according to the agricultural sector's survey at a fixed observation point was 7.9 percent between 2003 and 2007, while the average annual growth rate of the average wage of employed persons in urban units was as high as 14.9 percent. However, since 2008, the growth rate of migrant workers' wages has increased. According to dynamic monitoring reports by the National Bureau of Statistics over the years, the wages of migrant workers in 2014 were 2.14 times that of 2008, with an average annual growth rate of 13.49 percent. During the same period, the average annual growth rate of the average wages of employees in urban units was 10.13 percent. It is clear that the wages of the rural mobile labor force have been growing rapidly in recent years and are becoming increasingly differentiated.

Issues in the labor market have become increasingly complex with a variety of economic types and wage determination processes in various sectors. The bottom-up adjustment requirements in the market during this period prompted the state to introduce a series of systems and policy measures related to the wage determination process to protect the legitimate rights and interests of workers. The main wage systems and policies are listed in Table 3.9. Taken together, these policies and systems mainly cover the following aspects: First, increased incentives for management personnel. On the basis of the annual wage system implemented by many enterprise operators, some enterprises have tried out the equity incentive method and the enterprise annuity system and standardized claimable job expenditures. Second, efforts have been made to establish and improve income distribution incentive mechanisms for science and technology personnel and to implement the method of determining remuneration according to positions, tasks, and performance. Third, efforts have been made to deepen the reform of the internal distribution system of the enterprise and to establish a basic wage system with the position wage as the mainstay. Fourth, efforts have been made to explore distribution based on the contribution of production factors, and some enterprises have carried out pilot projects such as employee stock ownership within the enterprise and the inclusion of technological factors in equity initiatives. Fifth, efforts have continued to expand the implementation scope of the wage guideline, labor wage guide price, and labor cost information guidance systems, and to establish a minimum wage system on various fronts. Sixth, efforts have been made to further deepen the reform of the civil servant wage system and implement a job-level wage system, as well as to reform the system of distribution and implement a post- and performance-based wage system at public institutions.

Although the central government has issued a series of systems and policy measures to ensure the rights and interests of workers and has worked to reduce the income gap caused by the differentiation of wage determination mechanisms in different sectors, such as the minimum pay level, the Individual Income Tax Law, regulations on labor dispute arbitration, and regulations on paid employee annual leave, but differences in pay levels in both the private and state sectors continued to grow, and internally the structure has become more complex. In Table 3.10, we see how the average pay level in the state-owned economic sector has been higher than the national average pay level since 2000, and there has been an upward trend, while the average pay levels in other economic sectors have declined from 1.06 times the national average pay level in 2003 to only 98 percent of the national average pay level in 2010. The average pay level at collective economic units has long been equivalent to only over 60 percent of the national average. The average pay levels at

Table 3.9 Main wage systems after 2000

Year	*Wage system*
2000	The Ministry of Labor and Social Security issues and implements the Measures for the Implementation of Collective Wage Negotiation, which provides clear stipulations on the relevant principles, content, representatives, and procedures of collective wage negotiation as well as on wage agreement reviews
2000	The cooperative medical care system is abolished in the CPC Central Committee's The Outline of the 10th Five-Year Plan for National Economic and Social Development
November 2000	The Ministry of Labor and Social Security's Guiding Opinions on Further Deepening the Reform of the Internal Distribution System of Enterprises establishes a wage income distribution system that is compatible with the modern enterprise system together with an incentive and restraint mechanism for wage distribution
2001	The National Economic and Trade Commission, the Ministry of Personnel, and the Ministry of Labor and Social Security issues the Opinions on the Deepening of the Reform of Personnel, Labor, and Distribution in State-Owned Enterprises, introducing to SOEs market mechanisms for the employment of personnel and market allocation as well as the practices of competitive hiring and linking wages to job responsibilities
November 2001	The State Council issues the Circular on the Further Strengthening of the Minimum Subsistence for Urban Residents
May 2003	The Ministry of Labor and Social Security issues its Guiding Opinions on Participation in Basic Medical Insurance for Urban Flexible Employed Persons and Opinions on Several Issues Concerning Part-Time Employment, further regulating employer behavior with regard to part-time employment
2003	The State-Owned Assets Supervision and Administration Commission of the State Council introduces the Interim Measures for the Evaluation of the Operational Performance of Persons in Charge of Central Enterprises, which stipulates that the annual wage system is to be adopted to determine the labor remuneration of operators, that the operators of state-owned assets are to be restrained by quantitative indicators, and that remuneration is to be paid according to business performance
September 2003	The Ministry of Labor and Social Security and the Ministry of Construction issues the Circular on Effectively Resolving the Problem of Wage Arrears of Migrant Workers in Construction Enterprises

(continued)

Table 3.9 (continued)

Year	*Wage system*
September 2004	The Ministry of Labor and Social Security announces its Interim Measures for the Administration of Wage Payments for Migrant Workers in the Field of Construction
2005	The Ministry of Labor and Social Security, the Ministry of Construction, the Ministry of Public Security, and the Ministry of Supervision jointly issue the Notice on Further Steps to Resolve the Problem of Unpaid Migrant Workers' Wages, which requires local governments to adopt legal, economic, and the necessary administrative measures to urge enterprises that owe wages to migrant workers to pay these wages as soon as possible
October 2005	At the National Tripartite Work Conference on Coordinating Labor Relations, it is stipulated that from 2006 on, efforts are to be made to implement the Three-Year Action Plan for Labor Contract Work and to ensure that every employer signs labor contracts with its employees within this three-year period
December 2005	The State Council issues the Decision of the State Council on Improvements to the Basic Pension Insurance System for Enterprise Employees, ensuring that basic old-age insurance is paid in full and on time and expanding the scope of coverage of old-age insurance
2006	The State Council's Civil Servant Law puts in place a wage system that brings together the nationally uniform wage system that combines job responsibilities and grades
June 2007	The Standing Committee of the Tenth National People's Congress deliberates on and adopts the Labor Law of the People's Republic of China that would go into effect on January 1, 2008
December 2007	The Standing Committee of the Tenth National People's Congress deliberates on and adopts the Labor Dispute Mediation and Arbitration Law of the People's Republic of China that would go into effect on January 1, 2008
May 2007	The State Council issues its Circular on the Establishment of a Rural Subsistence Allowance System Across China, which stipulates that local authorities that have established a rural minimum living security system further improve the system, and that local authorities that have not done so are to promptly establish regulations and systems and to establish and organize implementation within the year
June 29, 2007	The Standing Committee of the Tenth National People's Congress deliberates on and adopts the Decision on Amending the Individual Income Tax Law of the People's Republic of China that would go into effect on January 1, 2008

(continued)

Table 3.9 (continued)

Year	*Wage system*
December 2007	The State Council promulgates its Regulations on Paid Annual Leave for Employees, which provides a clearer legal basis for the implementation of the paid employee leave system

state-owned economic units have remained the highest among the three economic types, and average wages for the other two economic types are below the national average. Now that the structure of the economy is becoming increasingly complex, it is not enough for us to only observe the changes in the pay levels across the three economic types. In Fig. 3.3, we see that since 2000, the "trumpet" in average wage distribution across various economic types has continued to grow. This means that the wage gap is growing. The units with much higher wages than the national average include joint stock companies, foreign-invested companies, and state-owned companies, and average wages at foreign-invested companies and companies limited by shares are higher than at state-owned companies. The average pay level at other economic units is lower than the national average pay level, with the average pay level of collectively owned units being the lowest. Clearly, a comparison of sub-economic types shows an increasingly differentiated wage structure, and the difference in wages by economic type means that the market is transitioning from a "dual" segmentation to a state of "multi-tiered segmentation."

To further examine the multi-tiered segmentation of wage determination, we will now examine average pay levels by economic type and industry. Table 3.11 shows the distribution of average pay levels by economic type and industry in 2008. Among the average wages by industry, the average pay level of non-state sectors was higher than that of state-owned units in eight industries, and in the information transmission, computer service industries, and the financial industry, average wages were about 20,000 to 30,000 yuan higher than the average pay level at state-owned units. The financial industry came with the highest average wage among the three economic types, and average pay levels were the lowest in agriculture, forestry, animal husbandry, and fishery among the three economic types. Among the state-owned and other economic units, there were 10 industries with average wages higher than the national average, while among the collectively owned units there were

Table 3.10 Average wages by economic types since 2003 (Unit: yuan)

Year	*2003*	*2004*	*2005*	*2006*	*2007*	*2008*	*2009*	*2010*
National average	13,969	15,920	18,200	20,856	24,721	28,898	32,244	36,539
State sector	14,358	16,445	18,978	21,706	26,100	30,287	34,130	38,359
State sector/National average	1.03	1.03	1.04	1.04	1.06	1.05	1.06	1.05
Collective economy	8627	9723	11,176	12,866	15,444	18,103	20,607	24,010
Collective economy/National average	0.62	0.61	0.61	0.62	0.62	0.63	0.64	0.66
Other sectors	14,843	16,519	18,362	21,004	24,271	28,552	31,350	35,801
Other sectors/National average	1.06	1.04	1.01	1.01	0.98	0.99	0.97	0.98

Source Zhang Dongsheng (ed.) 2009, Annual Report on Income Distribution among Chinese Residents (2009)

only two. The ratio of the highest waged to the lowest waged industry is 4.43, 2.34, and 4.69 in state-owned, collective, and other units respectively, indicating that the income gap is the largest in units of other economic types. However, in general, the average wage at state-owned units was the highest and higher than the national average pay level, while average wages at collectively owned units and other units were lower than the national average pay level. What this means is that the segmentation mechanism for wage determination based on ownership is multiple by industry, and at the same time, this also shows that segmentation by system is the most basic division, and segmentation by industry occurs on top of segmentation by system rather than segmentation by industry monopoly replacing segmentation by system.

3.4.2 Labor Mobility in Stage II of Marketization (2001–the Present)

Since 2000, labor mobility and transfer in China have primarily comprised rural labor, and for this reason, we have divided the study at this stage mainly based on the changes of rural labor mobility and transfers.[7] This division is based on the large scale of rural mobile labor force in China. Rural labor flows within the urban–rural dual structure are most sensitive to economic system reform, adjustments to the industrial structure, and changes in the relevant national policies. The direction of migration and mobility is often one of the weathervanes of changes in the economic structure. The composition of labor supply within the city has undergone major changes in this period. Here, we take 2004 as the boundary as it was a year of many notable changes. For the first time in China's history, there was a shortage of ordinary workers, wages for unskilled workers have continued to rise since then, and the cost of rural labor increased while labor inputs decreased (Cai 2011). The employment difficulties of college students have become more salient since then. Therefore, we divide these 10 years into two periods: the first is that of large-scale movement and the peak period for the reemployment of workers laid off from

[7] The migration of rural labor in China occurs when labor that is originally engaged in agriculture moves from rural areas to urban non-agricultural industries. For urban labor, however, there has hardly been any kind of systematic flow due to the constraints of the household registration system, the social security system, social protection network, and other public welfare benefits (Cai Fang 2010).

Table 3.11 Average wages by economic unit type and industry category in 2008 (Unit: yuan)

Industry	*Average wage across all units*	*Average wage at state-owned units*	*Average wage at collectively owned units*	*Average wage at other units*
Total	29,229	31,005	18,338	28,387
Agriculture, forestry, animal husbandry and fishery	12,958	12,798	13,656	17,134
Mining	34,405	35,822	19,837	34,361
Manufacturing	24,192	27,800	15,553	24,074
Electricity, gas, and water production and supply	39,204	39,394	27,805	39,405
Construction	21,527	23,862	15,820	22,041
Transportation, storage, and postal services	32,796	32,162	15,177	36,582
Information transmission, computer services, and software industries	56,642	40,897	28,975	67,423
Wholesale and retail	25,538	26,501	12,932	27,586
Accommodation and F&B	19,481	19,215	15,260	20,005
Financial services	61,841	56,652	31,996	80,328
Real estate	30,327	28,471	21,388	31,556
Leasing and business services	31,735	28,529	17,827	39,703
Scientific research, technical services, and geological surveys	46,003	43,259	30,691	58,817
Water conservancy, environment, and public facilities management	22,182	22,120	16,160	27,460

(continued)

Table 3.11 (continued)

Industry	*Average wage across all units*	*Average wage at state-owned units*	*Average wage at collectively owned units*	*Average wage at other units*
Residential and other services	23,801	28,598	16,619	20,815
Education	30,185	30,316	22,844	29,465
Health services, social security, and social welfare	32,714	33,652	24,223	28,023
Culture, sports, and entertainment	34,494	35,387	19,881	29,368
Public administration and social organizations	32,955	32,999	20,669	22,836
Industry highest/ lowest wage	4.77	4.43	2.34	4.69

Source China Labor Statistics Yearbook (2009)

state-owned enterprises between 2000 and 2004, and the second is the period from 2005 to the present, when there has been a shortage of "migrant workers" and college students are facing difficulties finding jobs.

First period (2000–2004): Large-scale rural labor flows and the reemployment of laid-off workers. In this period, the greatest flow of labor existed at the same time as the absorption of workers laid from as a result of SOE reforms. First of all, from the perspective of rural labor flows: according to estimates made by the Development Research Center of the State Council, during the Tenth Five-Year Plan period, rural labor mobility increased rapidly. As the numbers in Table 3.12 show, the growth of the number of migrant workers in 2000 and 2001 was relatively flat due to the impact of state-owned enterprise reforms on urban employment and the restrictions on the flow of migrant workers into the cities, in 2002, growth sprang to over 20 percent, and the 100-million mark was also crossed in 2002. Since then, more than one in eight rural residents has moved between rural and urban areas for employment and living, and the growth rate reached its peak in 2002 and 2003. By 2004, the growth rate of the rural labor "going out to work" declined slightly and the growth rate has remained more or less stable since then. While a large number of rural residents are employed in the cities and towns, it is clear that the industries in which these residents are employed have not changed much between 2000 and 2004 (Table 3.13).

This period was also a period of recovery from the impact of the restructuring of state-owned enterprises. By the end of 2003, there were 2.6 million laid-off workers in state-owned enterprises across the country,

Table 3.12 Number and growth rate of rural migrant workers and urban workers between 2000 and 2010

Year	*Rural migrant workers (×10,000)*	*Growth (percent)*	*Urban workers (×10,000)*	*Growth (percent)*
2000	7849	–	23,151	3.30
2001	8399	7.01	23,940	3.41
2002	10,470	24.66	24,780	3.51
2003	11,390	8.79	25,639	3.47
2004	11,823	3.80	26,476	3.26
2005	12,578	6.39	27,331	3.23
2006	13,212	5.04	29,630	8.41
2007	13,697	3.67	30,953	4.47
2008	14,041	2.51	32,103	3.72
2009	14,533	3.50	33,322	3.80
2010	15,335	5.52	34,687	4.10

Note The data for the period 2008–2011 was sourced from the *China Statistical Yearbook* (2011), while the number on employment and group data comes from "The Labor Statistics Report System," "The Labor Force Survey System," and "The Rural Social and Economic Survey Program" published by Department of Population, Social and Science Statistics, National Bureau of Statistics with some organizing and processing

Source Organization of Rural Socio-Economic Survey of National Bureau of Statistics, *2009 Report on the Monitor Survey of Migrant Rural Workers*, National Bureau of Statistics website

Table 3.13 Distribution of migrant workforce by industry (percent)

Year	*Industry*	*Construction*	*Transportation*	*Commercial services*	*Other*
2003	27.4	15.6	5.2	21.2	30.5
2004	28.9	15.6	5.3	21.1	29.1
2005	29.0	16.3	5.3	20.8	28.6
2006	28.7	16.3	5.4	20.6	2.0
2007	26.8	16.2	5.0	21.5	30.4

Source Cai Fang, The China Population and Labor Report, No. 11, July 2010

a decrease of 2.55 million from 2001, and reemployment service centers have been fully closed in seven provinces as a large number of surplus personnel generated by the reform of state-owned enterprises have been "digested" by the market. During this period, state-owned enterprises gained even greater autonomy in the hiring of workers, and they became able to employ more market mechanisms in the selection and hiring of workers.

The second period (2005–the present) has seen a shortage of migrant workers and employment difficulties for college students In this period, which saw the completion of the 11th Five-Year Plan period and the beginning of the 12th Five-Year Plan period, the number of rural migrant workers continued to grow. From Table 3.12, we see that although the growth rate of rural labor flows declined for a time in 2004, it then returned to a high growth rate of around 6 percent in 2005 and 2006 and a growth rate of around 3 percent for some time before returning to 5.4 percent in 2010. Then, after 2010, the growth rate of the total rural labor has been on a decline. According to data found in the "2014 National Monitoring Report on the Movement of Migrant Workers," between 2011 and 2014, the growth rate of the total number of migrant workers dropped by 1.0, 0.5, 1.5, and 0.5 percentage points respectively compared to the previous year, and in 2014, the growth rate of the total number of migrant workers in the country was only 1.9 percent. As a result, while large-scale rural labor mobility still exists in China's labor market, the pace of rural labor mobility has slowed. As the number of migrant workers increased substantially: First, there was no fundamental change in the industries that migrant workers were hired in. In Tables 3.13 and 3.14, we can see the industries in which migrant workers have been employed in recent years. Between 2001 and 2008, the proportion of the labor force going out to work in the secondary industry remained at around 43 percent, while around 5 percent were hired in the transportation industries and around 20 percent in the commercial services industries. From 2008 on, between 2008 and 2014, some structural changes have taken place in the employment of rural labor. Although the secondary industry was still the main employer of rural labor, the proportion of employees in the manufacturing industry declined rapidly, while the proportion of rural workers entering the construction industry and transportation industry increased. The proportion of employees in the tertiary industry has remained more or less unchanged. This means that the human capital level of the rural labor was low, and it was difficult to move across industries as they lacked the requisite skills. It also means that the opportunities for rural labor to enter the state sector were relatively few, and the opportunities to improve their human capital through "learning by doing" were scarce. Second, it is difficult for rural workers to integrate into the city. While the constraints imposed on the flow of rural labor across regions by the household registration system were reduced, the identity issues related to the household registration system meant that rural labor can only "flow" and not "migrate." Their ownership of rural land meant that minimum life support was but guaranteed for them, and the household registration system was not a constraint on the horizontal flow of rural labor. However, it has become an obstacle to the urbanization of rural labor and their upward mobility.

In addition, the problem of employment difficulties for college students emerged when the first cohort of students admitted under broadened admission quotas graduated and sought employment in 2003. Graduates from colleges and universities have become one of the groups with the most salient employment problems in the city, apart from migrant workers. In 2009, there were 6.1 million college graduates nationwide, and among the 4.95 million and 5.6 million who graduated in 2007 and 2008, one million and 1.5 million respectively did not find jobs. According to data from Mycos' University Student Employability Survey, taking 2009 as an example, about 12.6 percent of college graduates were still unemployed after half a year, of which 74.9 percent were continuing their job hunts and 17.5 percent were not seeking a job or undergoing further education. At the same time, a considerable number of college graduates earned little employment income. The monthly wage of the low-income "drifting population" six months after graduation among the graduates of 2009 was equivalent to about half of the national average monthly wage of the same class of graduates.[8] Most of these

[8] The monthly wage for graduates of 2009 that graduated from the so-called "211 Project" Universities six months after graduation was 2756 yuan, which was significantly higher than that for the class of 2008 (2549 yuan) but still lower than that for the class of 2007 (2949 yuan). The wage for graduates of 2009 from "non-211 Project" Universities was 2241 yuan after half a year, which was slightly higher than that for the class of 2008 (2030 yuan) but still lower compared to the class of 2007 (2282 yuan). The wage of the class of 2009 who had graduated from vocational colleges after half a year was 1890 yuan, which was a significant increase compared to the class of 2008 (1647 yuan) and significantly higher compared to the class of 2007 class (1735 yuan). Source: 2010 *China University Student Employment Report*.

Table 3.14 Changes in the employment of rural migrant workers in terms of industry across China, 2008–2014 (percent)

Year	*Manufacturing*	*Construction*	*Transportation, storage, and postal services*	*Wholesale and retail*	*Accommodation and B&F*	*Residential and other services*
2008	37.2	13.8	6.4	9	5.5	12.2
2009	36.1	15.2	6.8	10	6	12.7
2010	36.7	16.1	6.9	10	6	12.7
2011	36	17.7	6.6	10.1	5.3	12.2
2012	35.7	18.4	6.6	9.8	5.2	12.2
2013	31.4	22.2	11.3	6.3	5.9	10.6
2014	31.3	22.3	11.4	6.5	6	10.2

Source National Bureau of Statistics, *2014 National Monitoring Report on the Movement of Migrant Workers*

individuals were working in private enterprises and small and mid-sized enterprises in Beijing, Shanghai, and Shenzhen, and these college graduates tended to be from rural and migrant worker households hailing from poorer areas. Furthermore, most of these students tended to hail from the smaller cities or villages.

The central government has formulated and promulgated the corresponding policy measures to deal with the new phenomenon of labor mobility, and the key systems and policies that have been introduced since 2000 are shown in Table 3.15. These include: (1) To reform the system of urban–rural division, ensure fair treatment for workers of rural origin, lift unreasonable restrictions on the employment of rural residents in the cities, put in place urban–rural coordination when it comes to employment, facilitate labor mobility across various geographic locales, and advance trial-and-error reform of the household registration system in stages and various regions; (2) To put in place a more flexible employment system and promote employment creation in the private sector and informal employment through labor market policies; and (3) To create order in the labor market over time through various regulations, improve the labor contract system, form long-term mechanisms for the promotion of employment, establish new mechanisms for the quick handling of labor disputes, and protect the legitimate rights and interests of workers.

Although these institutional and policy adjustments have made the labor market more flexible and facilitated labor mobility, the household registration system continues to be an important factor constraining the labor force and therefore, it is necessary to review and analyze the changes that have occurred with the household registration system during this period.

In fact, as early as 2001, the city of Zhengzhou became a pioneer in efforts to fully liberalize the system of household registration. However, eventually, due to the rapid increase in the urban population, urban traffic congestion, the shortage of educational resources, and increased pressure on the social security agencies and the social security system, the city hastily reversed such liberalization in 2004. The failure of this experiment stopped the reform of the household registration system at one point. However, the overall construction of the urban and rural labor markets and the unlimited supply of labor led to more adjustments to the

Table 3.15 Key policies and systems related to labor mobility introduced since 2000

Date	*Issuing authority*	*Document name*	*Key policy thrusts*
July 30, 2000	Jointly issued by the Ministry of Labor and Social Security, the National Planning Commission, the Ministry of Agriculture, the Ministry of Science and Technology, the Ministry of Water Resources, the Ministry of Construction and the Development Research Center of the State Council	Notice on Further Pilot Work for the Development and Employment of the rural labor	Reform of the system of urban–rural division and removal of unreasonable restrictions on rural residents' employment in the cities
March 15, 2001	Fourth Session of the Ninth National People's Congress	Outline of the Tenth Five-Year Plan for National Economic and Social Development of the People's Republic of China	Breaking down the system of urban–rural division and establishing over time a new type of urban–rural relationship within the framework of the market economy
March 2002	The General Office of the State Council, forwarded to the Ministry of Education and other ministries	Notice on Opinions on the Further Deepening of the Reform of the Employment System for Graduates from Institutions of Higher Learning	Employment mechanisms that promote two-way choices between graduates and employers

(continued)

Table 3.15 (continued)

Date	*Issuing authority*	*Document name*	*Key policy thrusts*
August 2002	State Council	Small and Medium-Sized Enterprise Promotion Law	Regulating and promoting the development of small and medium-sized enterprises; encouraging workers to achieve employment in flexible ways; formulation of policies for part-time employment, medical insurance for temporary employees, and carrying out system construction in labor relations, wage payment, social insurance; and promoting and protecting the legitimate rights and interests of persons with flexible employment
2003	Ministry of Labor and Social Security	Notice on the Appropriate Handling of Problems Related to the Re-Employment of Workers Laid off from State-Owned Enterprises	Integrating the basic living security for laid-off workers from state-owned enterprises into unemployment insurance within three years
March 20, 2003	Ministry of Labor and Social Security	Letter of Response on Issues Relating to the Labor Laws Applicable to Rural Migrant Workers	Both the Labor Law and the Trial Measures for Work-Related Injury Insurance for Enterprise Employees are applicable to all migrant workers (including migrant workers on "rotation contracts") who have established labor relations with employers

Date	*Issuing authority*	*Document name*	*Key policy thrusts*
2005	Ministry of Labor and Social Security	Notice on the Abolishment of the Interim Provisions for the Management of Rural Labor Movements and Employment Across Provinces and the Supporting Documents	Abolishment of the Interim Provisions for the Management of Rural Labor Movements and Employment Across Provinces, the Emergency Notice on the Strict Prohibition of the Misuse of Migrant Employment Permits, and the Notice on Issues Concerning the Issuance and Management of "Employment Registration Cards for Outbound Persons"; halting of the implementation of the relevant provisions of the Notice on the Printing and Distribution of the "Opinion on the Work of Managing the Movement of Surplus Migrant Labor" issued by the General Office of the Ministry of Labor and Social Security regarding employment registration permits and migrant employment certificates; and calling for further improvements to the employment environment for rural residents entering the cities, and cleaning up and abolishing policies restricting the employment of such workers in the cities

(continued)

Table 3.15 (continued)

Date	*Issuing authority*	*Document name*	*Key policy thrusts*
March 27, 2006	State Council	Several Opinions of the State Council on the Resolution of the Problems of Rural Migrant Workers	Local governments and all directly affiliated institutions are to work to quickly resolve the outstanding problems faced by migrant workers and to form systems that fundamentally protect the rights and interests of migrant workers. In a favorable policy environment, the number of rural surplus workers leaving the countryside to work increases; and clear statement on how the problem of low wages for migrant workers must be resolved
August 30, 2007	Standing Committee of the Tenth National People's Congress	Employment Promotion Law of the People's Republic of China	Promoting employment across the country in accordance with the law

household registration system over time. Therefore, Chengdu (2007),[9] Shenzhen (2008),[10] and Chongqing (2010)[11] became the pilot areas for further reform of the system, and these three areas can also be used to illustrate the reforms undertaken in various regions and different stages of

[9] In 2007, Chengdu became a pilot area for comprehensive and coordinated urban–rural reform. Starting from the reform of the rural land use system and the equalizing of education, healthcare, and social security, Chengdu went on to carry out reform and innovation in several fields, including the introduction of the "land for identity, homestead for housing" policy. In November 2010, the "Opinion on the Unifying of Household Registration in the Urban and Rural Areas of Chengdu to Achieve the Free Migration of Residents" was issued, thus establishing a unified household registration system between one's household registration location and actual place of residence. Employment and unemployment registration were merged into a single system, and efforts were made to improve the employment assistance system as well as to improve the unified social insurance system for urban and rural areas as well as standardize resettlement compensation for retired soldiers and the preferential policy for urban and rural military conscripts' families. The urban and rural housing security system was standardized at the zone level, together with the support standards and subsistence allowance standards for persons classified as the "Three Withouts." Efforts were also made to make compulsory education fairer for all and to standardize the financial aid policy for secondary vocational students. A standard family planning policy for urban and rural areas was established, and urban and rural residents would go on to enjoy equal political rights and democratic management rights in their place of household registration. In January 2011, Chengdu introduced a residence permit system for the "floating population." According to the "Regulations on the Administration of Residence Permits in Chengdu" issued in July 2010, any person who intends to reside in Chengdu for a period of more than one year and who is engaged in local work and businesses, who has purchased or leased local housing, and who has paid social insurance for more than six months may apply for a residence permit. Permit holders would enjoy the same rights and protections as Chengdu residents in 12 areas, including employment, medical and healthcare, family planning, and legal aid.

[10] In 2008, the city of Shenzhen granted access to a comprehensive array of public services for the non-locally registered population through the implementation of the residence permit system. In addition, household registration-based restrictions concerning livelihood such as housing, medical care, pensions, and education were also lifted, meaning that the non-locally registered population would be more or less eligible for "citizen treatment." The success of the reform of the household registration system in major cities such as Chengdu and Shenzhen, after issues encountered in the Zhengzhou reforms, showed that the problems that hindered the household registration reform were solvable and that the unification of household registration was feasible with reasonable policies.

[11] The reform of the household registration system in Chongqing was officially implemented throughout the city starting from August 15, 2010. Chongqing thus put in place a bold plan of allowing three million rural residents to enter the city within two years and 10 million rural residents in ten. However, the reform of the household registration system in Chongqing still bore significant designing tendencies, particularly in the issue of how to handle rural land holdings.

development. The Shenzhen authorities used the residence permit system as a starting point and introduced the policy that would standardize social welfare regardless of household registration. In contrast, in Chengdu, reform of the rural land use system was linked to reform of the household registration system, and the policy of "land for identity, homestead for housing" was implemented. A unified household registration management system that combined the resident's household registration location with their actual domicile was established alongside measures such as residence permit management for the "floating population" in order to remove various additional benefits granted based on household registration status and promote actual household registration standardization. In Chongqing, the authorities referred to, and built upon, the experiences of both Shenzhen and Chengdu, with their most prominent innovation being the use of the "land ticket" system to deal with homesteads and contracted land following household registration transfer. The step-by-step and trial-and-error implementation undertaken shows the basic idea of exploratory reform of the household registration system.

As a result, since the beginning of the new century, the household registration system has changed from that of broad "household registration stratification" to a more limited "household registration inequality," and the significance of unequal household registration status is on the decline. The uneven piloting of local formal systems has, to some extent, mitigated the fragmentation caused by the household registration system. For example, authorities have abolished the review and approval system for household registration and replaced it with conditional access, gradually lowered thresholds for settlement in the city, reduced the level of economic benefits attached to household registration and even abolished the differences between agricultural and non-agricultural household registration to lower the institutional barriers associated with household registration and reduce the urban–rural differences caused as a result. In some provinces and cities, the agricultural and non-agricultural household registration has been abolished and residents have been unified into a standard "resident household registration" system instead. By 2009, 13 cities had abolished their binary systems though most of these local reforms did not go deep. In 2015, it was proposed in the "Opinions on the Key Work of Deepening the Reform of the Economic System in 2015" document that efforts be made to speed up reforms of the household registration system, and in many places local authorities came up with timetables for the abolishment of the distinction between agricultural and non-agricultural registration status and established and implemented residence permit systems. However, there is still a long way to go before true equality of treatment is fully realized, and apart from the new policy of household registration reform, now all benefits attached to the household registration system have been removed.

3.4.3 Summary

The period since 2000 has been a turning point when market reforms have achieved certain results and when the labor market has undergone significant changes that would affect the structure of labor supply and demand in the future. In this period of transition when the market is becoming increasingly diverse and the barriers to labor mobility are gradually being lowered, the market's ability to allocate resources is becoming increasingly important. In this stage, first of all, wage determination mechanisms have proliferated and become more individual or targeted, and wage pricing levels in both the state and private sectors have become less separate from each other. The combined effects of ownership structure and industry type have broadened wage distribution and increased the income gap. Second, while the free flow of rural labor into the cities remains a huge part of the labor market, as there are both a shortage of migrant workers and a struggle among college graduates to find jobs at the same time, the resulting supply-and-demand structure in the labor market has not afforded upward mobility despite free geographic mobility. Third, while the trial-and-error reform of the household registration system has advanced to some degree in some areas, there have not been reforms of the household registration system that would benefit migrant workers from other places, and apart from efforts to consolidate and standardize household registration, the place of origin is still a problem that has not been broadly resolved and continued to be the fundamental obstacle to rural labor mobility. In the 11 years since 2000, market reforms in the labor market have advanced rapidly. This has also been a time in which the multi-tiered segmentation characteristics of China's labor market have emerged. The incomplete reforms of the household registration system and the differences in the level of wage determination between ownership types are the fundamental reasons for such multi-tiered segmentation.

3.5 The Evolutionary Characteristics of China's Labor Market

China's journey to a major country has seen transition to the "dualistic" as well as institutional transformation, and correspondingly, players in the labor market have had to choose between retaining the traditional system and making various changes in response to such transition and transformation. In addition, the labor market involves people themselves, and is related to issues of social justice and social harmony, and the transition experienced by the labor market has been full of difficulties. Since its inception and introduction in China, the concept of the labor market has been deeply intertwined with both institutions and systems and the workers themselves.

The starting points for the establishment of the labor market in China were the strict urban–rural division and the planned economy, and therefore, the labor market has always had to contend with this "entanglement" between these two types of systems and the market system since its inception. It is precisely because of such characteristics that the evolution of China's labor market has combined the most powerful parts of the planning system and the market system. Of course, such "entanglement" is also the reason for the multi-tiered segmentation of China's labor market, and demographic transition has played the most important role in this evolution.

As we can see in Fig. 3.4, the course of the development of China's labor market from its infancy in more than 60 years can be divided into four stages: The first stage was the processes of labor employment and wage determination before the marketization stage. Within the urban–rural dual structure, there was almost complete segmentation due to the unified pricing and strict restrictions on mobility. In the second stage, the labor market was in the early stage of marketization. Market-oriented reforms had begun to advance and new economic types proliferated. Even as the wage determination mechanism remained unified, other types of income distribution began to appear, restrictions on labor mobility was slightly loosened, and the embryonic form of the labor market began to emerge as the employment and wage restrictions that had caused the near-complete segmentation of the market were slowly lifted. The third stage was stage I of market-oriented reforms which set the keynote for the market economy and formally established the existence of the labor market at the national level wage determination mechanisms proliferated due to market factors, and the rural labor began to flow on a large scale. Multi-tiered segmentation of the market based on a dual market segmentation emerged. In the fourth stage, the degree of marketization continued to increase, and the proportion of labor resources allocated by the market exceeded that of the centrally planned system. wage determination mechanisms further diversified, the labor force was able to flow freely across geographical space, and multi-tiered segmentation based on the double duality was formed. In these four stages, a fundamental factor that affected the direction of the labor market was China's demographic structure. The individual behavioral choices of the vast working-age population within the institutional framework were one of the important driving forces for the process of marketization.

From this, we can summarize the evolution of China's labor market as follows: The household registration system and the ownership type are the fundamental causes of what became a "dual" structure of the labor market, and the labor market became almost completely segmented prior to the introduction of the policy of reform and opening up. Due to the marketization, the market gradually evolved to one of multi-tiered segmentation based on household registration system and ownership, with multiple factors acting at the same time. Given the market allocation of labor resources, we can expect the double duality of China's labor market to be reduced in the future with greater integration of the labor market.

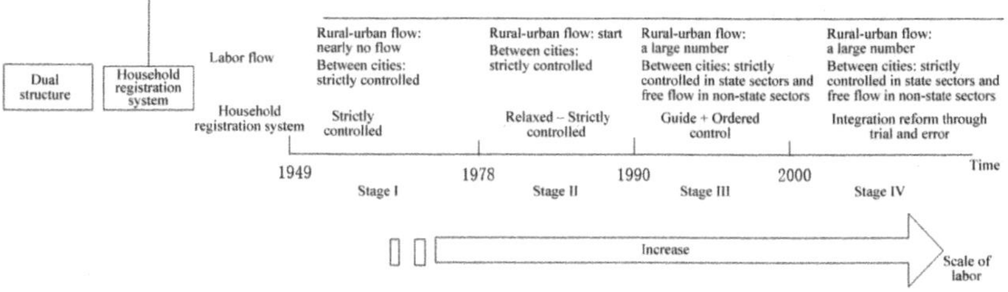

Fig. 3.4 The evolution of China's labor market

CHAPTER 4

A Theoretical Analysis of the Evolution of China's Labor Market from Segmentation to Integration: An Expansion of the Classic MP Model

Across various countries, there have been certain common factors related to the segmentation of the labor market, such as industry, occupation, and individual characteristics. Segmentation also differs depending on the specific conditions of each country. In contrast to other countries, the institutional background responsible for the formation of the labor market is distinctly Chinese in nature. The starting point of seeking a theoretical framework for the analysis of the evolution of China's labor market cannot be separated from China's ground realities. The main thrust of our enquiry here is to use the systems of household registration and ownership as a starting point as we build a theoretical analysis framework for the analysis of China's labor market.

4.1 China's Labor Market Segmentation and the Theoretical Framework

The starting point for examining the evolution of China's labor market in the context of its realities is labor market segmentation. In this part, we use segmentation as a starting point to analyze how the labor market has evolved from complete segmentation to multi-tiered segmentation

Y. Chen, *China's Labor Market in the Transition*,
https://doi.org/10.1007/978-981-99-9160-0_4

given China's special historical background and actual environment, and then theoretically discuss the possibility and conditions of evolution from multi-tiered segmentation to integration.

4.1.1 A Framework for the Theoretical Analysis of Segmentation in China's Labor Market: A "Synthesis" View

The non-competitiveness of the labor market is more pronounced compared to other factors. In China's labor market, labor shortages and difficulties in finding jobs are present at the same time. Contradictory phenomena such as easy employment of migrant workers and college graduates having difficulty finding jobs, and how certain groups having trouble gaining employment are seeing their situations worsen despite improvements in the overall employment situation are real situations that confirm the non-competitiveness of the labor market. However, theoretical research and government policy formulation have been insufficient in helping understand the labor market phenomena during China's period of transition, and a major reason for this is the lack of a theoretically consistent analytical framework (Cai, 2010). In a departure from the paradigm of traditional labor market theory, Western labor market segmentation theory strips the competitive part of the labor market out of the analytical framework and instead emphasizes the segmented nature of the labor market and the role of institutional and social factors on labor remuneration and employment, thus explaining the widening income gap between workers and various discrimination in the labor market. The basic assumptions of labor market segmentation theory are: (1) The labor market is divided into several different markets, each of which has different characteristics and has its own characteristics and methods of allocating labor and determining wages and (2) These sub labor markets are relatively closed, and the reasons for this is a combination of group forces and the constraints of institutional factors (Zhang & Yuan, 2007).

Chinese scholars have inherited the Western Lewis's "dual-sector" theory and labor market segmentation theory to demonstrate the causes of segmentation in China's labor market from multiple perspectives and further came up with various ways concerning how the market is segmented (Cai, 2002; Cheng & Ma, 2003; Lai, 1996; Li, 2002; Luo, 1998; Zhu, 2001; Yao & Li, 2005). Taken together, the work of these scholars can be classified into one of two camps: Based on Lewis's dualist structure and taking rural labor flow as a point of focus (Cai, 2002) and based on the institutional school using divisions in institutions or social group structure as a point of focus (Lai, 1996; Zhang, 2004; Zhu, 2001, 1999). In recent years, some scholars have put forward some new viewpoints on segmentation. For instance, Lu Ming (2011) believes that in Chinese cities, without local urban household registration, migrant workers face at least "three types of discrimination and one obstacle."[1] The short-term characteristics of labor mobility are obvious, but the trend is long-term, forming a "new dual structure" within the city, though there is no specific definition of said structure. Some scholars have further subdivided the segmentation and believe that the segmentation of China's labor market is a three-tier dual structure or believe that double duality exists in the urban labor market: urban–rural duality and internal and external duality, with the former nested in the latter (Zhang, 2009a). Among the divisions caused by institutional structures in China, there is also the division generated during the formation of the new system and the "path-dependent" division of the old system. Moreover, the different levels of the system are not balanced in the evolution process (Zhang, 2009a). Therefore, despite the continued exploration of Chinese scholars for nearly three decades, there are still many differences and difficulties in the theoretical analysis and empirical analysis of labor market segmentation in China.

With the dual structure as the hallmark, at the center of both domestic and foreign scholars' opinions as they analyze the segmentation of the labor market is that the system determines the operation of the labor market. However, it is precisely because of the special attention to the prominent role of the institutional framework that scholars have different opinions on the system and cannot come to a unified theoretical framework (Zhang & Qian, 2009). Combining the existing research on labor market segmentation at home and abroad, the main features are: First, the situation of perfect competition in the labor market has been stripped out

[1] Lu Ming (2011) believes that migrant laborers face at least "three types of discrimination and one obstacle," with the "three types of discrimination" being discrimination in the following areas: (1) Employment, mainly because it is almost impossible for non-local urban residents to enter the government's civil service system and high-income monopoly industries; (2) Social security, as all cities mainly serve local residents (even if some large cities have social security specially provided for migrants, the level of security is relatively low); and (3) Public services, especially as children's education, urban high school education, and higher education are not open to migrants. The "obstacle" here refers to the land system.

of the analytical framework, with scholars concentrating instead on the non-perfectly competitive part, and the competitive part and the non-competitive part in the labor market are completely separated. Second, scholars are using the analytical framework of the dual-sector model of the institutional school to study segmentation, especially segmentation in China, as it most directly reflects the nature of labor market segmentation. However, based on the market segmentation theory of macro analysis, it is difficult to incorporate micro behavior into the analytic framework, and workers' employment choices, that is, the micro behavior of economic agents, become unimportant in the analysis. Third, due to the separate application of mainstream economics and dual-sector economic theory, it is difficult for an analytical framework independent of mainstream economics to explain labor market phenomena at a specific stage when the characteristics of the dual-sector model and classical economics intersect. In particular, researchers are more likely to focus on institutional segmentation while ignoring the results of the economic behavior of micro subjects in the labor market as it is the primary form of segmentation in China's labor market. China's economic development, which has been accompanied by demographic transition and economic transition, calls for efforts to explore a fusion model that combines both the dual-sector model and classical economics.

In this chapter, we argue that understanding labor market segmentation should integrate neoclassical economic theory on the basis of the dual-sector model and analyze from the following three aspects: (1) The labor market of a certain country or region is to be regarded as a complete whole composed of several "silos" in which there are supply and demand sides engaged in perfect competition and imperfect competition, and there are divisions caused by market competition or monopoly; (2) There should be the introduction microeconomic agents, i.e., enterprises and workers. Within a stable institutional framework, the preferences of enterprises and workers and their economic behavior in the labor market have become important driving forces that affect the degree of labor market segmentation; and (3) Institutional and geographical features that affect the labor market are an important driving force for the choice of economic behavior by micro actors. Established geographic and institutional characteristics are embedded in the labor market like wedges and inhibit the integration of the labor market. Therefore, the analysis of labor market segmentation should be based on the economic behavior of workers and micro-individual enterprises in the labor market, and based

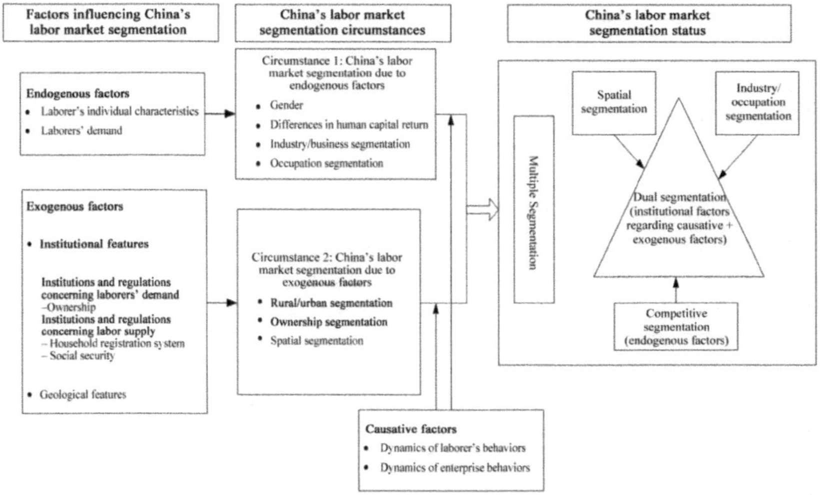

Fig. 4.1 Factors affecting labor market segmentation and their effects

on this a theoretical analysis framework for labor market segmentation under the influence of workers' or enterprises' individual characteristics, institutional, and geographical characteristics can be established. In terms of analytical method and perspective, this method of analysis can be said to be a compromise or synthesis of classical economics and traditional labor market segmentation theory.

Based on this understanding, China's labor market cannot simply be divided into several parts for analysis. Instead, it is necessary for us to start with the factors that cause segmentation of the labor market and to analyze the results and their interrelationships to reveal the state of segmentation in China's labor market. Therefore, the following analytical framework is considered (Fig. 4.1).

Analysis of Influencing Factors with China's Labor Market Segmentation

Considering the realities of China and the basic factors of labor market operations, in this chapter we have divided the factors that affect the degree of labor market segmentation in China into three types: endogenous factors, exogenous factors, and causative factors.

In Chapter 2, we discussed the relationship between integration (or fragmentation) and competitive equilibrium from a conceptual perspective. This analysis is based on the results of price (wage) formation arising from the effect of labor supply and demand and does not involve the characteristics and behaviors of micro subjects within the labor market structure. In this chapter, the characteristics of micro actors and their behavior will be introduced in our discussion of their impact on labor market segmentation or integration, with the former regarded as an endogenous factor and the latter a causative factor. The former will be discussed first, and the causative factor will be discussed after we have analyzed the exogenous factors.

Situation I: Labor Market Segmentation with the Influence of Endogenous Factors

The first factor type, endogenous factors, originates from both the supply and demand sides of the labor market. They reflect the influence of workers and firms in the labor market on the competitiveness and segmentation of the labor market. We divide these endogenous factors into two categories according to whether they will create a monopoly in the labor market: Individual characteristics on the supply side, such as gender, education level, ethnicity, and other differences; and enterprise characteristics on the demand side, such as industry characteristics, employment needs, and other differences. We attribute these factors to endogenous factors that have been extensively discussed in past literature. Therefore, segmentation in the labor market through the action of endogenous factors is reflected as (1) The segregation of employment opportunities and income differences of workers due to gender, age, and education level and (2) Differences in employment needs and incomes arising from differences in the industries and jobs provided by firms.

It can be said that the endogenous factors of labor market segmentation are the inherent influencing factors of micro actors, and that the resulting labor market segmentation does not change due to changes in other influencing factors. In other words, the segmentation generated by endogenous factors does not change over time over the course of the evolution of the labor market, and even in a highly integrated labor market, endogenous factors will still cause inequality and mobility barriers in the labor market.

Situation II: Segmentation of the Labor Market with the Influence of Exogenous Factors

Another type of factors that affect segmentation are exogenous factors. If the inherent and stable nature of endogenous factors can be changed by the behavior of workers or enterprises, then, the inherent and stable nature of exogenous factors is difficult to change to a great extent due to the economic behavior of micro subjects. In this text, we divide the exogenous factors of labor market segmentation into two categories: The first is the institutional segmentation that arises from institutional factors and the other is the geographic segmentation arising from spatial factors.

First, institutional fragmentation resulting from institutional factors. Up till now, institutional factors have been the most critical and major factor in the segmentation of China's labor market. The dual structure and economic system have had the greatest impact on China in the past three decades, among which the household registration system and the ownership played a key role. The household registration system differentiates labor supply, and the biggest distinction here is the binary distinction between urban and rural workers. On the other hand, ownership type divides labor demand into two parts: the state sector and the non-state sector. The desire of rural workers for employment and better lives has always been the driving force behind the reform of the labor market, i.e., reform of the household registration system. The labor demand of units in the private sector has been the leading force in driving reform of the labor market, i.e., reform of the economic system. Whether it be the state or non-state sector or between urban and rural areas, these two types of systems are intertwined with the marketization process, producing a labor market with more complex segmentation characteristics.

Second, spatial factors have created geographic divisions. The geographic segmentation of the labor market caused by spatial factors is affected by transportation costs and land rent. The geographic segmentation comes from two levels: the first is the segmentation of the labor market between regions, and the other is the segmentation of the labor market within cities, especially within the larger cities. The combined result of the two is "spatial mismatch," which is caused by the asymmetric distribution of demand and supply of labor skills in space. In the first situation, unemployed workers in one area cannot freely and easily fill vacant positions in another area; in the second situation, there is a spatial separation between the concentration of unemployed workers in the city center and the concentration of low-skilled jobs in the suburbs; and in the third situation, there is a geographic segmentation created by institutional barriers due to China's system of distribution.

The Role of Causative Factors: Consolidation or Attenuation

From the analysis above, we can see that labor market segmentation caused by endogenous factors is inherent. However, the results of spatial factors in labor market segmentation caused by exogenous factors are similar to endogenous and inherent. Institutional factors, on the other hand, are quite different from time to time, so the division between endogenous factors and spatial factors is of universal significance, while the segmentation caused by institutional factors is often difficult to alleviate in a long period of time due to the stability and dependence of the system, or can become even more stable.

Would it be possible to reduce the segmentation of the labor market or would such segmentation become even more stable? To answer this question, it is necessary to consider how causative factors affect the segmentation of the first two types of factors:

First, the effect of causative factors on the segmentation results caused by endogenous factors. For the worker, segmentation due to personal characteristics can be reduced through individual effort. For example, the level of education produces income differences, and the level of personal human capital can be improved through formal education, on-the-job training, or learning by doing, which helps to narrow income differences as a result. However, at the same time, factors such as occupational segmentation and industry monopoly-related segmentation are often made even more stable by micro-individual economic behaviors. From the perspective of the worker, choosing better positions in monopoly industries to maximize their utility though constrained by personal conditions would naturally mean that only a small number of workers actually enter such positions while most workers take on relatively poor jobs. On the other hand, the enterprise chooses workers who can maximize its expected profits and sets screening conditions according to different industries or occupations. The matching result after the two parties search and select each other naturally makes such an endogenous segmentation even more stable.

Second, the influence of causative factors on the segmentation caused by exogenous factors. Institutional and spatial factors divide the labor market into different segments, and workers can arbitrage between different segments of the labor market. When institutional factors are beneficial for a certain type of workers, the same type of workers will have a group effect under the protection of the system due to the consistency of their individual characteristics. The maximization of the employment search utility of workers is largely restricted to the same group and thus, the segmentation effect of institutional factors is made more stable. Differences in employment income between spaces promote the flow of workers to places with high yields, i.e., arbitrage. When institutional factors constrain the occurrence of spatial arbitrage, the labor force is completely isolated, and once the institutional factors that act on space are lowered, the opportunity for spatial arbitrage will be attenuated in the flow process though the group effect of institutional factors would be maintained. Therefore, although spatial segmentation will weaken through the action of causative factors, the resultant group effect stabilizes institutional segmentation.

As a result, the segmentation results caused by endogenous and exogenous factors are reinforced or diminished by the influence of causal factors, and the labor market then becomes more segmented or integrated as a result.

In Chapter 2, we defined labor market integration as the transfer of labor overdemand and supply overdemand between different markets in an environment of labor market search friction (i.e., transaction costs). When markets are integrated, supply and demand in one market can affect prices and/or labor mobility in another market. In the absence of endogenous and exogenous factors, there is no division of the labor market, which is competitively balanced and integrated. However, reality is always imperfect, and the ideal integration is always absent. Based on the sufficient and necessary conditions for labor market integration, we believe that (1) When the differences in pay levels between the divisions tend to converge, the arbitrage opportunities between segments decrease and (2) When the barriers to the flow of labor between different markets are lowered, the labor market has a tendency to integrate when these two conditions are met.

The Segmentation of China's Labor Market and the Possibility of its Integration

Given China's context in transition, we believe that there are the following problems in analyses of the segmentation of China's labor market from the viewpoint of the "dual" structure: First, scholars who have adopted the segmented labor market (SLM) approach have also followed the view of foreign scholars that there are major sectors and minor sectors in China's labor market, or they all say that there is a distinction between "primary sectors" and "secondary sectors." We do not deny that such segmentation must exist in China's labor market. The fundamental premise of using the above analytical method is that there are "good" jobs and "bad" jobs in the labor market. A "good" job in China often means a "good" unit or employer. The difference is that even a "bad" job in SLM theory can become "better" than a "good" job in a "bad" unit when one is employed by a "good" unit, and therefore, following such a dual classification method may not fully explain China's labor market. Second, scholars who have adopted Lewis's dual-sector theory have inherited the analytical methods and viewpoints of the urban–rural dual structure. The dual-sector theory reflects three important features of the economic structure: interactions between modern and traditional sectors, the abundance of labor, and the maintaining of differences in the labor market. The situation in China points to the existence of the latter two characteristics, and in particular, due to the division between urban and rural areas caused by the household registration system, the strict restrictions on rural–urban migration have been maintained. This is something that has been widely recognized. However, in the context of the continued reform of the system of household registration, in the process of the transformation from the duality of urban and rural household registration to the unity of the household registration system, the constraining role of the household registration system in resource allocation will become more prominent. In addition, it may be more appropriate to discuss the interactions between the modern sector and the traditional sector on the ground in China as the interactions between the private and state sectors. The difference between the work in "good" and "bad" units is also the difference between the work in the state and private sectors. When we combine segmentation theory and urban–rural dual-sector theory and apply them to the analysis of China, it is clear that thinking of the segmentation of China's labor market through the household registration system and the ownership is the fundamental way that effectively integrates the two theories.

The household registration system and the ownership are the most influential systems in China's economic and social life, and also the first institutional constraints that enterprises or units and workers face in the labor market. We know that workers choose jobs to maximize their utility, and that firms choose their workers to maximize their profits. In the context of China's realities, workers and enterprises or agencies will first consider the choices available in the context of these two types of systems. For instance, workers with urban household registration or local household registration are more willing to choose job vacancies in entities within the state sector, or entities within the state sector are more willing to look first at locally registered workers. The influence of other factors should then be considered on this foundation. Obviously, the household registration system and the ownership divide labor supply and demand into two categories, that is, labor demand in the state and private sectors and labor supply in urban and rural areas. When the urban–rural division meets the state-private division, the flow of rural workers from the urban private sector to the urban state sector will naturally meet with the corresponding obstacles. The labor demand of the private and state sectors allocates workers with different household registration statuses to various economic sectors, and wage determination is different due to the ownership type while labor mobility is differentiated due to the household registration system. The resulting segmentation is what we call double duality. Based on this, combined with the segmentation results caused by endogenous factors and spatial factors, we have produced the multi-tiered segmentation results for China's labor market.

China's labor market is in a state of multi-tiered segmentation due to the above three types of factors. This multi-tiered segmentation has at its foundation the duality arising as a result of the household registration system and the ownership type and the further influence of endogenous segmentation and spatial segmentation. However, the individual behavior of micro subjects can strengthen or weaken such divisions. This view combines the basic ideas of classical economics, segmentation theory, and the model of the urban–rural dual structure, so we call it a "synthesis" view.

This view suggests that any analysis of China's labor market should use duality as a starting point to better understand the evolution of the labor market. Therefore, in the second half of this chapter, we establish a framework of theoretical analysis to discuss the results of this double duality and the related trends.

4.1.2 *Theoretical Analysis Framework of China's Dual Labor Market: Matching Equilibrium in a State of Bilateral Heterogeneity*

Reich et al. (1973) viewed labor market segmentation as a historical process in which changes in political power lead to the double duality of the labor market into secondary markets with varying market characteristics and rules of conduct. Thus, in this chapter we argue that labor market segmentation generated by institutional factors is a crucial aspect, and that the interaction of the three types of factors affecting labor market segmentation over time leads to various patterns of labor market segmentation depending on the strength or weakness of each influencing force. For example, the complete segmentation that was in place in China prior to the introduction of the policy of reform and opening up is the type of segmentation that occurs without endogenous and causative factors; however, the market segmentation in the early stage of reform and opening up is a kind of segmentation produced by causative factors and institutional effects. Today, due to the effect of systems old and new and various market forces working at the same time, the state of segmentation in China's labor market is multiple and complex. At the same time, there have been changes in the institutional factors, and thus causative factors, which act as a bridge linking endogenous and exogenous factors, have become crucial in the analysis of labor market segmentation.

In this text, we posit that causative factors—enterprises and workers—are the most important agents in the labor market. Within a limited time window, workers search for jobs and decide which type of jobs they would accept to maximize their utility while firms, the employers, decide what kind of workers they would accept to maximize their profits. Therefore, the introduction of causative factors into labor market segmentation needs to be based on the analytical framework of Mortensen and Pissarides (1994, 1999) and Pissarides (2000) and labor market modeling has to be characterized by double duality.

There are various transaction costs in labor market transactions, and in particular, where information is incomplete, it takes time for workers or firms to search for suitable jobs or maximize their utility or profit. In this way, market frictions have created a situation where vacancies and unemployed workers exist at the same time in the labor market. Unlike standard supply–demand models, the introduction of job search theory emphasizes fixed friction during the exchange process, and this opens up many new perspectives. Mortensen and Pissarides (1994, 1999) have used a matching function that determines employment based on labor supply and demand to represent the transaction costs that exist in the labor market, thus providing us with strong explanations for unemployment, income disparities, and job creation in firms as well as making it possible for us to analyze the Beveridge curve. The classical job search-and-matching theory is based on the analysis of the ex-ante situation where both workers and firms are homogeneous to obtain unemployment at equilibrium, tightness in the labor market, and wage determination mechanisms and their dynamic changes. Because of its parsimony and flexibility, it has been expanded considerably in recent years: (1) The introduction of the ex-ante heterogeneity of workers or firms, especially the introduction of skill-biased heterogeneity between firms and workers, has been discussed in numerous literature (Acemoglu, 1999, 2001; Albrecht et al., 2002; Shimer & Smith, 2000) and (2) The idea of exogenous shocks that lead to job destruction or new job creation, including aggregate shocks and heterogeneous shocks, has also been introduced (Merlino, 2009; Mortensen & Nagypál, 2007; Shimer, 2005; Sala & Silva, 2009a, 2009b). New developments in these studies, especially in the labor market segmentation or the duality of labor markets, are an excellent reference for theoretical research on China.

The existence of the double duality undoubtedly increases the transaction costs of labor market participants and increases the friction between workers and firms in job search and matching. This makes it difficult to find a unique equilibrium in the classical MP model and implies the existence of multiple equilibria. Merlino (2009) argues that the existence of multiple-equilibrium characteristics in job search models is mainly due to the role of two types of externalities. The first stems from the externalities of job search friction. Job seeker activity reduces the matching rate of other job seekers, which is a congestion externality, and therefore increases the matching opportunity for the enterprise, i.e., a thick market externality.[2] The second is the existence of a coordination externality

[2] Thick market externality means that the presence of such forces leads to more exchange opportunities in the market and expands the market size. There are a large number of buyers and sellers in a thick market, and thus search cost is relatively low. Everyone chooses the employment opportunities that would maximize their utility, but the fact is that what they do leads to an overall outcome for society as a whole. As a result, thick markets can be considered to occur more frequently in times of economic boom, and less frequently at times of recession (Dimond, 1982).

in the search strategies from both sides of the market. This is because firms determine the types of vacancies they will advertise in the labor market, and workers determine the kinds of jobs they will accept. Within a dual structure, search and consistency externalities have an impact on matching outcomes through additional entry (exit) costs under institutional constraints and arbitrage behavior between market segments. To do this, we consider individually the cost of employee dismissal and entry, arbitrage conditions among segmented sectors, with the former affecting congestion externality while the latter changing the behavior of consistent externalities. As the ability of workers to search for vacancies is affected, segmentation is produced. Therefore, when firms or units and workers are heterogeneous, we consider the equilibrium result of the dual[3] structure and its dynamic changes.

4.2 The Evolution of China's Labor Market in the Context of "Double Duality": A Benchmark Model

4.2.1 Transactions in the Labor Market: The Job Matching Process

Transactions in the labor market are achieved through the matching between workers and vacancies through an overall match function (Blanchard & Dimond, 1989; Pissarides, 1989). A well-behaved match function can be formed by giving the number of workers looking for jobs and the number of firms looking for workers at any point in time, and it reflects the trade and congestion externalities in the search process of the labor market. Assuming that the total labor force in the labor market is 1 and that an amount ρ of labor is produced at each time point, and the rate of exiting the labor market at the same time (including resignation, retirement) remains the same.

[3] While we have drawn on Zhang Zhaoshi (2007)'s point of view that the dual labor market in China [should be taken] as the starting point for theoretical analysis, as explained in Sect. 4.1, in this chapter, we also argue that there is no nested relationship within this duality. Yao Yang (2011) believes that the household registration system is no longer an issue of basic rights but rather of resource allocation, and therefore, this duality is a process that affects resource allocation. We believe that duality acts on both the supply and demand sides of the labor market and as a result it affects the search behavior of workers and leads to the existence of multiple equilibria in the labor force, thereby causing the labor market to be segmented.

There are a large number of labor supply sources or "silos" in the economy, denoted by i or j, respectively, and given the matching process of the labor market, the state of labor from the labor supply source is either employed (E_i) or unemployed (U_i), and firms from category j also have two states in the labor market: either their job vacancies filled by workers (J_j) and thus with output, or the firm has announced vacancies and is searching for workers (V_j).

4.2.2 Labor Market Policies

After the transformation of the systems and institutions, the most distinctive labor market policies in China's transition period are as follows: the exertion of influence by old and new systems alike, and the "dual-track system" of enterprise employment and the household registration system that separates urban and rural areas.

First of all,[4] the "dual-track system" means that the employment decisions of enterprises are differentiated according to the type of ownership, which determines the types of jobs accessible by workers. There are sectors in the market that provide two types of jobs, state-owned (I) and private or non-state-owned (O), denoted by j, $j = (I, O)$. Non-state-owned enterprises are free to enter and exit the labor market, that is, there are no entry and exit costs. When a state-owned enterprise dismisses a worker, it must pay the dismissal cost f, where f represents the loss of income after matching, in other words, f is the red-tape cost imposed by policy (Costain, 2011). The total number of firms or units in the labor market is 1, the number of vacancies is V, which gives us $V_I = V - V_O = \phi V, 0 < \phi < 1$. Here, ϕ stands for the vacancy ratio at state-owned firms on the market, V_I stands for the number of vacancies at state-owned firms, and V_O stands for the number of vacancies at non-state-owned firms.

Secondly, one of the institutional conditions for the segmentation of China's labor market—the household registration system—is now no

[4] Ye et al. (2011) used enterprise data from the first national economic census in 2004 to test two representative views on the wage gap of enterprises, and found that both ownership type and industry monopoly were factors that played a role in the enterprise wage gap. However, the influence of ownership was greater than that of behavioral monopoly, and industry monopoly could only bring direct wage premiums to employees of state-owned enterprises with no direct impact found with other types of enterprises. *Management World*, 2011, No. 4.

longer a fundamental issue involving individual rights, but a problem involving the allocation of resources (Yao, 2011). The household registration system divides workers searching for jobs in the market into two categories: the labor force with urban household registration (denoted by C) and the labor force with rural household registration (denoted by R).[5]

Within the dual structure, workers in the market are in one of four states: either employed in or looking for jobs in the state sector, or employed in or looking for jobs in the non-state sector.[6] Combined with the heterogeneity of workers due to the household registration system, a worker may exist in one of the following eight states:

Unemployment status: U_{RI} U_{RO} U_{CI} U_{CO}. These four states represent the expected utility of workers with urban and rural household registration from withdrawing from unemployment from the state-owned and non-state sectors. No matter what sector the unemployed come from, the expected utility of unemployment is the same, and in addition, for those from the state sector, long-term fixed labor contracts ensure that there is little or no unemployment in the sector and therefore, we can assume that there is no unemployment in the state sector, $U_{RI} = U_{CI} = U_{RO} = U_{CO} = U$. In short, the expected value of unemployment status has nothing to do with whether one is looking at the state-owned/non-state sectors and the household registration system.

Employment status: E_{RI} E_{RO} E_{CI} E_{CO}. These four states represent the expected utility of workers with rural and urban household registration matched with state-owned and non-state-owned entities. The employment expectations of workers with rural and urban household registration are the same for both sectors, and there are $E_{RI} = E_{CI} = E_I$, $E_{RO} = E_{CO} = E_O$.

Within this dual structure, the labor force with urban and rural household registration searching for work in enterprises in the state-owned and non-state sectors of the labor market forms four possible match states as shown in Table 4.1.

The matches of the labor force with urban household registration with the vacant positions in state and non-state sectors are represented by (O, C) and (I, C), respectively; the matches of the labor force with

[5] In this chapter, the labor force with rural household registration is taken as workers with rural household registration who are engaged in non-farm employment.

[6] For the convenience of analysis, in this chapter we do not consider the status of workers who are idle or who perform domestic work.

Table 4.1 Job matching types within the dual structure

Match result		*Worker type*	
		Urban household registration (C)	*Rural household registration* (R)
Job vacancy type	Non-state-owned (O)	(O, C)	(O, R)
	Change of status[a]	↓	↓
	State-owned (I)	(I, C)	(I, R)

[a]Due to the difference in wages and the related benefits between the state and non-state sectors as well as between various household registration systems, status changes from state-owned to non-state-owned entities and from urban household registration to rural household registration have not been included in the consideration here. This change is considered to be one-way and irreversible

rural household registration with the vacant positions in state and non-state sectors are represented by (O, R) and (I, R), respectively. At the same time, the combination of ownership and the household registration system makes the conversion of the two types of workers between the three states a one-way conversion. That is, workers from non-state sectors will accept workers from the state sector, not vice versa. The labor mobility of enterprises in the state and non-state sectors is definitely closely related to the household registration system. The location or nature of one's household registration status determines the sector one enters.[7] The household registration system increases part of the expenses that workers need to bear for their identity conversion in addition to the search cost. For the sake of simplicity, in this chapter we only consider the conversion cost arising from the household registration system. That is, the cost of converting one's labor household registration during job hunting, Z, that is, the arbitrage condition from the state sector to the non-state sector.

[7] The management and technical personnel that China's big cities are willing to accept are posted by the human resources department, and they and their families can obtain household registration at their destination. Other jobs that can be supplied by the local labor market are also closed to labor from other places, especially those with rural household registration. The labor and employment plan of the employer must be approved by the labor and human resources departments, and local household registration is a prerequisite. Only jobs where the local labor supply cannot meet or the government has not intervened in can be filled with "outside" labor. Yang Yunyan and Chen Jinyong (2000), "Layers and Competition in a Labor Market Amidst Transformation: An Empirical Analysis That Takes Wuhan as an Example," *Social Sciences in China*, No. 5.

Assume that the job-finding rate (or vacancy-filling rate) of each segment of the labor market or "silo" depends on the number of vacancies available $v = \sum v_j = v_I + v_O$ and the number of unemployed workers in the market, u, i.e., how "tight" the labor market is. $\theta = \frac{\sum v_j}{u}$ and $\theta_j \equiv \frac{v_j}{u}$, $j = I, O$. The overall match function is written as $m = m\ (u,\ v)$. The unconditional probability of matching each job vacancy with an unemployed worker is $q(\theta_j) = \frac{m(u,v_j)}{v_j} = m(\theta_j, 1)$, $q'(\theta_j) < 0$, $q''(\theta_j) > 0$, which satisfies the Inada condition, and furthermore, $\lim_{\theta_j \to 0} q(\theta_j) = \infty$, the job-acquisition rate of unemployed workers or the unemployment exit rate is $\theta_j q(\theta_j) = \frac{m(u,v_j)}{u} = \frac{\theta m(u,v_j)}{v_j}$, and both the vacancy matching rate and the job-finding rate fall within the Poisson distribution. And throughout the analysis, it is assumed that on-the-job search is unavailable.

4.2.3 Job Destruction and Job Creation

Job creation occurs when firms and workers meet and enter into employment contracts. Until then, the firm must create a new job opening and seek out potential employees, while the unemployed worker seeks out potential employers. The employment contract is simply a rule for a given wage rate at a given time. The working hours are fixed and there is no termination cost for either party at any time.

There are two types of firms in the economy that produce homogeneous products: state-owned enterprises (I) and non-state-owned enterprises (O). Assume that the labor productivity of the firm is y_I, y_O.[8] Firms create job vacancies until their growth profits are exhausted, i.e., firms

[8] Zhang Jie, Li Ke, and Liu Zhibiao (2011). "Market Transformation and Enterprise Productivity: A Study of the Chinese Economy," *China Economic Quarterly*, Vol. 10, No. 2. The results of a January 2011 empirical study show that there were significant differences in productivity between state-owned and non-state-owned enterprises, with the productivity of foreign-invested enterprises significantly higher than that of Hong Kong, Macao, and Taiwan-invested enterprises as well as private and state-owned enterprises. However, the productivity difference between private enterprises and the Hong Kong, Macao, and Taiwan-invested enterprises was relatively small, and the productivity of state-owned enterprises is significantly lower than the other three types of enterprises. However, in recent years, strategies such as allowing the private economy to step up and the loosening of micro-level control have improved the labor productivity of state-owned enterprises. In 2007, the average total factor productivity (TFP) of state-owned enterprises

create new job openings until their value $V(y)$ drops to 0. The cost of vacant positions at each time point is C, and the benefit of vacant positions is the new match generated using probability $q(\theta_j)$. This new match is hired in a state-owned or non-state-owned firm, so the value of the job filled with the match is J^I, J^0, or 0 if the firm does not hire to fill the vacancy.

China's unique system of transformation is characterized by two types of job destruction and job creation with the following characteristics:

Type 1: State-owned actors have two distinct characteristics in the labor market, which are industry monopoly and administrative monopoly. First, administrative monopoly means that the economic behavior of an enterprise is under the jurisdiction of the administrative agency, and this kind of jurisdiction is reflected in obvious differences in ownership, and the work of enterprises within such jurisdiction is stable and long term. The wage determination mechanism is based on a fixed post wage. Within an administrative monopoly, the barriers to entry are relatively high for workers, and exit mechanisms basically do not exist. At the same time, enterprises enjoy comparatively greater protection from the system and can pass on their production costs to consumers while having zero incentives to control their costs. Secondly, industry monopoly[9] is manifested as the restriction of market entry and exit in an environment with imperfect competition, which enables enterprises in monopolized industries to have significant price control power and significant pricing power in the labor market. With the protection afforded by administrative monopoly, state-owned actors harness their industry monopoly to bring about wage premiums compared to firms in competitive industries. Therefore, it is assumed that state-owned actors adopt a fixed quotation mechanism to determine their pay level w_I^P.

was 6.92, and the average TFP of private enterprises and Hong Kong, Macao, and Taiwan-invested enterprises were 6.74 and 6.91, respectively. The TFP of state-owned enterprises has surpassed that of private enterprises and Hong Kong, Macao, and Taiwan-invested enterprises, indicating that the productivity gap between state-owned and non-state-owned enterprises is getting smaller and smaller. Given such circumstances, for the convenience of analysis and the proximity to reality, in this chapter, we take that there is no difference in productivity levels between state-owned and non-state-owned enterprises.

[9] There is evidence that monopolists and other firms that can influence prices pay higher wages than competitive wages. Workers employed in highly concentrated industries earn wages higher than their peers in competitive markets. Bauhaus (2010), *Labor Economics*, p. 221.

In steady state, the income stream when the jobs offered by state-owned actors are filled comes from the average gains from the productivity of the jobs and the changes in the status of these jobs, as well as the average gains from the jobs transitioning from non-state sectors to state sectors. Therefore, the Bellman equation for this income stream is as follows:

$$rJ_I = y_I - w_I^P + \lambda[V_I - J_I - f] \tag{4.1}$$

$(1-\varphi)\psi$ is the conversion cost of the labor force from rural household registration to urban ones, λ is the probability of job destruction from external heterogeneous shocks, and f is the cost of employee dismissal.

The Bellman equation for the income stream for the corresponding state-owned vacancy is:

$$rV_I = -C + q(\theta_I)(J_I - V_I) \tag{4.2}$$

C is the unit time cost of the vacant position, representing the cost incurred (advertising fees, agency fees, consulting services fees) resulting from vacancies and the recruitment of the appropriate employees to fill the vacancies. Profit maximization and free entry require all gains from new jobs to be exhausted. That is to say, the condition for job creation, for state-owned actors, is that the value of unfilled vacancies is exactly equal to the fixed entry cost, with $V_I = k$.

Therefore, from Formula (4.2) and the condition of free entry, we have:

$$\frac{c + rk}{q(\theta_I)} = \frac{y_I - W_I^P - r(f + k)}{r + \lambda} \tag{4.3}$$

Equation (4.3) is the job creation equation (JC) for state-owned actors. The above formula shows that in addition to the impact of productivity and pay levels, the labor demand of these actors is also affected by the cost of opening up new job positions "within the system."

Type II: Job positions in the non-state sector. The typical differences between positions in a state sector and a non-state sector are in the wage determination mechanism, whether firms enjoy administrative monopoly, and whether in the absence of administrative monopoly there are jobs with industry monopoly and competition in the market. The former receive wage premiums due to their monopoly power, while the latter are at a market-clearing level.

The Bellman equation for the income stream for a non-vacant position in the non-state sector is:

$$rJ_O = y_O - w_O^B + (\lambda + \gamma)(V_O - J_O) \tag{4.4}$$

Equation (4.4) shows the value stream for non-vacant jobs in the non-state sector is equal to the immediate profit ($y_O - w_O^B$). Add to that the average earnings associated with positions that have the potential to change status $(\lambda + \gamma)(V_O - J_O)$, this profit is actually due to the separation of personnel and positions, and the ratio of positions in the non-state sector to be destroyed is $(\lambda + \gamma)$, with $\gamma > 0$ being the excess job destruction rate that reflects the city's ability to enforce laws with both state-owned and non-state sectors.

The Bellman equation for the income stream of a vacant job position is:

$$rV_O = -C + q(\theta_O)(J_O - V_O) \tag{4.5}$$

If the conditions for creating work in the non-state sector have been met, $V_O = 0$, then:

$$\frac{C}{q(\theta_O)} = \frac{y_O - W_O^B}{r + \lambda + \gamma} \tag{4.6}$$

Equation (4.6) shows that in addition to the productivity level, wage cost, interest rate level, and external heterogeneity shocks, the labor demand of the non-state sector is also affected by legal discrimination that benefits the state sector.

According to Eqs. (4.3) and (4.6), there are differences in the entry conditions for state-owned and non-state-owned firms. As a result, there are two different labor demand curves in the market:

Proposition 1 (the labor demand curve) There are two different demand curves in what is a dual labor market, namely, the labor demand curves of the state sector: $\frac{c+rk}{q(\theta_I)} = \frac{y_I - W_I^P - r(f+k)}{r+\lambda}$ (4.3) and of the non-state sector: $\frac{c}{q(\theta_O)} = \frac{y_O - W_O^B}{r+\lambda+\gamma}$ (4.6).

4.2.4 *Workers' Employment and the Value of Unemployment*

Workers influence the resulting equilibrium through their job search and, consequently, wage decisions. In the labor market policy analysis section, we believe that the policy variable affecting workers is mainly the household registration system. This exogenous institutional variable acts on workers and changes their job search strategies in the labor market.

Assume that the individual worker is risk-neutral, then $W_j^t, t = B, P, j = I, O$ represents the expected income from employment. The worker's unemployment insurance income is b; assume that it is the average unemployment insurance income level in society. Unemployed workers from the private sector can obtain the average unemployment insurance benefits in society, while the amount of unemployment insurance benefits of unemployed workers from the state sector is $b[1 + \eta \times 1(j = I)]$), and η represents the benefit excess obtained by workers from the state sector compared to workers from the private sector.

Situation 1: Employed in the State Sector. A worker with rural household registration is eligible for urban household registration once they are employed by an employer in the state sector. For workers with rural household registration, when they are employed in the state sector, the expected utility of workers' unemployment is the same as U_I, and therefore, the immediate utility streams for workers employed in the state sector are:

$$rE_I = w_I^P + \lambda(U_I - E_I) \tag{4.7}$$

Equation (4.7) shows that the immediate utility streams for workers employed in the state sector come from the sum of the utility of wage income and changes in employment status.

Situation 2: Employment in the private sector.

The immediate utility streams for workers employed in the private sector are:

$$rE_O = w_O^B + (\lambda + \gamma)(E_O - U) \tag{4.8}$$

The immediate utility stream for the expected utility of unemployment within a dual structure is:

$$\begin{aligned} rU = b[1 + \eta \times 1(j = I)] + \varphi\theta_I q(\theta_I) \times \ [E_I - U] \ \times 1(j = I) \\ + (1 - \varphi)\theta_O q(\theta_O) \ \times (E_O - U) \times 1(j = O) \end{aligned} \tag{4.9}$$

Equation (4.9) shows that the reservation wage in the labor market is determined by unemployment benefits (including unemployment-related benefits such as unemployment insurance and social welfare transfer payments), and the average income brought about by changes in the employment status of workers in the state-owned and private sectors, that is, the loss suffered by workers due to leaving their jobs, with $\theta_j q(\theta_j)$, $j = I, O$ as the unemployment exit rate.

4.2.5 Wage Determination, Reservation Wage, and Match Reminder

Wages in China are often determined by the correlation between the factor and product markets and the corresponding institutional arrangements throughout the process of reform. The dual-track path to liberalization has greatly promoted the development of marketization in China. Its essence is that prices are liberalized at the margin, though ultra-marginal planned prices and quotas remained for some time before they were phased out (Rodrik, 2009). The development of the labor market has also followed this path. However, the difference is that the dual-track system in the labor market faded out more slowly and therefore, the coexistence of the "dual-track system" of market pricing in the commodity market and market prices in the labor market became a unique feature in China's labor market. It is due to the long-standing existence of the dual price system in China's labor market that a dual wage determination structure naturally emerged in the labor market.

Wage Determination Mechanisms and Reservation Pay Level
Neoclassical economists believe that given the conditions of labor competition, wages are determined by the marginal productivity of labor following the interaction between labor supply and demand; where search friction exists in the job search, quasi-rents are generated when workers maximize their search returns due to their time and other costs. The existence of quasi-rent means that market wages are not the only form of wages present in this environment. The distribution of quasi-rent becomes the result of the game between workers and enterprises as they seek to maximize their respective benefits. Thus, the residual distribution that happens through bargaining becomes the main way of wage determination. In a multi-level labor market, wages are determined not only by skill differences but also by institutional arrangements and the degree of

market segmentation. To a certain extent, the latter has a greater impact on the allocation of labor between regions and the distribution of income among employees (Démurger et al., 2009). As such, wage determination in China's labor market differs between two sectors: the state sector and the non-state sector.

The state sector has inherited the wage determination mechanism of the planned economy era, though the state sector—building on the flexible wage system[10] that was introduced in 1985—has become increasingly market-oriented. However, the wage determination mechanism of the planned employment system has retained enough influence that cannot be ignored. With the restructuring of state-owned enterprises, a more market-oriented approach to wage payment, employment, and employee disposal is now in place. However, wage decisions are still made based on the mechanism of reporting the total wage budget of the enterprise to the relevant administrative department for review, and in this sense, wage determination at state-owned enterprises has retained the methods of the planned economy to a certain extent. Apart from state-owned enterprises, total wages and wage growth at other state-owned entities, such as administrative institutions, are still regulated by the government. A substantive system for employees to negotiate wages and employment with their employers has yet to be formed in the state sector. As far as SOEs are concerned, the government still plays a key role in their wage decision and employment (Lu, 2004). As a result, wage decisions in the state sector, especially in large and medium-sized state-owned enterprises with monopoly power and the public sector, still have strong institutional characteristics. That is, wages in the state sector are similar to wage posting in economics. Therefore, we assume that any worker i would have w_I^P, in which P stands for the wage determination mechanism in the form of a wage offer and I stands for the state-owned employer. What this means is that enterprises that make wage offer commitments have an advantage in bargaining; at the same time, the state sector knows exactly what kind of applicants will be hunting jobs within the sector, and therefore imposes constraints on the applicant's entry. Applicants who meet these criteria decide whether to accept or reject such positions.

[10] In 1993, the state introduced inflexible wages. In 1995, the labor department released Notice on Improving Flexible wages, which stipulated that the annual flexible increment in wages is $H = H_0 \times \beta + \alpha$, where H is the increment in wages, H_0 last year's total wages, β adjustment coefficient of wages, α special adjustment coefficient.

Due to the necessity of analysis and the promotion of reform in China in recent years, in this chapter we assume that the state sector's ex-ante wage offer is the pay level that maximizes its profits, that is, max $(p - w_I^P)G(w_I^P)$, $G(w)$ being the labor supply function. If $G(w_I^P) = (w_I^P - \underline{w}_I^P)^\varepsilon$, then, $w_I^P = \frac{\varepsilon}{1+\varepsilon}p + \frac{1}{1+\varepsilon}b_0$ in which ε is the price elasticity of labor supply, p is the product price, and $\underline{w}_I^P$ is the minimum pay level at which a worker accepts employment. If $\frac{\varepsilon}{1+\varepsilon} = \beta$, we then have

$$w_I^P = \beta p + (1 - \beta)\underline{w}_I^P,$$

where $\underline{w}_I^P$ is the reservation wage in the job search model, that is, rU. Then, the equation above may be rewritten as follows:

$$w_I^P = \beta \times P + (1 - \beta)rU \tag{4.10}$$

The non-state sector has grown and developed from nothing to what it is today. Although the power of China's workers in the bargaining process is still weak, in recent years, with the advancement of the collective bargaining system, workers are now beginning to use collective bargaining to determine wages in some regions. At the same time, since the non-state sector has a higher degree of marketization, the formation of wages is determined by the comparison of supply-and-demand forces on both sides of the labor market. We can consider that the surplus distribution of the non-state sector follows the principles of classical economics and adopts the method of bargaining, that is, the bargaining pay level of enterprises is w_O^B. Here, B indicates that the pay level is determined by the bargaining mode, and O stands for private-sector units, reflecting the dependence of wages or wages on labor productivity. This precludes the possibility that a firm's wage decision is based on the types of workers, that is, the firm's wage offer does not depend on the true value of the worker to the firm. The reason for this is that it is difficult to fully describe the types of workers in demand at the time of job posting, although wage bargaining can be done by taking into account some observable individual characteristics such as education.

Wages in the non-state sector are determined by bargaining, that is, an ex-post wage determination mechanism after the worker is matched with the firm. According to Mortensen and Pissarides (1994, 1999) and Pissarides (2000), job matching generates economic rent that is exactly equal to the sum of the firm's and worker's search costs (including foregone wages and profits). In addition to compensating for the cost of the work, wages are a form of allocation to this partial monopoly rent of the economy. Assuming that monopoly rent is allocated according to the Nash solution to the bargaining problem, then the maximization of wage w_{ij}^{B} is the weighted result of the net earnings of the worker and the firm after post-matching. To get a match between an unemployed worker with a firm, the worker gives up U with E while the enterprise gives up V with J. Therefore, the wages of workers in this case satisfy:

$$w_{O}^{B} = \arg\max(E_{O}^{B} - U_{O}^{B})^{\beta}(J_{O}^{B} - V_{O}^{B})^{1-\beta}$$

The first-order conditions (FOC) is followed by:

$$\alpha(J_O - V_O) = (1-\alpha)(E_O - U_O) \Rightarrow E_O - U_O = \beta(J_O + E_O - V_O - U_O)$$

Here, α stands for the worker's bargaining power, and also their share in the total surplus produced by job matching.

From the above formula, it can be inferred that the wages of workers outside the system are produced by them:

$$w_{O}^{B} = \alpha y + (1-\alpha)b \tag{4.11}$$

Match Remainder

Workers can be separated without cost in the state sector regarding job matching, that is, the surplus of workers working in the state sector is $E_I - U_I$. On the other hand, the firm has to pay for layoffs when the job matches are separated in the state sector f. Therefore, when there is external selection, the match reminder of the state sector is: $J_I - V_I + f$.

The total surplus of the state sector is: $S_I = E_I - U_I + J_I - V_I + f$.

The market power of the state sector is β, which gives us:

$$J_I - V_I + f = (1-\beta)S_I \tag{4.12}$$

$$E_I - U_I = \beta S_I \tag{4.13}$$

As for job matching in the non-state sector, workers and firms can be separated without cost, and the surplus of workers working in the non-state sector is $E_O - U_O$; the remaining enterprise vacancies are $J_O - V_O$, meaning that the total match reminder for the non-state sector is:

$$S_O = E_O - U_O + J_O - V_O$$

Wages at non-state-owned firms are determined by the Nash bargaining mechanism between firms and workers and staff separation is treated as an exogenous choice. The bargaining power of the worker is α. This means that the remainder allocation rules for the non-state sector are:

$$J_O - V_O = (1 - \alpha)S_O \tag{4.14}$$

$$E_O - U_O = \alpha S_O \tag{4.15}$$

Thus, the total surplus, both state-owned and non-state-owned, is: $S = S^I + S^O$.

4.2.6 *The Wage Curves of the Dual Labor Market*

We now turn to the analysis of the wage determination mechanism of the dual labor market. There are two distinct wage curves due to differences between the state-owned and non-state sectors.

Solving the wage curve begins by specifying the reservation pay level in the dual labor market. Using the unemployment value expression (4.10) and match surplus expressions (4.13) and (4.15), we have:

$$rU = \begin{cases} \dfrac{b[1 + \eta \times 1(j = I)] + \varphi\theta_I q(\theta_I)\beta[y_I + rf - rV_I]}{r + \lambda + \varphi\theta_I q(\theta_I)\beta} & j = I \\ \dfrac{b + (1 - \varphi)\theta_I q(\theta_I)\alpha y_O}{r + \lambda + (1 - \varphi)\theta_O q(\theta_O)\alpha} & j = O \end{cases} \tag{4.16}$$

Then, by using the expression for the match remainder, we can obtain the expressions for the wage curves of state-owned and non-state-owned enterprises, respectively (refer to Appendix A for the specific derivation processes):

Proposition 2 (wage curves for dual markets) In equilibrium, the wage offer function of state-owned and non-state-owned firms is given by the Nash bargaining function for vacant positions and worker types $i \in [R, C]$, which gives us:

The wage curve in the state sector:

$$w_I^P = \beta P + [1 - \Gamma(\theta_I)]b(1 + \eta) + [\Gamma(\theta_I) - \beta]y + [\Gamma(\theta_I) - \beta]r(f - k) \tag{4.17}$$

Here, $\Gamma(\theta_I) = \frac{r+\lambda+\varphi\theta_I q(\theta_I)}{r+\lambda+\varphi\theta_I q(\theta_I)\beta}\beta$, the cost of dismissal by state-owned employers under institutional constraints is greater than the fixed entry cost for vacant posts $(f - k) > 0$.

The wage curve in the non-state sector:

$$W_O^B = b + \Gamma(\theta_O)(y_O - b) \tag{4.18}$$

Here, $\Gamma(\theta_O) = \frac{r+\lambda+\gamma+(1-\varphi)\theta_O q(\theta_O)}{r+\lambda+\gamma+(1-\varphi)\theta_O q(\theta_O)\alpha}\alpha$

Formulas (4.17) and (4.18) indicate that the wage functions of state-owned employers are $W_I^P(r, \lambda, \theta_I q(\theta_I), \varphi, \eta, b, f, k)$ and $W_O^B(r, \lambda, \gamma, \theta_O q(\theta_O), \varphi, b)$, respectively. The exit rate or job match rate of the state-owned and non-state sectors in Eqs. (4.17) and (4.18) $\theta_j q(\theta_j), j = I, O$ is the increasing function of labor market tightness with these two types of firms θ_j, and therefore, $\Gamma(\theta_j), j = I, O$ increases along with θ_j. This function shows the actual influence of workers in the two sectors. When θ_j increases, it means that the number of vacancies in this type of firm in the labor market increases and the wage determination process benefits the worker. This is because the probability of exiting unemployment and the expected utility of opportunities after unemployment increase together, and as a result, workers are optimistic about the prospect of unemployment, while the opportunities for firms to hire suitable workers are relatively reduced, thus improving the bargaining power of workers and raising the pay level.

Comparing Eqs. (4.17) and (4.18), we see that institutional segmentation leads to a great variance in workers' compensation obtained from Nash bargaining. Equation (4.17) shows that, in addition to compensating workers for giving up their leisure utility and deducting the compensation per unit of output from the level of leisure utility, wages paid by state-owned firms must also account for termination costs in addition to the fixed entry costs for creating the vacancy. Equation (4.18), on the other hand, shows that wages paid by non-state-owned actors are the sum of the leisure utility that workers give up and the compensation per unit of output that is deducted from the leisure utility. Thus, we see clearly that there is $W_I^P > W_O^B$. Moreover, when $\theta_j \to \infty, j = I, O$, there is $W_I^P = W_O^B + (y_I - y_O) + r(f - k)$. Therefore, if non-state-owned firms always match workers with higher labor productivity, the pay level at state-owned firms will not always be higher than that of their non-state-owned counterparts. This also corresponds with the difference in pay levels seen with different ownership types in reality. If the labor productivity of the state-owned concern is the same, then the difference in pay levels between the two types of enterprises comes from the difference in cost compensation arising from the matching of state-owned firms with workers.

4.2.7 Flow Balancing and the Beveridge Curve in the Dual Labor Market

The reallocation of labor resources in the dual labor market covers the unemployment inflow and outflow of labor with urban and rural household registrations between state-owned and non-state-owned enterprises, respectively, as well as the flow of the labor force whose household registrations converse due to employment from the non-state sector to the state sector. Therefore, flow balance involves two aspects: first, the overall labor force unemployment inflow, unemployment outflow and job inflow and job flow in the market are at equilibrium; and second, the flow from the non-state sector to the state sector is at equilibrium.

First, we look at the balance of unemployment flows in the market as a whole. Assume that U represents the stock of the unemployed, L represents the number of employed persons, N represents the scale of the labor force in a given period, and the scale of labor supply is fixed in a certain period. Thus, $N = 0$. The change in the number of the unemployed is as follows:

$$\dot{U} = [\lambda\varphi + (1-\varphi)(\lambda+\gamma)]L - [\varphi\theta_I q(\theta_I) + (1-\varphi)(1-\varphi)\theta_O q(\theta_O)]U$$

The first is for workers who have lost their jobs, and the second is for those who have been added to each cycle of employment.

Use $u = {}^{U}/_{N}$, $N = L + U$, and the rate of change in employment is

$$\dot{u} = [\lambda\varphi + (1-\varphi)(\lambda+\gamma)](1-u) - [\varphi\theta_I q(\theta_I) + (1-\varphi)\theta_O q(\theta_O)]u \tag{4.19}$$

In steady state, the unemployment inflow equals unemployment outflow in the economy as a whole, $\dot{u} = 0$, and we can use this to calculate the steady-state unemployment rate.

Proposition 3 (Beveridge curve) The steady-state unemployment rate in the dual labor market is:

$$u = \frac{[\lambda\varphi + (1-\varphi)(\lambda+\gamma)]}{[\lambda\varphi + (1-\varphi)(\lambda+\gamma)] + [\varphi\theta_I q(\theta_I) + (1-\varphi)\theta_O q(\theta_O)]} \tag{4.20}$$

It has the following characteristics:

1. $\frac{\partial u}{\partial \lambda} > 0$, $\frac{\partial u}{\partial \gamma} > 0$, $\frac{\partial u}{\partial \theta_j} < 0$
2. The impact of the ratio of vacant posts in the state-owned and non-state sectors on the unemployment rate is uncertain and depends on the size of $[\theta_I q(\theta_I) - \theta_O q(\theta_O)] \times [\gamma\theta_O q(\theta_O) - \lambda - (1-\varphi)\gamma]$

Equation (4.20) describes the relationship between the unemployment rate and the vacancy rate in the labor market and the equilibrium relationship between unemployment flows and employment flows. The change in the unemployment rate comes from the negative relationship between vacancies and employment as shown by the Beveridge curve.

Secondly, we look at the flow balance between systems. When the market is in a steady state, there is no net flow in the state-owned or non-state-owned systems, that is, inflows and outflows are equal. This implies that employees in the non-state sector decide whether to keep their jobs in the sector or to search for jobs in the state sector. To ensure flow balance at steady state, the expected utility of working in the non-state-controlled sector must be kept equal to the expected utility value of job searching in the state sector after deducting turnover costs Z.

$$U(j = I) - Z = J^O$$

Using Eqs. (4.4), (4.7), and (4.9), we get (refer to Appendix B for more details):

$$Z = \frac{T_3 - (y_O - W_O^B)T_1 + \varphi\theta_I q(\theta_I) W_I^P T_2}{[rT1 - (r+\lambda)\varphi\theta_I q(\theta_I)]T_2} \tag{4.21}$$

Here, $T_1 = r + \lambda + \varphi\theta_I q(\theta_I)$, $T_2 = r + \lambda + \gamma$, $T_3 = b(1+\eta)(r+\lambda)T_2$

Proposition 4 (no arbitrage) When the turnover cost paid by the worker satisfies Eq. (4.21), there is no arbitrage between the state-owned and non-state sectors, that is, there is no difference for job seekers whether they choose a vacancy in the state sector or the other.

4.3 Steady-State Equilibrium and Dynamic Analysis of the Double Duality of the Labor Market

Based on the standard MP model, the equilibrium of the labor market characterized by double duality satisfies three basic relations: demand for labor, the wage curve, and the Beveridge curve. Apart from these, a necessary condition is that there is no net flow of labor between the state-owned and non-state sectors in this double duality system, that is, the labor flow of enterprises between the two systems should be balanced.

According to the analysis in Sect. 4.2, the market equilibrium of the labor market characterized by double duality is defined as:

Definition 1: Steady-state equilibrium is the solution to the wage functions $W_I^P(r, \lambda, \beta, \theta_I, f, k)$ and $W_O^B(r, \lambda, \alpha, \theta_O)$, the labor demand equation, the Beveridge curve, and the balance of flows between the state-owned and non-state-owned systems, and satisfies the following conditions:

1. Wage determination mechanisms: Formulas (4.17) and (4.18).
2. Labor market demand (or entry at equilibrium): Formulas (4.3) and (4.6).
3. Beveridge curve: Formula (4.20).
4. No-arbitrage condition: Formula (4.21).

4.3.1 Wages, Unemployment Rate and Mobility in the Double Duality of the Market

In the traditional competitive equilibrium model, the intersection of the labor supply-and-demand curves determines the equilibrium value of wages and employment. In the equilibrium model for the labor market characterized by double duality, the wage curve replaces the labor supply curve and the job creation curve replaces the labor demand curve, and therefore, the intersection of the wage curve and the job creation curve determines the equilibrium value of wages and employment.

According to conditions (1) and (2) of Definition 1, we have drawn the supply-and-demand curves of the labor market for the state-owned and non-state sectors (as shown in Fig. 4.2). Along the plane coordinate (θ_j, W_j), $j = I, O$, the equilibrium values of labor market tightness and wages correspond to the intersection of the wage curve and the labor demand curve defined by Eqs. (4.3), (4.6), (4.17), and (4.18), respectively. According to Eqs. (4.3) and (4.6), the job creation curve is a downward sloping curve in a space of market tightness and the wage rate. That is, high wage rates are less profitable for companies to create new jobs, and the result is a lower job-to-worker equilibrium ratio. Equations (4.17) and (4.18) show that at higher labor market tightness points, the relative bargaining power of market participants changes in favor of the workers. Looking at the supply and demand of labor in the state-owned and non-state sectors, respectively, we see that compared to non-state-owned firms the wage creation/labor demand for state-owned firms is relatively flat. However, the wage curve/supply curve is relatively steep, reflecting the low motivation for state-owned units to create new jobs as they face institutional constraints and high-welfare levels. The demand for labor is relatively rigid, and workers are more willing to search for jobs in the state sector than the non-state-owned counterpart.

Figure 4.2 shows the two equilibrium points at (0.24, 0.905) and (1.09, 0.893). When comparing the results of the two equilibrium points, we see that: (1) There is lower labor market tightness in the state sector, where there are also fewer vacancies available in the market. In the face of higher labor search willingness, the matching result is formed with a lower degree of labor market tightness and a relatively high pay level. (2) In contrast, the labor market at equilibrium for the non-state sector is relatively tight, and there are more vacancies available in the market. At equilibrium: $\theta_O = 1.09$, and job seekers have at least 1.09 vacancies to choose from, which meets with a relatively low willingness to search for work. A higher degree of labor market tightness and a relatively low pay level form the matching result. (3) When we compare the pay levels of the two equilibrium points, based on the above equations, we can obtain the average level of reservation wages at the equilibrium of the labor

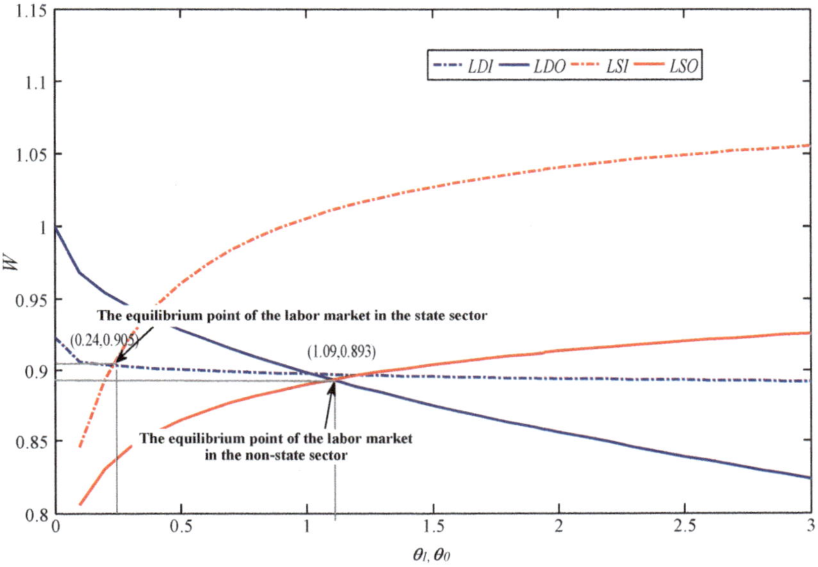

Fig. 4.2 Wage rate and market tightness at the equilibrium points of the labor market characterized by double duality (*Note* $y_I = y_O = 1, r = 0.025, \alpha = 0.5, \beta = 0.18, c = 0.35, b = 0.4, \eta = 0.675 \quad m(\theta_I) = 1.35 \times \theta_I^{-0.18}, m(\theta_O) = 1.35 \times \theta_O^{-0.5}, \varphi = 0.48, f = 4, k = 1.5, \lambda = 0.01, \gamma = 0.2, P = 1$)

market[11] as $\underline{w}^* = 0.84$, and $\underline{w}^* < W_O^{B^*} < W_I^{P^*}$ at equilibrium. This is consistent with the real-world data referred to in Chapter 3. (4) In addition, the small blue circles in Fig. 4.2 represent where job creation in the state-owned/non-state sectors and workers searching for vacancies in the state-owned/non-state sectors meet, and the intersections are (1.2, 0.896) [(0.4, 0.944)]. The results of these two intersections suggest that if institutional segregation eases, the benefits to society as a whole for job seekers in the labor market will improve. However, the chances of such two intersections appearing within the dual market structure are very low.

[11] The reservation pay level is the average level of reservation wages in the labor market as a whole obtained using weighted calculation based on equilibrium conditions, the reservation pay levels for the state and non-state sectors, the results from the parameter calibration section, and following calculations of the average level of reservation wages for the state and non-state sectors.

Thus, according to the definition of equilibrium and the results in Fig. 4.2, we can easily see that there are separate points of equilibrium in the labor market characterized by double duality for the state-owned and non-state sectors. Since search is difficult to match across sectors, it means that the labor market is segmented and that there are at least two equilibrium points.

Proposition 5 The steady-state equilibrium of the labor market characterized by double duality is multiple equilibria, and the labor market is segmented.

After having considered unemployment inflow and unemployment outflow, we can easily obtain the equilibrium unemployment rate within the double-duality market structure. Figure 4.3 shows the Beveridge curve in the steady state on the plane coordinate (U, V). The curve starting from the origin and the slope of $\theta_j^*, j = I, O$ is the vacancy supply curve. This represents the supply of jobs and the number of job seekers that can maximize the profit of the firm at equilibrium. It is clear that there are more jobs in the non-state sector than in the state sector, though the proportion of job seekers in the former is also much lower.

Finally, according to the no-arbitrage condition for mobility between the state-owned and non-state sectors, the relationship between labor turnover costs and labor market tightness is shown in Fig. 4.4. The turnover cost is the highest when the degree of labor market tightness is around 10 percent in the state-owned and non-state sectors, and then it rapidly decreases, and the cost decreases at a steeper rate in the state sector. When the two sectors are aggregated, the turnover cost is the highest when labor market tightness rises to close to 20 percent, and then rapidly decreases. However, the turnover cost does not decrease to zero when labor market tightness is at its lowest.

4.3.2 *Mathematical Simulation of the Double Duality*

In this section, we will first calibrate the key parameter values for the model based on the model results in Sects. 4.2 and 4.3, and then use mathematical simulation to try to explain the evolution process of the unemployment rate, labor demand, and pay level in China's labor market by using the degree of segmentation of the dual market as a variable to try to uncover the possibilities and necessary conditions for the greater

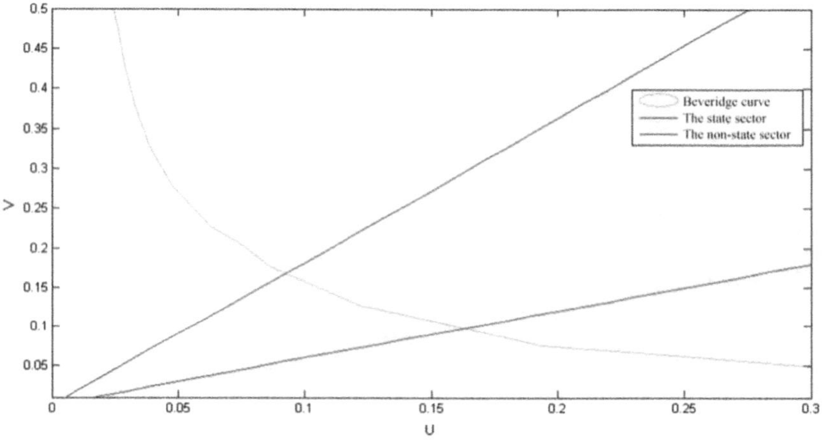

Fig. 4.3 The Beveridge curve in the labor market characterized by double duality (*Note* $y_I = y_O = 1, r = 0.025, \alpha = 0.5, \beta = 0.18, c = 0.35, b = 0.4, \eta = 0.675 \quad m(\theta_I) = 1.35 \times \theta_I^{-0.18}, m(\theta_O) = 1.35 \times \theta_O^{-0.5}, \varphi = 0.48, f = 4, k = 1.5, \lambda = 0.01, \gamma = 0.2, P = 1$)

integration of China's labor market characterized by double duality in the future.

We will calibrate our model using the year as our time unit. The parameter values for the model come from three sources: First, the research results from domestic scholars; second, from the input of statistical data; and third, data endogenously obtained through a series of fits with the labor market. The key values are set as follows (see Table 4.2).

(1) Productivity level and interest rate level: According to domestic research on the labor productivity of China's state-owned firms, the labor productivity of the state sector has more or less been the same as that of the non-state sector in recent years. Therefore, we set the labor productivity of both the state-owned and non-state sectors as 1. Based on the reality in China, in this chapter, we set the annual interest rate level r as 0.025.

(2) Match function $m(\theta_j) = \frac{q(\theta_j)}{\theta_j}$: In the absence of evidence of the match function in China's labor market, we draw on domestic and foreign

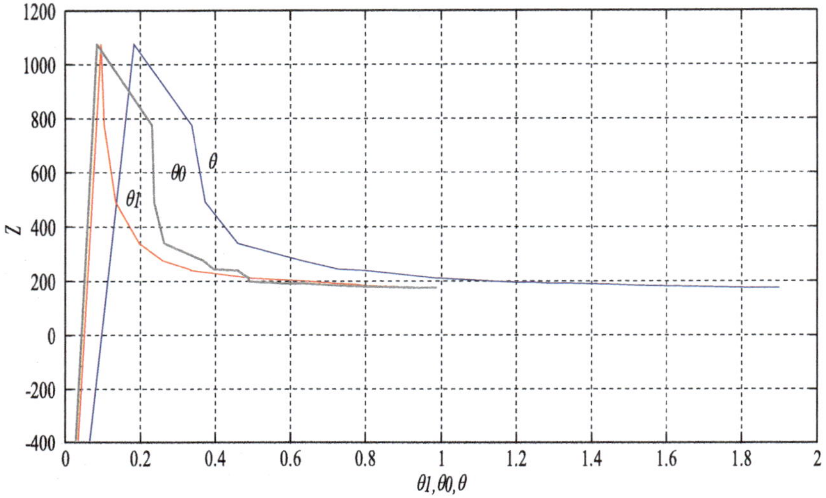

Fig. 4.4 Turnover costs in the context of equilibrium in the labor market characterized by double duality (*Note* $y_I = y_O = 1, r = 0.025, \alpha = 0.5, \beta = 0.18, c = 0.35, b = 0.4, \eta = 0.675 \quad m(\theta_I) = 1.35 \times \theta_I^{-0.18}, m(\theta_O) = 1.35 \times \theta_O^{-0.5}, \varphi = 0.48, f = 4, k = 1.5, \lambda = 0.01, \gamma = 0.2, P = 1$)

Table 4.2 Calibration parameters for the dual search-and-matching model

Description	*Parameter*	*Value*
Effective interest rate	r	0.025
Unemployment benefits	b	0.4
Percentage of state-owned firms	φ	0.48
Job destruction rate in the state sector	λ	0.01
Destruction rate of additional positions in the non-state sector	γ	0.2
Job vacancy cost	C	0.35
Bargaining power of workers		
State sector	β	0.18
Non-state sector	α	0.5
Vacancy entry cost	k	1.5
Cost of dismissal	f	4
Match function elasticity		
State sector	τ_I	0.18
Non-state sector	τ_O	0.5

research and our match function takes the form of a Cobb–Douglas function with fixed returns, that is $m(\theta_j) = v_j^{\tau_j} u^{1-\tau_j} = \Pi \times \theta_j^{1-\tau_j}, j = I, O$.

Then, we also drew on Tang Kuang's work on job vacancies based on a survey sample of Beijing (2007) and foreign theoretical literature on job matching in the United States, Spain, and other countries to calibrate our base values. Shimer's analysis of data from the US (2005b) shows the average job arrival rate to be close to 1.35, and thus the constant of the match function was set at 1.35. This constant is subsequently set as $m(\theta_j)u = 1.35\theta^{1-\tau_j}$ for United States and various European countries based on the Hiosos theorem match function. Pertrongolo and Pissarides (2001), by summarizing previous research on the job match function, found that the estimated results of match functions show unemployment in the system to be in the range of 0.5–0.7. In the estimation using total employment as the dependent variable, the coefficient of unemployment is relatively low, ranging from 0.3 to 0.4, while the coefficient of the corresponding vacancies is relatively high. In most literature, 0.5 is often used as the elasticity value of the match function (Gobillon et al., 2007), and some researchers have also used the upper limit of generalized results, 0.72 (Merlino, 2009). Within the dual structure, matching elasticity values vary between the state-owned and non-state sectors. First of all, for the convenience of analysis, we set the matching elasticity value for the non-state sector as 0.5. According to Hoisos (1990), the matching elasticity value of the state sector is equal to the bargaining power of workers. Wage setting at state-owned firms is related to the market power within the system, which gives us $\tau_I = \beta = \frac{\varepsilon}{1+\varepsilon}$. Here, ε is the elasticity of labor supply for the state sector, and some research estimates show the labor supply elasticity of this sector to be 0.2113. In the absence of other calculations and references, we use this value, which gives us $\tau_I = \beta = 0.18$. The choice of this value is also in line with the fact that state-owned firms are not sensitive to labor market tightness. Correspondingly, according to the Hosios rule (1990), $\tau_O = \alpha = 0.5$ and the match functions of the two sectors are $m(\theta_I) = 1.35\theta_I^{1-0.18}$ and $m(\theta_I) = 1.35\theta_0^{1-0.5}$, respectively, meaning that the match function of the labor market characterized by double duality is $m(\theta) = 1.35[\varphi\theta_I^{1-0.18} + (1-\varphi)\theta_O^{1-0.5}]$.

(3) The exogenous separation rate of the labor market: The destruction rate of vacancies varies by ownership type, and apart from the impact of the reform of the state-owned system, there has been stability with the state sector in other years as well as a lower separation rate. Let us assume the separation rate at state-owned firms to be $\lambda = 0.01$, meaning that work at these units are lifelong job. Let us also assume the separation rate at non-state-owned firms to be $\lambda + \gamma = 0.1 + \gamma$, with γ standing for the separation rate at non-state-owned firms affected by external shocks, $\gamma = 0.2$.

(4) Vacancy cost (c) and unemployment benefits (b): The values of (c) and (b) are set relative to the average productivity across sectors. The cost of post vacancies is assumed to be 0.35 of average labor productivity, which is the midpoint from all estimated literature. For Shimer (2005a, 2005b) this estimate was 0.213, and for Hall and Milgrom (2008), 0.43 was used.

(5) Quantity structure of state-owned and non-state-owned firms (φ): As there is no monitoring data on labor market tightness in China, we have had to use data from surveys and other related statistics to determine the value of the parameter φ for the distribution of vacancies in the state-owned and non-state sectors. We have, in this chapter, derived the number of vacancies by unit type using Tang Kuang's work (2008) on the results of a survey of 161 public institutions in Beijing. The number of vacancies in the 11 entities in the survey sample was 106 or 2.43 percent of the total; the number of vacancies in the 30 public institutions surveyed was 1378 or 31.68 percent of the total; and the number of vacancies in the 120 surveyed enterprise units was 2865 or 65.89 percent of the total. Moreover, according to the China Statistical Yearbook and the China Labor Statistics Yearbook (2010), in 2010 the proportion of employment in the state sector was 52.6 percent while in the non-state sector it was 44.3 percent. In this chapter, we take the values for the two sectors together as $\varphi = 0.4$.

(6) Vacancy cost (c) **and unemployment benefit parameters for the state and non-state sectors** (b, η): The parameters c and b are relatively fixed. In the existing literature, it is considered that the vacancy costs published include: 0.213 (Shimer, 2005), 0.43 (Hall & Milgrom, 2008), and 0.3 (Costain, 2011). When searched in a certain direction, the vacancy cost is 0.03, otherwise, the vacancy cost is 0.17 (Merlino, 2009). In view of the realities of China, in this chapter we set the value of c at 0.35. Typically, in studies of the United States, the unemployment benefit stream b is often set at 70 percent of average productivity (Costain & Reiter, 2008; Hall & Milgrom, 2008; Pissarides, 2009) while for Spain where labor protection is more severe the value of 80 percent is used

(Costain, 2011) while in other literature it is 40 percent (Merlino, 2009). In China, according to the 1999 Regulations on Unemployment Insurance, unemployment insurance payouts were to be lower than the local minimum wage standard and higher than the minimum "living security" standard of urban residents and to be determined by the people's government of the respective provinces, autonomous regions, and municipalities directly under the central government. When comparing unemployment insurance and minimum pay levels in major cities (see Appendix C), we see that in 2011, the minimum wage in Hangzhou was 1310 yuan and unemployment insurance payout was set at 768 yuan or 58 percent of minimum wage; in 2011, the minimum wage in Shanghai was 1280 yuan and unemployment insurance payout was set at 730 yuan (57 percent); and in 2010, Sichuan Province stated that its unemployment insurance payment standard was 70 percent of the minimum wage standard as determined by the local government. However, we should also note that the unemployment insurance coverage rate in our country is less than 40 percent of the urban employed population. Taking 2009 as an example, we see that the number of people covered by unemployment insurance in China was 127 million or only 40 percent of the 313 million urban labor, while the number of migrant workers covered by insurance was 16.43 million or only about 7 percent of the 230 million migrant workers. Considering the structural characteristics of the labor market characterized by double duality, in this chapter we set b as the unemployment insurance income from employment in the non-state sector with the value of 0.4 and at the same time, if the unemployment insurance income of workers employed in the state sector is set to 0.7, then $\eta = 0.675$.

(7) Cost of dismissal (f) and cost of entry (k): As for the cost of dismissal (f) and the cost of vacancy entry (k), Costain. J (2011) uses 1.93. In this chapter, we set the cost of dismissal f at 4 and the cost of vacancy entry k at 1.5.

According to the above parameter values, the main variable values at equilibrium can be calculated as follows (Table 4.3).

In the calibrated equilibrium result, the wage differential between the state and non-state sectors is 0.012, while the utility value of unemployment is $\underline{W}_I^{P*}$ and $\underline{W}_O^{B*}$, respectively. For those seeking a job in the non-state sector, the need to leave the sector requires a short-term trade-off of lost income $W_O^{B*} - \underline{W}_O^{B*} = 0.0847$, and there is also a turnover cost of 250.16 to move from the non-state sector to the state sector, and the possible benefit in the long run is $W_I^{P*} - W_O^{B*} = 0.012$. For workers

Table 4.3 Steady-state equilibrium in the dual market

$\theta_I{}^*$	0.24
$\theta_O{}^*$	1.09
W_I^{P*}	0.905
W_O^{B*}	0.893
$\underline{W}_I^{P*}$	0.864
$\underline{W}_O^{B*}$	0.8083
$\underline{W}$	0.825
$m(\theta_I)^*$	0.4189
$m(\theta_O)^*$	1.4094
$U*$	0.11
$U*$	0.11N
VI *	0.027N
V_O*	0.1239N
Z	250.16

from rural areas, relative to their marginal productivity and turnover benefits, excessively high mobility costs have become the biggest restriction for workers with rural household registration seeking to enter the urban system. Of course, the choice of parameter calibration value will change this result to some extent, and as such, in the process of calibrating our parameter, we have carried out various experiments bearing in mind domestic and foreign literature and the actual situation in China, and the result is that there is essentially no change or little change.

4.3.3 *Dynamic Analysis of the Double Duality*

The discussion in the previous section has focused entirely on steady-state analysis. Search behavior in the labor market clearly captures the evolutionary dynamics between unemployment, pay levels, job creation, and job destruction, and from this, we can look for the expected behavior of firms and workers in job creation and wage determination. Therefore, our aim is to find the dynamic behaviors of unemployment, vacancies, and wages when there is a matching function. Here, we will ignore the impact of the capital market and focus on the following multidimensional parameter dynamics $(\lambda, \gamma, u, w_j^t, z)$, $j = I, O; t = P, B$.

In the steady-state model, we deduce the equilibrium value of labor market tightness from the expected return of creating a new job k and

0, respectively. Now assume that this property still exists, to make sure that our assumption holds, vacancies and therefore market tightness are in two different states, that is, the former is relatively flat and the latter is a relatively steep variable. For the latter, it is a must to create or destroy vacancies immediately to ensure that new vacancies always have a value of 0.

The same assumptions apply to wage determination. In steady state, wages are introduced by the firm and the worker in the matching of the share of the remaining distribution (4.3)–(4.6). Now, assume that the same holds true when dynamic, meaning consistent with our assumption. Employers and workers in the state and non-state sectors are able to renegotiate prices based on new information, and therefore, the pay level will increase continuously and show rigidity. If a firm or unit meets a worker, the overall level of matching information is determined by the matching technology. Matching technology does not allow for a jump in job information; instead, it describes a slow, steady, and backward-looking process created by the difference between job creation and job disruption flows. This makes unemployment a predetermined variable at all times.

To get the dynamic equation for wages and market tightness, we need firms and workers to outperform dynamic expectations. The net value of work and workers is now an explicit function of time. The arbitrage equation determines that their value is similar to the value 1 while remaining stable.

Therefore, the benefit flow equations in dynamic time are as follows:

$$rJ_I = y_I - w_I^P + \lambda[V_I - J_I - f] + \dot{J}_I$$

$$rV_I = -C + q(\theta_I)(J_I - V_I) + \dot{V}_I;\ V_I = k,\ \dot{V}_I = 0$$

$$rE_I = w_I^P + \lambda(U - E_I) + \dot{E}_I$$

$$rJ_O = y_O - w_O^B + \lambda[V_O - J_O] + \dot{J}_O$$

$$rV_O = -C + q(\theta_O)(J_O - V_O) + \dot{V}_O,\ V_O = \dot{V}_O = 0$$

$$rE_O = w_O^P + (\lambda + \gamma)(U - E_O) + \dot{E}_O$$

$$rU = b[1 + \eta \times 1(j = I)] + \varphi\theta_I q(\theta_I)\,[E_I - U - z \times 1(i = r)]$$

$$+ (1-\varphi)\theta_O q(\theta_O)\,(E_O - U) + \dot{U}$$

The above differential equation for asset value is not balanced due to arbitrage and perfect expectation. Wages are determined by the wage offer and wage bargaining mechanisms, respectively, as indicated by the aforementioned distribution rules. We allow wages to be renegotiated continuously, and the aforementioned distribution rules maintain the rate of change. By making the same replacement for the wage equation, we can get the same wage equation as before, valid for both steady-state inflows and outflows. Thus, given productivity and income during periods of unemployment, wages outperforming steady-state dynamics are purely driven by the tightness of the labor market.

The remaining matches in the state and non-state sectors are, respectively, S_I, S_O,

$$\dot{J}_I = \frac{c + [r + q(\theta_I)]k}{q(\theta_I)}$$

$$S = \frac{c + [r + q(\theta_I)]k}{(1-\beta)q(\theta_I)} \Rightarrow \dot{S} = -\frac{(c + rk)q'(\theta_I)}{(1-\beta)[q(\theta_I)]^2}\dot{\theta}_I$$

$$rU(j = I) - \dot{U}(j = I) = b(1+\eta) + \frac{\varphi\beta[c + rk + q(\theta_I)k]}{1-\beta}$$

Hence, $(r+\lambda)S_I = \dot{S}_I + y + \dot{U}(j = I) - rU(j = I) - rk - \dot{f}$.

The dynamic equation for the state sector after substitution is as follows:

$$\frac{(c + rk)q'(\theta_I)}{(1-\beta)q^2(\theta_I)}\theta_I' + \frac{[c + rk + q(\theta_I)][r + \lambda + \beta\theta_I q(\theta_I)]}{(1-\beta)q(\theta_I)} - y + b(1+\eta) + r(f - k) = 0 \quad (4.23)$$

At steady-state, the steady-state values for labor market tightness $\theta_I' = 0$ can be defined as θ_I^*. The above differential equations are solved after linearization at $\theta_I' = 0, \theta_I = \theta_I^*$, with no analytic solution.

Similarly, we can obtain the dynamic equations for the non-state sector as follows:

$$\frac{cq'(\theta_O)}{(1-\beta)q^2(\theta_O)}\theta_O' + \frac{c(r + \lambda + \gamma + \beta\theta_O q(\theta_O))}{(1-\beta)q(\theta_O)} - y + b = 0 \quad (4.24)$$

Similarly, there is no analytic solution following linearization. The graphical solutions for $\theta_I(t), \theta_O(t)$ in Eqs. (4.23) and (4.24) are shown in Fig. 4.5. On the left is the dynamic change in labor market tightness in the state sector, and on the right is the dynamic change in labor market tightness in the non-state sector.

As shown in Fig. 4.5, there is a big difference in the dynamics of labor market tightness between the state and non-state sectors. In the former, there is a gradual increase while in the latter rises almost vertically after remaining at 0 for a certain period of time. There are significant differences in the dynamics of labor market tightness between the two sectors. We know that $\theta_j = \frac{v_j}{U}, j = I, O$. Assume that U is a constant value. The creation of jobs in the state sector has always been strictly controlled by the government, and job creation within this sector in the early days was limited and increased only slightly. As the marketization process advanced, state-owned actors, especially the state-owned enterprise units, adapted to the needs of the market and the inherent enterprise need for profit maximization, and the number of jobs created increased. In contrast, non-state employers faced strict policy or institutional constraints for a considerable period of time, and job creation in the non-state sector was close to zero, which is consistent with the lack of a non-state sector prior to reform and opening up. As shown in the figure, after the critical point of $t = 3.5$, labor market tightness increases rapidly, which means that the labor

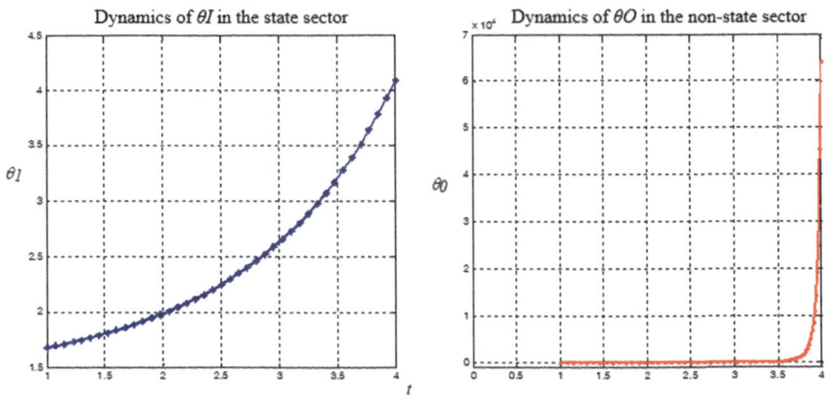

Fig. 4.5 Graphical solutions for the θ_I and θ_O differential equations

market had sufficient motivation to create new jobs following the liberalization of the system, and a large number of vacancies emerged as a result. The labor tightness faced by the state and non-state sectors is very similar to the changes before and after China's reform and opening up, and it also shows the difference between the creation of vacancies in the two sectors as in the former there were higher job creation costs while in the latter there was a transition point due to institutional constraints.

The dynamics of labor market tightness can be used to express the dynamics of pay levels and their variations both within and outside the state sector. As we can see from Fig. 4.6, as the pay levels in the state-owned and non-state sectors are both monotone functions of their respective labor market tightness, both increase over time. Further, we also see that the growth rates of the two have changed significantly, with the pace of the former catching up after some time while in the latter the change has occurred at a stable rate. As such, pay levels within the state sector will be higher than in the non-state sector for a certain period of time. Empirical studies by domestic scholars have also borne out this observation: According to Ye Linxiang et al. (2011), on average, wages at state-owned enterprises are 30.5–35.9 percent higher than at private enterprises, while foreign-funded enterprises on average pay 19.8–20.6 percent more than private enterprises, while the pay level at collectively owned enterprises is 3.8–6.0 percent lower than in private enterprises and the pay level in monopolistic enterprises is only 4.8–13.0 percent higher than at their counterparts in competitive industries. However, over time, the average pay level in the non-state sector catches up with the speed at which wages increase in the state sector. This is highly consistent with the current trend of rising labor costs in China and the rapid rise in wages in the non-state sector, such as in private enterprises. The difference in the rate of change of pay levels in the state and non-state sectors leads to the trend that we see in Fig. 4.6, i.e., the difference in pay levels gradually narrows over time. In this way, we simply infer that *ceteris paribus*, with dual market segmentation the difference in pay levels between the state and non-state sectors will narrow, meaning that such segmentation has a tendency to converge or integrate over time.

Similarly, by using the dynamics of labor market tightness in the state and non-state sectors we can also obtain the dynamics of unemployment and mobility costs. As we can see from Fig. 4.7, on the left side is the dynamic result of the unemployment rate, and on the right side is the dynamic result of the current cost, both of which show a decreasing trend.

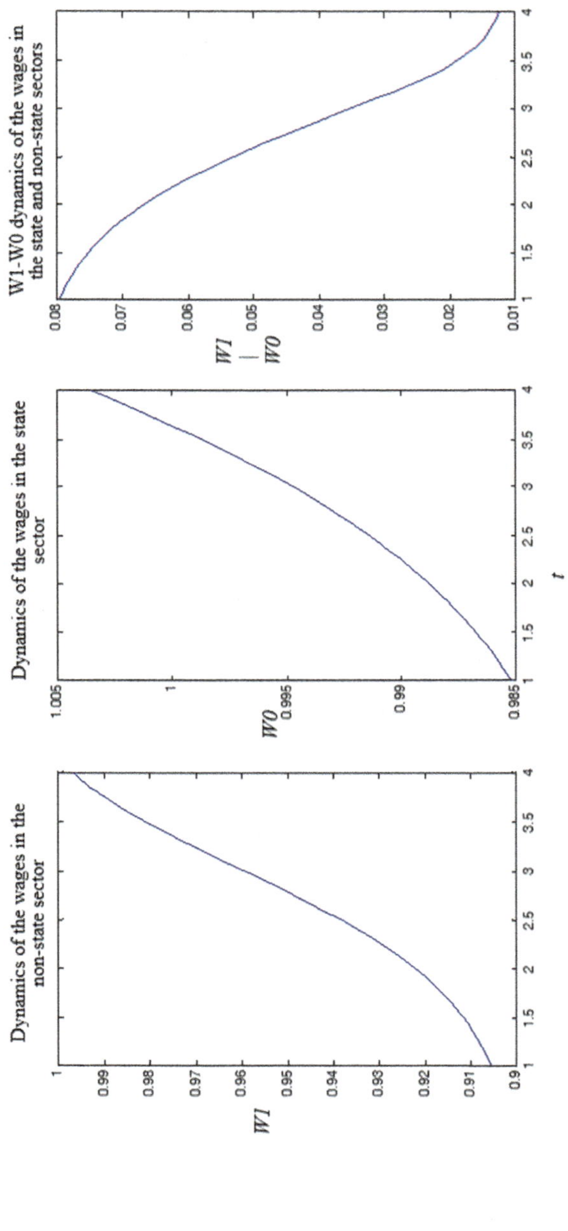

Fig. 4.6 The dynamics of wages and wage differentials in the state and non-state sectors

As the unemployment rate within the dual structure decreases over time, the barriers to entry or mobility that imply the existence of a dual structure will reduce unemployment due to increased labor market tightness in the market and as more newly created vacancies attract job seekers. On the right side, the dynamic changes in the mobility cost allow us to predict that the barriers for rural labor to enter the state sector will gradually weaken in the future. However, we also see that it is difficult for this mobility cost to approach zero within the dual structure, that is, for any worker, the expected benefits of vacancies in the state and non-state sectors are equal, and under these conditions, we can consider the double duality to be completely eliminated and a higher degree of labor market integration, achieved. The fact that the current cost dynamics do not approach zero indicates that the double duality can be reduced within a certain range though the double duality will continue to exist given China's current circumstances and policies.

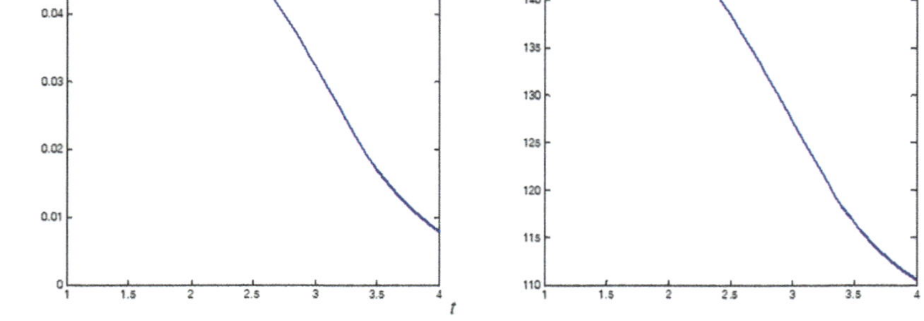

Fig. 4.7 The labor market unemployment rate and mobility cost dynamics

4.4 Summary

Following our examination in Chapter 3 of the evolution of China's labor market since the founding of the People's Republic of China, we believe that China's labor market has, following a period of near-complete segmentation, come to a state of double duality due to a combination of market factors and the household registration system and enterprise ownership, a phenomenon that has to be further verified and discussed on the theoretical level. In this chapter, we began with the issue of segmentation and embarked on a review of existing research and understanding on the part of Chinese and foreign scholars alike regarding the issue of segmentation in China's labor market. Given that existing research has focused on the non-perfectly competitive part of the labor market with the competitive and non-competitive parts completely excluded, any use of the analytical framework of dual-structure theory (including SLM theory and Lewis's urban–rural dual-structure theory) to study segmentation issues, especially segmentation in China, would fail to reflect workers' employment decision-making. In this chapter, we have divided the factors affecting the division of the labor market into three categories: endogenous factors, exogenous factors, and causative factors. The first two result in segmentation that is reinforced or diminished by the influence of causative factors, and consequently, the labor market becomes more segmented or integrated.

Based on the understanding that "good" jobs in China are equivalent to "good" units (employers) and that the barriers to mobility posed by the household registration system have lowered while barriers to resource allocation remain, we have proposed that China's labor market is in a state of multi-tiered segmentation, a state that has come about as a result of the double duality caused by institutional factors and the superposition of endogenous segmentation and spatial segmentation. These divisions can be reinforced or weakened by the choice of individuals on the micro level.

We then introduced worker and enterprise behavior into the labor market segmentation model based on the job search theory of Mortensen and Pissarides (1994, 1999) and Pissarides (2000) in order to model China's labor market characterized by double duality. As the double duality distinguishes between labor supply and demand, for this chapter we constructed a job search model that also incorporates the heterogeneity of firms and workers. Within a dual structure, search and consistency externalities have an impact on matching outcomes through additional entry (exit) costs under institutional constraints and arbitrage behavior between market segments. To model this, we separately considered the cost of dismissal and entry cost in each sector within this "duality" as well as the arbitrage conditions between the two sectors.

The equilibrium results of the model show that this double duality has led to multiple equilibria in China's labor market and thus, there are various wage determination mechanisms and labor demand conditions as well as higher turnover costs, enterprise dismissal costs, and entry costs in this market. Through numerical calibration we also found the equilibrium result within this double duality, which show us that the existence of this "duality" does lead to differences in pay levels and that the labor flow, especially rural labor flow, that exists between the state and non-state sectors has to bear both the conversion cost and the higher flow cost. Excessively high mobility costs have become the greatest constraint for rural labor seeking to enter the urban system.

The results of our dynamic analysis show that the indicator reflecting the flexibility of the labor market—a dual structure in terms of labor market tightness—to be fairly significant. While wages in the state sector have grown at a steady rate, with wages in the non-state sector we have seen explosive growth at reform and opening up following years of strict constraints. The results also show that the other influencing factors have not changed, and that the difference in pay levels between the state and non-state sectors will narrow. What this means is that the double duality has a tendency to converge or integrate, although the barrier to labor mobility—the mobility cost—can only be reduced within a certain range and can never reach zero. That is, the double duality can be reduced within a certain range though the double duality will continue to exist given China's current circumstances and policies.

In this chapter, we have attempted to propose an analytical framework for the segmentation in China's labor market by integrating the understanding of segmentation in classical economics, institutional economics, and development economics, and it was on this basis that the Mortensen and Pissarides (2000) model was used to construct a two-way heterogeneous search model for a better understanding of how China's labor market has evolved over time. However, there are a number of flaws in this part of the model. First, according to Merlino (2009), labor market segmentation is determined by the ability of workers to directly search for special vacancies, and this is not covered in this model. Second, according to the idea of the theoretical analysis framework, the multi-tiered segmentation based on the double duality is the basic feature of China's labor market. In this chapter, we have conducted only a preliminary discussion of this double duality and without considering other factors that cause segmentation, we have come to the inference that this segmentation has the tendency of integration or convergence. However, if we are to take into account the group effect of spatial segmentation and institutional factors, whether there is a tendency for integration of multiple segments, and under what circumstances will integration occur, are questions that are worthy of further research.

CHAPTER 5

An Empirical Study on the Evolution of China's Urban Labor Market Segmentation: Confirmation by Data from Various Sources

The theoretical analyses in Chapter 4 have proved that the dual structure is the cause of multiple equilibria in China's labor market. If it is not influenced by other factors, the multiple equilibria will converge over time, the wage gap will narrow, the intersectoral labor flow rate will increase, the cost of labor mobility will reduce, and the labor markets tend to integrate with each other. Nevertheless, in reality, some phenomena we have observed are different from the results of the theoretical analyses. We believe that sectoral segmentation and regional segmentation have not been analyzed in the theoretical framework and the long-term existence of China's dual structure has generated new social stratums, thereby making it possible for multi-tiered segmentation to exhibit hyperstability. The dynamic effects of the model may change if the two factors above are considered, thereby changing the equilibrium solution of the dual structure. Hence, this chapter empirically expounds on the existence of the dual structure and whether multi-tiered segmentation can be intensified or reduced due to the effects of industry factors and social structure. This chapter focuses on the verification of the existence and changes of the dual structure and its state of multi-tiered segmentation under the additional effects of industry factors.

Y. Chen, *China's Labor Market in the Transition*,
https://doi.org/10.1007/978-981-99-9160-0_5

Since the 1970s, scholars at home and abroad have measured the segmentation and integration of the labor market by using a large number of methods and standards. These researches are conducted in the two ways below in accordance with features of data: First, based on micro data, segmentation resulting from characteristics of individuals, work, industries, and job levels are separately or collectively tested, and the obstacles to the labor mobility between different parts are tested; second, based on macro data, the degree of integration of the labor market is tested by using the time-series data of wage. The temporal characteristics of segmentation and integration indicate that the first way tests the state of segmentation of the labor market at different time points of evolution. If the segmentation at different time points is observed in succession, the second way can be tested by judging whether the labor markets integrate with each other or experience further segmentation. Macro data equalize the information on individual heterogeneity, hence, using survey data at multiple time points helps gain a deep understanding of the state of evolution of the labor market.

China's labor market has evolved from the "dual" state of complete segmentation, which started in the era of planned economy, to the state of multi-tiered segmentation of the dual structure at present. The empirical survey on the evolution needs to be conducted at the following two aspects: (1) The difference and tendency of pay level generated by double duality; (2) The intersegmental mobility in the dual structure. This chapter consists of the following four sections. The first section further explains the data and empirical approaches used in this chapter; the second section tests the existence of the dual structure and obstacles to the flow of labor; the third section tests the degree of segmentation of the dual structure and answers the variability of pay level difference; and the fourth makes a summary of this chapter.

5.1 Sources of Data Validating the Evolution of China's Labor Market and the Empirical Approach

To test the evolution of China's labor market, in view of the characteristics of data availability and matching, this paper selects national sample survey data at two time points (2002, 2006) since China's launch of reform and opening up to give a general description of the evolution of China's labor market in the process of marketization. The data for 2002 are from the "China Household Income Project Survey" [CHIPS (2002)] of the Institute of Economics, Chinese Academy of Social Sciences. CHIPS data have been extensively adopted for study on China's income distribution and have unique meanings as they are normative social survey data that are hardly found at the initial time point of urban reform. The data of 2006 are from "Chinese General Social Survey" [CGSS (2006)], which was jointly launched by the Department of Sociology of Renmin University of China and the Social Survey Center of Hong Kong University of Science and Technology. CGSS uses a sampling frame for demographic census, by using this method, residents' committees in urban areas of China (excluding Xinjiang, Tibet, and Qinghai) are randomly selected, and household samples are taken by sample surveyors using the equidistant sampling method according to the residents' committee's household register book, and the sample surveyors conduct random questionnaire-based surveys on respondents by using household random sampling table.

It is a long-standing problem to test whether the labor market is segmented. In consideration of selectivity bias, which is caused by the fact that workers are indirectly connected with primary or secondary sectors, there are the following two most important estimation methods in the studies: (1) The estimation method, which was proposed by Dickens and Lang (1985) and has been used up to now, namely the labor market characterized by double duality theory is tested in the framework of the wage determination mechanism transformation model; (2) The study was conducted by Heckman and Hotz (1986) by using the income equation in the sample selection model. Later on, Launov (2004) tested the existence of the labor market characterized by double duality by using classified count models based on the intersectoral transfer of workers.

It has been made clear in the distinction of concepts that wage convergence is a necessary condition for the integration of the labor market, while flow of labor is the necessary and sufficient condition for the integration of the labor market, therefore, segmentation and integration of the labor market can be tested from the following two perspectives: (1) Integration of pay levels, namely the realization of the law of one price with competitive equilibrium; (2) Full flow of labor. The labor market is integrated if the flow of labor is free and full and intermarket interest arbitrage is impossible, but this condition basically does not exist in reality. Hence, as long as two sectors feature free choice, the labor market with two different wage equations is not segmented (Dickens & Lang, 1985; Maloney, 2004).

Therefore, the evolution characteristics of China's labor market shall be tested from the following two aspects: (1) Use the switching regression model to test the labor mobility between different segments. (2) Build a segmentation index based on the Mincer wage equation, and test the convergence of difference between wages.

5.2 Validating the Evolution of China's Labor Market from Double Duality to Integration (I): Flow of Labor Between Segments

5.2.1 Theoretical Assumption

There are three fundamental principles on labor market segmentation, namely the existence of a limited number of good jobs; quota restrictions on these jobs lead to limited mobility; one's income or wage can neither be increased though he/she has raised his/her skill level nor make him/her secure a good job. Compared with a segmented labor market, in an integrated labor market, one of its most important symbols is free intersectoral labor mobility. Actually, labor mobility involves two aspects: (1) horizontal mobility, namely a laborer changes his/her job between different sectors or regions; (2) vertical mobility, namely the mobility of the socioeconomic status of a laborer.[1] The former is the research focus of labor economics, while the latter is the research focus of sociology. If the concept of social capital is introduced, the latter can be analyzed in the framework of economics, which is necessary for understanding the flow of labor. The household registration system and the ownership are two "hurdles" that must be crossed to achieve a flexible mechanism for labor allocation in China's labor market. Although the current household registration system hardly restrains the horizontal mobility of labor, it does divide the population into urban residents and rural residents,

[1] All Chinese and foreign scholars recognize and accept the concept of socioeconomic status, Li Lulu (2008) believes that scholars traditionally and simply identify this concept with occupational status and it is impossible to reflect the institutional characteristics of structural barriers. Li believes that occupation has the meaning of resource content as a position indicator, but unit and regional barriers may cause that the resource contents of the same occupational status differ between different structures.

and different groups on the basis of their registered permanent residence, causing segmentation between locals and non-locals. Typically, the urban public sector tends to recruit people with local permanent residence, which has the nature of labor market segmentation and expands the non-local populations to include rural migrant workers and those who have received higher education but have not local permanent residence, indicating that the restriction of the household registration system on horizontal mobility is shifting to barriers to vertical mobility. In addition, the ownership or the unit system that acts together with the household registration system restricts horizontal mobility of labor, moreover, it has become the largest barrier to upward mobility of labor. Employers with different types of ownership adopt different systems in terms of recruitment, wage income, and social insurance, restricting free mobility of labor. Therefore, this paper focuses on to what extent the labor mobility will be influenced by the dual structure under the effects of the household registration system and the ownership type, and this section tests dual factors of intersectoral flow of labor and their changes.

5.2.2 Test of Labor Mobility Changes in the Segmented Dual Structure

Model Setting

The switching regression model is considered as the optimal solution for the labor market characterized by double duality theory to empirical research issues. By using the model, we can discuss the distribution of labor resources between the primary labor market and secondary labor markets. The method of Dickens and Lang (1985, 1992) indicates that if the observed value cannot be used to classify the market mechanisms, switching regression may be used to include wages of the two sectors, moreover, normal distribution hypothesis is used for residuals of the segmentation equations of the two sectors, and the maximum likelihood switching regression model is used for each segment to estimate segmentation equations and probability function for mechanism identification. Subsequently, a scholar (Goldberger, 1983) believed that this selection model questions the normal distribution hypothesis and parameter estimation is sensitive to the distribution hypothesis. Distribution hypotheses applied to residuals play a vital role in intersectoral allocation of workers, hence, applying different distribution hypotheses to the residual is very likely the hypotheses existing in the two sectors of the labor market.

Heckman and Hotz (1986) have also raised the same question. Baffoe-Bonnie (2003) said that the switching regression with different income distributions and disturbance term distributions will result in (1) different propositions in the labor market characterized by double duality and (2) Significant differences in income for workers in any profession and industry.

The dual structure in China's labor market indicates that the household registration system results in low labor mobility as it makes laborers have to pay high cost of labor mobility if they choose to be employed in the sector with segmented ownership. Therefore, if there are local and non-local laborers with registered residences at the levels of township, county, and city living in the sectors, the cost of labor mobility is zero, namely the probability of mobility is close to 1, we can verify the level of the labor market segmentation from the perspective of mobility, and furthermore, use the estimated results at different points of time to verify the changes in the level of labor market segmentation. By referring to the empirical thoughts of John Baffoe-Bonnie (2003), we assume that the market-oriented allocation mechanism is used in the non-state sectors, therefore, the sector enjoys a higher pay level than other sectors due to the rich experience and strong educational background of its employees. Meanwhile, we assume that an individual rationally chooses his/her job in the labor market, and his/her economic behaviors in the labor market aim to maximize the effects of his/her lifecycle. Assuming that effectiveness progressively increases with the net present value (NPV) of the lifecycle income, if the non-monetary preference for work does not change with the lifecycle, and the worker is fully familiar with all features of work, we can infer that the worker may start his/her career in a sector and works in the sector until his/her retirement. If the two sectors have similar non-monetary characteristics, it is predicted that the worker will stay in the sector generating the highest lifecycle income. Hence, assuming that the probability of the worker working in the state sectors is shown below:

$$p = \Pr\{\ln(NPV_I) - \ln(NPV_O) > C\} \tag{5.1}$$

In order to modelize the NPVs in the two sectors, we write out the Mincer wage equations of the two sectors:

$$\ln(W_{iI}) = XB_I + Ya_I + e_I \tag{5.2}$$

$$\ln(W_{iO}) = XB_O + Ya_O + e_O \tag{5.3}$$

$$Z_i^* = \delta(\ln w_{1i} - \ln w_{2i}) + D_i\Pi + e_i \tag{5.4}$$

Equations (5.2) and (5.3) are wage equations of state-owned/non-state-owned enterprises, respectively, wherein X is the individual's characteristic vector; Υ is work experience; w_{ij} is the pay level of individual i in sector j, w_{iI} is the pay level of an individual not in the state sector; e_I is the unobserved normally distributed error that affects the wage of state-owned enterprises; B_I and a_I are estimated parameters; w_{iO}, e_O, B_O, a_O are similar terms of non-state-owned enterprises. Equation (5.3) determines the tendency or possibility of individual's choice of the state sectors, Z_i^* is unobserved latent variable measuring individual's employment tendency in the state sectors. If $Z_j^* > 0$, the pay level of the laborer is determined by Eq. (5.1), otherwise, if $Z_j^* \leq 0$, the pay level of the laborer is determined by Eq. (5.2).

Through observations, we found that dual realization of latent variable Z_j^* indicating whether the individual i works in a certain sector has the following forms:

$$\begin{aligned} Z_i &= 1 \quad \text{if} \quad Z_i^* > 0 \\ Z_i &= 0 \quad \text{otherwise} \end{aligned} \tag{5.5}$$

The switching regression equation implies that regression of the full sample may result in sampling bias. In the dual structure considered in this paper, regression of full sample may produce such a result, namely an urban or local laborer may be estimated to not work in the state sectors or the non-state sectors though he/she does work in the state sectors or the non-state sectors, and the result is biased and inconsistent. Meanwhile, wage determination does not depend on the household registration system, but directly depends on the nature of enterprises or units with different types of ownership. Hence, indiscriminate full sample regression may cause the problem of sample selection bias. According to econometrics, endogenous sample selection bias is corrected neither by Heckman's sample selection bias nor the endogenous switching econometric model. As for our research issues, we not only need to make clear the existence of the dual structure and based on it infer the degree of integration of the labor market, but also must answer such questions such as whether the hypothesis of the dual structure is endogenous (i.e., discerning whether the sample selection bias is endogenous), as well as obstacles to flows generated by the dual structure. Switching regression discerns whether a sample selection bias is endogenous or exogenous by estimating residual-related coefficients of each wage equation and selection equation. If the unobservable factors entering the state sectors or the non-state sectors have nothing to do with those of the wage equation, the choice is exogenous. In this case, for laborers, it is random for them to enter the state sectors or the non-state sectors and there is no sample selection bias, that is, the dual structure we assume is wrong. The endogenous switching econometric model also provides key information on the indirect influence of ownership on wages. Hence, for each wage equation, it is likely to make clear whether the selection of ownership is independent or interactional. By means of the united the conversion effects of observed and unobserved factors of the wage equation, we can obtain wage penalties or premium after entering sectors with different types of ownership through the household registration system.

Descriptions of Data and Variables

In China's labor market, the emphases of the two databases differ, in the CHIPS (2002), rural migrant labor force is included in the CHIPS database for the first time, respondents are divided by local and non-local rural/non-rural permanent residence, and it involves the ownership of employers of urban and rural migrant labor force in 10 provinces. CGSS (2006) involves urban and rural populations (divided by rural/non-rural permanent residence) in 30 provinces, autonomous regions, and municipalities directly under the central government except for Tibet, further distinguishes the respondents by the administrative rank, and covers respondents divided by unit type, ownership, and the administrative rank of unit. In addition, CGSS (2006) distinguishes the respondents based on the information on social structure such as main management type and administrative rank of the unit, as well as the structure of personal social capital. Although the two databases reflect the information on the labor market from different sides, the information can be used to examine and test the evolution and influence factors of double duality in China's labor market.

To ensure the external validity of data use (namely the internal consistency of the results of two samples), main variable data are selected: First, as this paper focuses on the issues of employment selection and income difference of working-age laborers in the labor market, males aged 15–60 and females aged 15–55 are included into the working-age population according to China's Labor Law; second, this paper targets job seekers and sets individuals' current situations in both the databases, but does not involve students at school, dropout students, those who have lost their labor capacity and soldiers. After treatments, we have finally obtained 17,800 CHIPS (2002) samples and 8608 CGSS (2006) samples for research.

On the basis of the "dual" hypothesis, we use two methods for the two classes of data of the household registration system, respectively, and make the data serve as substitution variables of labor supply segmentation, and make types of ownership serve as substitution variables of labor demand segmentation. Specific descriptions of variables are shown in Table 5.1.

Tables 5.2 and 5.3 provide the main statistical information on CHIPS and CGSS data, respectively. In CHIPS data samples, respondents with urban permanent residence account for 76.92 percent, with local nonrural permanent residence account for 75.76 percent, and with high school education background and above account for 56.1 percent. CHIPS data directly involve individual's specific years of schooling. In this paper, the level of education is converted into years of schooling, and the average years of schooling of the samples are 10.4 years, equivalent to the high school level. In addition, CHIPS directly involves years of working in urban and rural migrant labor force, which has an average work experience value of 17.05 years. For data of pay level, this paper restores the level of wage covering endowment insurance, medical insurance, and unemployment insurance. The per-hour wage of a sample individual is 5.77 yuan on average, but the wage gap between individuals is relatively large, and the per-hour wage of the individuals at 90 percent is nearly 10 times that of the individuals at the remaining 10 percent.

Among CGSS data samples, survey respondents with urban residency account for 49.72 percent, and a total of 4208 or 49.7 percent of respondents take surveys based on their registered permanent residence, and respondents at the county and prefecture levels account for the most, reaching 48.21 percent collectively; 50.21 percent of the respondents have received education at senior high school and above. For years of schooling of the respondents, similar to CHIPS, CGSS makes a direct survey of their specific years of schooling. This paper does not measure education on the basis of years of schooling, which is 9.29 years on average for such samples, equivalent to the junior high school level

Table 5.1 Descriptions of main variables tested by double duality

Variable name	*Variable description*	*CHIPS*	*CGSS*
Pay level	Convert the data of annual or monthly income into per-hour wage in accordance with working hours	Including various wages, allowances, subsidies, tax expenditures, benefits, and insurance expenses	Including the proportions of fund and insurance expenses to wage, based on which labor price is calculated
Education	The conversion is made on the basis of the final education degree, specifically: uneducated = 0; literacy class = 1; primary school = 6; junior high school = 9; senior high school = technical secondary school = 12; junior college = 14; undergraduate = 16; postgraduate = 19; unit: year		
Work experience	Years of working provided by the respondent		
Gender	Male = 1, Female = 0		
Age	Date of birth provided by the respondent		
Registered permanent residence: (1) Urban/rural	1 = rural, 0 = non-rural		
(2) Local/non-local	1 = local non-rural, 2 = local rural, 3 = non-local non-rural, 4 = non-local rural		–
(3) Administrative setup and geographic administrative divisions	1 = township, 2 = county and county-level city, 3 = prefecture-level city, 4 = provincial capital, 5 = municipality directly under the central government	–	1 = township, 2 = county and county-level city, 3 = prefecture-level city, 4 = provincial capital, 5 = municipality directly under the central government
Type of ownership	1 = state-owned, 0 = non-state-owned		
Industry	1 = primary industry (including agriculture, forestry, husbandry, and fishery); 2 = manufacturing industry (including the manufacturing industry and supplies of electric power, coal, and water); 3 = mining industry and construction industry; 4 = service industry I (including information transmission, computer services, geological survey, education, health, social security, social welfare, culture, sports and entertainment, public administration, social organization, and international organization.); 5 = service industry II (other service industries except for what is listed above)		

Note – means the variable is not set in the database

Table 5.2 Statistical descriptions of main variables of CHIPS (2002) data

Variable	*Observed value*	*Percentage (percent)*	*Mean value*	*Standard deviation*	*Variable*	*Observed value*	*Percentage (percent)*	*Mean value*	*Standard deviation*
Registered permanent residence					Education				
Urban = 1	13,691	76.92	–	–	≤6	1824	10.27	10.39	3.31
Rural = 0	4109	23.08			7–9	5954	33.54		
Local non-rural	13,486	75.76	–	–	10–12	5915	33.31		
Local rural	1455	8.17			More than 12 years	4060	22.87		
Non-local non-rural	205	1.15			Work experience				
Non-local rural	2654	14.91			0–10	4763	26.76	17.05	10.331
Marital status					10–20	4061	22.81		
Unmarried = 1	14,373	82.09	–	–	20–30	3955	22.21		
Married = 0	3136	17.91			≥30	1850	10.39		
Gender					Ownership				
Male = 1	9190	48.37	–	–	State-owned = 1	7387	44.79	–	–
Female = 0	8610	51.63			Non-state-owned = 0	5993	55.21		
Region					Industry				
Eastern China	6533	36.70	–	–	1	146	1.06	3.74	1.338
Central China	6421	36.07			2	4143	30.2		
Western China	4846	27.22			3	673	4.91		
Age	17,800	100	37	10.85	4	3494	25.47		

(continued)

Table 5.2 (continued)

Variable	*Observed value*	*Percentage (percent)*	*Mean value*	*Standard deviation*	*Variable*	*Observed value*	*Percentage (percent)*	*Mean value*	*Standard deviation*
Per-hour wage	13,667	76.78	5.77	22.6	5	4701	34.27		
Number of working hours per day	13,527	75.9	8.65	2.18	6	562	4.1		

Note 1 = primary industry (including agriculture, forestry, husbandry, and fishery); 2 = manufacturing industry (including the manufacturing industry and supplies of electric power, coal, and water); 3 = mining industry and construction industry; 4 = service industry I (including information transmission, computer services, geological survey, education, health, social security, social welfare, culture, sports and entertainment, public administration, social organization, and international organization.); 5 = service industry II (other service industries except for what is listed above); and 6 = other industries

Table 5.3 CGSS (2006) data main variables description

Variable	*Observed value*	*Percentage (percent)*	*Mean value*	*Standard deviation*	*Variable*	*Observed value*	*Percentage (percent)*	*Mean value*	*Standard deviation*
Registered permanent residence	Education								
Urban = 1	4280	49.72	–	–	≤6	1750	21.98	9.29	3.438
Rural = 0	4328	50.28			7–9	3006	37.83		
Town and township	603	14.09			10–12	1990	24.99		
County and county-level city	948	22.15			More than 12 years	1217	15.28		
Prefecture-level city	1111	25.96			Per-hour wage	4413	51.27	181.67	212.49
Provincial capital	801	18.71			Daily working hours	8608	100	8.93	2.25
Municipality directly under the central government	817	19.09			Age	8608	100	38.7	11.03
Marital status					Work experience				
Unmarried = 0	1463	17.00	–	–	0–10	3535	41.06	10.55	9.58
Married = 1	7145	83.00			10–20	1226	14.24		
Gender					20–30	772	8.39		
Male = 1	4129	47.97	–	–	≥30	237	2.75		
Female = 0	4479	52.03			Industry				
Ownership					1	69	0.8	–	–
State-owned = 1	2571	31.87	–	–	2	1775	20.62		
Non-state-owned = 0	2724	33.76			3	615	7.14		
Region					4	1463	16.99		
Eastern China = 1	3439	39.95	–	–	5	1564	18.17		
Central China = 2	3337	38.77							
Western China = 3	1832	21.28							

and slightly lower than that of CHIPS. From the perspective of sample proportion, the proportion of rural samples of CGSS data is higher than that of CHIPS data, and the average year(s) of schooling of CGSS data is slightly lower than that of CHIPS data, conforming to the composition of sample. Likewise, CGSS makes a direct survey of the working years of non-rural laborers. In addition, CGSS covers the duration of the first job, the duration of working in the present occupation, and the duration of working in the last occupation. By using the data in three aspects, as well as the education background and the final time of education, it is estimated that CGSS respondents have a work experience value of 10.55 years on average, slightly lower than that of CHIPS data. For pay level data of the samples, CGSS involves data about the income of the previous month and the gross income of the year and its structure, and both of them have a big deviation in CGSS. Meanwhile, some of the data are missing. In this paper, the data about the sum of wage and bonus are used as gross annual income and its structure, the data of missing samples of gross annual income are restored by using those of monthly income. After the sample outliers have been processed, the average per-hour wage of sample individuals is 181.67 yuan, a significant increase over the CHIP data in 2002, and the wage gap between individuals is relatively large.

We need to test the relevance of the variables before making an empirical study on the model. Table 5.4 lists correlation coefficient matrices related to this paper in CHIPS and CGSS data. As shown in the table, except for age and empirical variables which have significant correlation, all other variables have very low correlation coefficients in between. As age growth is generally accompanied by an increase in work experience, we do not incorporate empirical variables in the estimation of the switching regression model, and add the variable of square of age.

Empirical Results and Analyses

This paper aims to test the existence of the dual structure and its changes, and switching regression shows the obstacles to flow of labor generated by labor market segmentation from the perspective of flow of labor, which is different from the study of Zhang Zhaoshi (2007) who considers the dual structure as a nest. This paper considers that the dual structure acts on the supply and the demand sides in the labor market, the household registration system acts on laborers and influences labor supply behaviors, and the ownership acts on the employer and influences the labor demand behaviors, resulting in differences of the pay levels. Hence,

Table 5.4 The Spearman/Pearson correlation coefficient matrix between CHIPS (2002) and CGSS (2006) variables

	CHIPS (2002)				*CGSS (2006)*			
	Per-hour wage	*Education*	*Experience*	*Industry*	*Per-hour wage*	*Education*	*Experience*	*Industry*
Per-hour wage	1.0000				1.0000			
Education	0.3766*	1.0000			0.4077*	1.0000		
Work experience	0.3676*	0.1074*	1.0000					
Industry type	−0.2126*	−0.1348*	−0.2705*	1.0000	0.1217*	0.0921*	−0.1085*	1.0000

Note The significance level of *5 percent

we use the household registration system as an important variable for securing jobs with different types of ownership and include it in the selection equation, rather than including it in the master equation. The household registration system has a great influence on laborers' selection or their participation in the labor market, but the household registration system does not have a direct influence on the pay level, and the purpose is similar to that of the instrumental variable method, namely, the household registration system is not the determinant of wage, while the difference between different types of ownership is a key factor for wage determination; in addition, CHIPS data involve 12 provinces, while CGSS data involve 30 provinces, autonomous regions and municipalities directly under the central government except for Tibet, for this, we introduce dummy variables of eastern China, central China, and western China in the equation to control interregional differences. Meanwhile, in recent years, quite a few scholars have regarded industrial monopolization as the principal cause for wage gaps between different industries and enterprises (Luo & Li, 2007; Nie, 2004), and therefore this paper includes industry factors in the model. By referring to the industrial classification method of Zhang Yuan and Gao Han (2011), we classify the industries into six types and introduce industrial dummy variables to control industrial effects.

The estimated results are shown in Tables 5.5, 5.6, 5.7 and 5.8, of which Tables 5.5 and 5.6 are estimated results of 2002 CHIPS data, and Table 5.7 and 5.8 are estimated results of 2006 CGSS data.

(1) **If the labor market is unified, it means that the results of the two switching regressions are consistent with OLS; if the labor market is segmented, there are two wage equations in the market**

We have proposed testing hypotheses about whether the segmentation of the dual structure exists.

Original hypothesis $H_o : \beta_I = \beta_o, \alpha_I = \alpha_o$, alternative hypothesis: $H_1 : \beta_I \neq \beta_o, \alpha_I \neq \alpha_o$

First of all, we analyze the situation regardless of registered permanent residence and administrative division. Based on the comparative results of Tables 5.5 and 5.7, the results of 2002 CHIPS data show that, whether regional and industrial differences are controlled or not, the coefficients of education, age, gender, and marital status are close to each other in the

Table 5.5 Estimated OLS and RSM results of CHIPS data (registered permanent residence, excluding the place of origin)

Variable	*OLS*	*Switching regression equation (1)*			*Switching regression equation (2)*		
		State sectors	*Non-state sectors*	*Transformation equation*	*State sectors*	*Non-state sectors*	*Transformation equation*
Registered permanent residence: urban				1.028*** (0.0332)			1.026*** (0.0327)
Education	0.0966*** (0.00186)	0.0556*** (0.00336)	0.0657*** (0.00425)	0.0864*** (0.00428)	0.0522*** (0.00315)	0.0595*** (0.00418)	0.0864*** (0.00428)
Experience	0.0603*** (0.00561)	0.0509*** (0.00837)	0.0517*** (0.00942)	−0.0265** (0.0124)	0.0553*** (0.00819)	0.0506*** (0.00921)	−0.0289** (0.0123)
Square of experience	−0.000485*** (6.97e−05)	−0.000478*** (9.99e−05)	−0.000553*** (0.000119)	0.000542*** (0.000151)	−0.000574*** (9.81e−05)	−0.000565*** (0.000116)	0.000584*** (0.000151)
Gender	0.0200 (0.0209)	0.124*** (0.0160)	0.221*** (0.0192)	0.0392 (0.0242)	0.131*** (0.0157)	0.235*** (0.0188)	0.0341 (0.0241)
Marital status	−1.213*** (0.0970)	0.0656* (0.0386)	0.0845** (0.0418)	0.236*** (0.0560)	0.118*** (0.0380)	0.128*** (0.0410)	0.209*** (0.0560)
Region		Uncontrolled			Controlled		
Industry		Uncontrolled			Uncontrolled		
Constant term		−0.135 (0.169)	−0.904*** (0.162)	−1.622*** (0.217)	0.0793 (0.162)	−0.637*** (0.160)	−1.661*** (0.217)
$\ln\sigma_{1,2}$		−0.373*** (0.0148)	−0.313*** (0.0107)		−0.380*** (0.0143)	−0.334*** (0.0108)	
$r_{1,\ 2}$		−0.635*** (0.0516)	−0.226*** (0.0458)		−0.732*** (0.0463)	−0.233*** (0.0459)	
Observed value	13,553	13,148			13,148		
Logarithmic likelihood value	−14,457	−20,806			−20,430		
Wald		437.9			1058		

(continued)

Table 5.5 (continued)

Variable	*Switching regression equation (3)*		
	State sectors	*Non-state sectors*	*Transformation equation*
Registered permanent residence: urban			0.840***
			(0.0364)
Education	0.0562***	0.0580***	0.0417***
	(0.00290)	(0.00364)	(0.00475)
Experience	0.0624***	0.0501***	−0.0270**
	(0.00782)	(0.00891)	(0.0131)
Square of experience	−0.000633***	−0.000556***	0.000494***
	(9.33e–05)	(0.000113)	(0.000160)
Gender	0.134***	0.189***	−0.0360
	(0.0152)	(0.0185)	(0.0261)
Marital status	0.102***	0.113***	0.187***
	(0.0362)	(0.0397)	(0.0591)
Region	控制		
Industry	控制		
Constant term	−0.314*	−0.470**	−0.213
	(0.164)	(0.205)	(0.266)
$\ln\sigma_{1,2}$	−0.464***	−0.375***	
	(0.0141)	(0.00959)	
$r_{1,\,2}$	−0.473***	−0.0872	
	(0.0643)	(0.0596)	
Observed value	13,145		
Logarithmic likelihood value	−19,261		
Wald	1377		

Note (1) The values in parentheses are standard deviations, (2) The significance levels are, respectively, $^{***}p < 0.01$, $^{**}p < 0.05$, $^{*}p < 0.1$; (3) The equation setting controls regional and industrial differences, and this table does not give the results

Table 5.6 Estimated OLS and RSM results of CHIPS data (registered permanent residence, including the place of origin)

Variable	*Switching regression equation (4)*			*Switching regression equation (5)*		
	State sectors	*Non-state sectors*	*Transformation equation*	*State sectors*	*Non-state sectors*	*Transformation equation*
Local non-rural			1.040***			1.034***
			(0.0380)			(0.0373)
Local rural			−0.0491			−0.0523
			(0.0521)			(0.0513)
Non-local non-rural			0.246**			0.265**
			(0.108)			(0.106)
Education	0.0567***	0.0654***	0.0848***	0.0530***	0.0586***	0.0849***
	(0.00339)	(0.00423)	(0.00429)	(0.00316)	(0.00416)	(0.00429)
Experience	0.0517***	0.0517***	−0.0313**	0.0560***	0.0504***	−0.0333***
	(0.00835)	(0.00942)	(0.0124)	(0.00818)	(0.00922)	(0.0124)
Square of experience	−0.000485***	−0.000553***	0.000588***	−0.000579***	−0.000566***	0.000626***
	(9.96e–05)	(0.000119)	(0.000152)	(9.79e–05)	(0.000116)	(0.000151)
Gender	0.124***	0.221***	0.0413*	0.131***	0.235***	0.0361
	(0.0159)	(0.0192)	(0.0242)	(0.0157)	(0.0188)	(0.0242)
Marital status	0.0617	0.0859**	0.251***	0.114***	0.130***	0.223***
	(0.0385)	(0.0419)	(0.0562)	(0.0379)	(0.0411)	(0.0562)

(continued)

Table 5.6 (continued)

Variable	*Switching regression equation (4)*			*Switching regression equation (5)*		
	State sectors	*Non-state sectors*	*Transformation equation*	*State sectors*	*Non-state sectors*	*Transformation equation*
Region	Uncontrolled			Controlled		
Industry	Uncontrolled			Uncontrolled		
Constant term	−0.178	−0.901***	−0.465**	0.0470	−0.630***	−0.511**
	(0.169)	(0.162)	(0.225)	(0.162)	(0.160)	(0.225)
$\ln\sigma_{1/2}$	−0.379***	−0.312***		−0.384***	−0.333***	
	(0.0148)	(0.0107)		(0.0143)	(0.0109)	
$r_{1/2}$	−0.610***	−0.232***		−0.715***	−0.248***	
	(0.0529)	(0.0455)		(0.0470)	(0.0456)	
Observed value		13,148		13,148		
Logarithmic likelihood value	−20,776			−20,401		
LR	445.0			1065		

Variable	*Switching regression equation (6)*		
	State sectors	*Non-state sectors*	*Transformation equation*
Local non-rural			0.831***
			(0.0414)
Local rural			−0.0897
			(0.0564)
Non-local non-rural			0.301**
			(0.117)
Education	0.0567***	0.0577***	0.0409***
	(0.00292)	(0.00364)	(0.00477)
Experience	0.0629***	0.0501***	−0.0294**
	(0.00781)	(0.00891)	(0.0131)
Square of experience	−0.000636***	−0.000556***	0.000517***
	(9.32e−05)	(0.000113)	(0.000160)
Gender	0.134***	0.190***	−0.0341
	(0.0152)	(0.0185)	(0.0261)
Marital status	0.0996***	0.113***	0.195***
	(0.0361)	(0.0397)	(0.0593)
Region	Controlled		
Industry	Controlled		
Constant term	−0.334**	−0.471**	0.712***
	(0.164)	(0.205)	(0.275)
$\ln\sigma_{1/2}$	−0.467***	−0.375***	
	(0.0141)	(0.00964)	
$r_{1/2}$	−0.453***	−0.0941	
	(0.0663)	(0.0598)	
Observed value	13,145		
Logarithmic likelihood value	−19,248		
LR	1379		

Note (1) The values in parentheses are standard deviations, (2) The significance levels are, respectively, $^{***}p < 0.01$, $^{**}p < 0.05$, $^{*}p < 0.1$; (3) The equation setting controls regional and industrial differences, and this table does not give the results

Table 5.7 Estimated OLS and RSM results of CGSS (2006) data (registered permanent residence, regardless of administrative rank)

Variable	*OLS*	*Switching regression equation (7)*			*Switching regression equation (8)*		
		State sectors	*Non-state sectors*	*Transformation equation*	*State sectors*	*Non-state sectors*	*Transformation equation*
Registered permanent residence: urban				0.910*** (0.0482)			0.869*** (0.0460)
Education	0.210*** (0.00757)	0.0802*** (0.0125)	0.142*** (0.0140)	0.0479*** (0.00737)	0.0558*** (0.0128)	0.125*** (0.0133)	0.0552*** (0.00712)
Experience	0.113*** (0.0184)	0.00266 (0.0297)	0.0983*** (0.0289)	0.0465*** (0.0167)	0.0133 (0.0298)	0.0967*** (0.0268)	0.0369** (0.0159)
Square of experience	−0.00141*** (0.000228)	−0.000688* (0.000360)	−0.00156*** (0.000373)	−0.000133 (0.000206)	−0.000844** (0.000360)	−0.00150*** (0.000344)	−4.67e–05 (0.000196)
Gender	0.366*** (0.0476)	0.482*** (0.0720)	0.377*** (0.0768)	−0.0274 (0.0425)	0.469*** (0.0724)	0.307*** (0.0717)	−0.00899 (0.0408)
Marital status	−0.222*** (0.0802)	−0.125 (0.128)	−0.479*** (0.118)	0.0242 (0.0716)	−0.123 (0.129)	−0.409*** (0.111)	0.0551 (0.0687)
Constant term	0.150 (0.328)	5.642*** (0.571)	0.844* (0.500)	−2.482*** (0.302)	6.225*** (0.577)	1.304*** (0.470)	−2.557*** (0.292)
Region		Uncontrolled			Controlled		
Industry		Uncontrolled			Uncontrolled		
$\ln\sigma_{1/2}$		0.637*** (0.0180)	0.463*** (0.0268)		0.658*** (0.0182)	0.468*** (0.0248)	
$r_{1/2}$		−1.578*** (0.0585)	−0.745*** (0.0678)		−1.643*** (0.0579)	−0.729*** (0.0631)	
Observed value	4098		3841			4090	
Logarithmic likelihood value	−6215.61		−8819			−9455	
LR			394.8			443.1	

Variable	*Switching regression equation (9)*		
	State sectors	*Non-state sectors*	*Transformation equation*
Registered permanent residence: urban			0.936***
			(0.0497)
Education	0.0807***	0.129***	0.0337***
	(0.0130)	(0.0132)	(0.00781)
Experience	0.0288	0.126***	0.0269
	(0.0295)	(0.0273)	(0.0168)
Square of experience	−0.000971***	−0.00185***	5.23e–05
	(0.000357)	(0.000353)	(0.000207)
Gender	0.528***	0.393***	−0.0574
	(0.0726)	(0.0756)	(0.0439)
Marital status	−0.112	−0.410***	0.0800
	(0.127)	(0.111)	(0.0721)
Constant term	5.643***	0.879	−2.259***
	(0.668)	(0.567)	(0.367)
Region	Controlled		
Industry	Controlled		
$\ln\sigma_{1/2}$	0.621***	0.441***	
	(0.0179)	(0.0243)	
$r_{1/2}$	−1.601***	−0.720***	
	(0.0614)	(0.0645)	
Observed value		3976	
Logarithmic likelihood value		−8963	
LR		553.1	

Note (1) The values in parentheses are standard deviations, (2) The significance levels are, respectively, $^{***}p < 0.01$, $^{**}p < 0.05$, $^{*}p < 0.1$; (3) The equation setting controls regional and industrial differences, and this table does not give the results

Table 5.8 Estimated OLS and RSM results of CGSS (2006) data (registered permanent residence, based on administrative rank)

Variable	*Switching regression equation (10)*			*Switching regression equation (11)*		
	State sectors	*Non-state sectors*	*Transformation equation*	*State sectors*	*Non-state sectors*	*Transformation equation*
Registered permanent residence: township						
County and county-level city			0.0200			0.0345
			(0.0593)			(0.0468)
Prefecture-level city			0.0835			0.133***
			(0.0576)			(0.0450)
Provincial capital			−0.0106			0.107**
			(0.0609)			(0.0464)
Municipality directly under the central government			−0.242***			0.0393
			(0.0637)			(0.0492)
Education	0.180***	0.258***	0.0826***	0.0632***	0.186***	0.0432***
	(0.0131)	(0.0249)	(0.00983)	(0.0139)	(0.0209)	(0.00804)
Experience	0.0635**	0.234***	0.0682***	−0.0346	0.194***	0.0559***
	(0.0316)	(0.0549)	(0.0222)	(0.0330)	(0.0457)	(0.0182)
Square of experience	−0.000909**	−0.00183***	−0.000267	−0.000279	−0.00155***	−0.000224

Variable	*Switching regression equation (10)*			*Switching regression equation (11)*		
	State sectors	*Non-state sectors*	*Transformation equation*	*State sectors*	*Non-state sectors*	*Transformation equation*
	(0.000371)	(0.000692)	(0.000276)	(0.000397)	(0.000569)	(0.000222)
Gender	0.563***	0.497***	0.0523	0.449***	0.283**	−0.0538
	(0.0691)	(0.135)	(0.0529)	(0.0774)	(0.116)	(0.0444)
Marital status	0.255**	−0.119	0.105	0.0315	−0.225	0.00431
	(0.128)	(0.218)	(0.0884)	(0.138)	(0.188)	(0.0757)
Region	Uncontrolled			Controlled		
Industry	Uncontrolled			Uncontrolled		
Constant term	1.155*	−1.297	−2.603***	7.026***	0.337	−2.034***
	(0.686)	(0.995)	(0.413)	(0.645)	(0.847)	(0.349)
$\ln\sigma_{1/2}$	0.415***	0.891***		0.655***	0.869***	
	(0.0193)	(0.0377)		(0.0181)	(0.0330)	
$r_{1/2}$	0.262***	2.083***		−2.288***	2.080***	
	(0.0964)	(0.0998)		(0.0672)	(0.0885)	
Observed value		2,703			2,864	
Log likelihood value		−6246			−6491	
LR		380.6			422.9	

(continued)

Table 5.8 (continued)

Variable	*Switching regression equation (12)*		
	State sectors	*Non-state sectors*	*Transformation equation*
Registered permanent residence: township			
County and county-level city			0.116**
			(0.0573)
Prefecture-level city			0.224***
			(0.0550)
Provincial capital			0.270***
			(0.0596)
Municipality directly under the central government			0.276***
			(0.0654)
Education	0.0829***	0.108***	0.0207**
	(0.0143)	(0.0194)	(0.00907)
Experience	−0.0141	0.171***	0.0350*
	(0.0330)	(0.0408)	(0.0201)
Square of experience	−0.000480	−0.00229***	−5.06e–06
	(0.000396)	(0.000526)	(0.000244)
Gender	0.568***	0.533***	−0.132***
	(0.0773)	(0.105)	(0.0485)
Marital status	0.00366	−0.354**	0.0656
	(0.138)	(0.156)	(0.0829)
Region	Controlled		
Industry	Controlled		
Constant term	6.310***	0.593	−1.687***
	(0.760)	(0.869)	(0.453)

Variable	*Switching regression equation (12)*		
	State sectors	*Non-state sectors*	*Transformation equation*
$\ln\sigma_{1/2}$	0.609***	0.382***	
	(0.0179)	(0.0390)	
$r_{1/2}$	−2.213***	−0.292*	
	(0.0726)	(0.169)	
Observed value		2,800	
Log likelihood value		−6234	
LR		565.1	

Note (1) The values in parentheses are standard deviations, (2) The significance levels are, respectively, $^{***}p < 0.01$, $^{**}p < 0.05$, $^{*}p < 0.1$; (3) The equation setting controls regional and industrial differences, and this table does not give the results

process of wage determination of state and non-state sectors; the results of 2006 CGSS data show that controlling regional and industrial differences does not significantly change main coefficients of the Mincer wage equation, but there is a great significant difference between the wage equation coefficient of state sectors and that of non-state sectors. The education efficiency of non-state sectors is 1.5 times that of state sectors. There is a very great difference in wage return to lifecycle between state sectors and non-state sectors. The age coefficient of state sectors is not significant. The age earning the highest wage in the non-state sector is 34, after which the marginal changes to age decrease. The gender coefficient of the state sector is 1.34 times that of the non-state sector. Both the coefficients of marital status are negative values, the marginal income ratio of the unmarried is higher than that of the married, and the marginal income ratio of non-state sectors nearly triples that of state sectors.

In the switching regression equation, the results of CHIPS data (2002) indicate that all coefficients other than gender, including the household registration system, education, age, and marital status, are relatively significant, and the household registration system, together with other factors, becomes important factors influencing laborers to enter state and non-state sectors. Nevertheless, the results of CGSS data (2006) indicate that the coefficients of all variables other than the household registration system are not significant, and the role of the household registration system in determining one entering state or non-state sectors is more significant. By contrasting the data of the two years, the coefficient of the household registration system of 2002 decreases when the regional and industrial differences are controlled, while that of 2006 increases to some extent. According to preliminary judgment, the impact of the household registration system on employment choice is increasing.

Likelihood ratio test is adopted. The likelihood ratio statistics of 2002 and 2006 are $LRT_{2002} = 2 \times (-14457 + 19261) = 9608$ and $LRT_{2006} = 2 \times (-6215.61 + 8963) = 5494.78$ respectively. This conforms to the x^2 distribution at a degree of freedom of 23, and the critical value at a 1 percent significance level is $x^2(23) = 41.638$. Thus, H_0 is rejected, meaning that two equations provide greater explanatory power than one. According to the results of likelihood ratio tests, labor market characterized by double duality was clearly present in both years. However, as CHIPS (2002) came out with very similar estimates for the pay levels of state-owned and non-state-owned companies, it is fair to conclude that the wage gap was not wide between the two sectors although they had separate mechanisms for wage determination.

Secondly, we discuss about the cases based on permanent residence and administrative division, respectively. In the CHIPS data results of 2002, the estimated coefficients of wage equation for state and non-state sectors in the master equation are close to each other and significant at the level of 1 percent. In the transformation equation, with regional and industrial differences controlled, all other variables than gender are significant, which is consistent with the estimated results of the urban–rural household registration system. There is a significant difference between local laborers and non-local laborers choosing to enter the state sectors or non-state sectors, which will be analyzed later; among the CGSS data results of 2006, the regression results of main variables have proved the estimated results of the urban–rural household registration system. In the above two cases, the coefficients are consistent with each other in terms of direction and size, highlighting the fact that the effect of the level of human capital on the pay level in non-state sectors is more significant than that in state sectors. The measured results prove the statement of competitive pay level of non-state sectors in reality, and the function of human capital has been reflected. In the switching regression equation, the coefficients of the household registration system increase progressively, which is consistent with the understanding of reality. Likewise, the likelihood ratio is used to construct LR statistics for testing. However, the CHIPS (2002) data is shown below:

$LRT_{2002} = -2 \times (-14457 + 19248) = 9582$, the freedom of obedience is the x^2 distribution of 23, therefore, it is significant at the level of 1 percent, rejecting the original hypothesis. Despite the influence of permanent residence, two wage equations still have greater explanatory power than one equation.

$LRT_{2006} = 2 \times (-6215.61 + 6243) = 36.78$, the freedom of obedience is the x^2 distribution of 27, and is $x^2(27) = 36.74 < 36.78$ at the level of 10 percent, rejecting the original hypothesis H_0. . Comparatively speaking, CGSS (2006) considers that the explanatory power of the last two wage equations of different administrative divisions declines, if the significance level is 5 percent, $x^2(27) = 40.113 > 36.78$, accepting the original hypothesis.

The analyses of the coefficients of main variables and LRT testing indicate the double duality featuring coexistence of the household registration system and the ownership. Although the sources of the two databases vary, but as the distributions of their main variables are basically consistent with each other, we may consider that the results of the two databases at the two points of time have external validity, namely, the conclusions made from the estimated results of the two databases can be promoted. Hence, this paper holds that, between 2002 and 2006, the "dual" characteristics of China's labor market were significant, however, due to the finiteness of data in the period of time, it cannot be verified whether such segmentation can become integrated.

(2) If obstacles to flow between labor market segments are weakening, then the labor market has a tendency of integration

One of the key marks for judging whether the labor market is integrated is the mobility ratio of labor between different segments. The transformation equation of the switching regression model indicates the impacts of the household registration system on employment, based on which intersegmental barriers to flow can be analyzed.

First of all, Tables 5.5 and 5.7 show that the urban–rural differences of the household registration system vary with the logarithmic generation ratio for laborers entering the state or non-state sector. As the CHIPS (2002) data show, if regional and industrial differences are uncontrolled, compared with laborers with rural permanent residence, the logarithmic generation ratio of laborers with urban permanent residence entering the state sectors is 1.028, and the odds ratio is 2.79. With controlled regional differences, there is no difference; while with controlled industrial and regional differences, the logarithmic generation ratio is 0.840, and the odds ratio is 2.31. The CGSS (2006) data indicate that, if regional and industrial differences are uncontrolled, compared with laborers with rural permanent residence, the logarithmic generation ratio of those with urban permanent residence entering the state sectors is 0.91, with an odds ratio of 2.48, which fell slightly with regional differences controlled, but the logarithmic generation ratio has not changed significantly with controlled industrial and regional differences compared with that with uncontrolled industrial and regional differences. The estimated results show that it is easier for laborers with urban permanent residence to enter state sectors. Comparatively, the possibility for laborers with rural permanent residence to work in state sectors is merely about 40 percent.

Secondly, Tables 5.6 and 5.8 show, respectively, the conversion of labor mobility caused by the differences between permanent residence and administrative division in the household registration system. Table 5.6 indicates that, as the CHIPS (2002) data show, with industrial and regional difference uncontrolled, compared with laborers with non-local rural permanent residence, the logarithmic generation ratio for local non-rural laborers to work in state sectors is 1.04, with a probability of occurrence of 39 percent, that for non-local non-rural laborers to work in state sectors is 0.246, with a probability of occurrence of 6.7 percent, and that for local rural laborers to work in state sectors is −0.049, with a probability of occurrence of −10.6 percent; with industrial and regional difference controlled, compared with the logarithmic generation ratio of laborers with non-local rural permanent residence, that of local non-rural laborers working in state sectors is 0.831, with a probability of occurrence of 30.81 percent, that of non-local non-rural laborers working state sectors is 0.301, with a probability of occurrence of 8.15 percent, and that of local rural laborers working in state sectors is −0.0897, with a probability of occurrence of −3.6 percent. The comparative results show that barriers do exist for the migrant labor force to enter state and non-state sectors. However, such flow barriers have been reduced after regional and industrial differences have been controlled. Particularly, the controlled industrial differences signify that barriers to local and non-local labor flow driven by the market forces are greatly reduced, and barriers to urban–rural labor flow are also reduced.

According to Table 5.8, the estimated results of CGSS (2006) indicate that regional and industrial factors may change the possibility for laborers from different administrative regions to enter the state sector. However, only when both industrial and regional factors are considered, the impacts of the factor of permanent residence based on administrative division are significant for working in the state or non-state sector. Therefore, we focus on the influences of permanent residence on sectoral selection after industrial and regional factors are controlled. Compared with the occurrence ratio of laborers whose household registration is at the level of township, that of those whose household registration is at the levels of county and county-level city working at state sectors is 0.116, with a probability of occurrence of 6 percent, that of those whose household registration is at the prefecture level working in state sectors is 0.224, with a probability of occurrence of 8.9 percent, and those of those whose household registration is at the level of provincial capital and municipality directly under the central government working in state sectors are 0.27 and 0.276, respectively, very close to each other, with the former slightly lower than the latter, and the probabilities of occurrence of them are about 9.6 percent. The results show that the level of administrative division is one of the barriers to the flow of labor.

The transformation equation analyses in Tables 5.5, 5.6, 5.7 and 5.8 show that the household registration system and the ownership type are indeed barriers to flow of labor, and the barriers of the dual structure to flow of labor are shown as follows: (1) urban labor < rural labor; (2) local non-rural labor < non-local non-rural labor < non-local rural labor < local rural labor; (3) labor of provincial capital ≈ labor of municipality directly under the central government < labor of prefecture-level city < labor of county\county-level city < labor of town/township.

(3) **Whether the dual structure is endogenous**

After testing the existence of the characteristics of the dual structure and the obstacles to its flow of labor, it is necessary to discuss whether such a dual structure is endogenous. In other words, it is necessary to verify the degree of correlation between the residuals of the unobservable part of the wage equation and those of the mechanism transformation equation of the two sectors. The coefficient has been estimated by using the switching regression model, so we only list relevant coefficients with controlled industrial and regional differences.

In accordance with the characteristics of the switching regression model, whether the residuals of the regression equation are correlated to that of the switching regression equation of the two sectors in the master equation is an important basis for judging whether the transformation equation is endogenous (Berardi, 2009). Relevant coefficients in Table 5.9 indicate that, whether in CHIPS data or CGSS data, the correlation coefficient between the residuals of the wage equation and the transformation equation for the state sectors and non-state sectors is significant at the level of at least 5 percent. It implies that we assume that the dual structure is endogenous.

Table 5.9 The endogenous coefficient of the dual structure in switching regression

System sector	*Data source*			
	CHIPS (2002)		*CGSS (2006)*	
	The household registration system: urban–rural	*The household registration system: permanent residence*	*The household registration system: urban–rural*	*The household registration system: administrative division*
ρ_1: State sectors	−0.54432*** (0.03722)	−0.4241*** (0.05438)	−0.92174*** (0.00923)	−0.9763*** (0.00339)
ρ_2: Non-state sectors	−0.2282*** (0.0431)	−0.0938** (0.05925)	−0.61719*** (0.03991)	−0.28357** (0.15550)

Note (1) The values in parentheses are standard deviations, (2) the significance levels are ***p < 0.01, **p < 0.05, and *p < 0.1, respectively

5.2.3 *Brief Summary*

In this part, we use data in CHIPS (2002) and CGSS (2006) and the switching regression method to test the "dual" hypothesis in Chapter 4, and analyze obstacles to the flow of labor generated by the dual structure. The main conclusions are shown below: (1) The dual structure does exist in China's labor market. It does not cause differences of wage determination in early stage, but results in differentiation of the wage mechanism in later stage, namely the intersectoral wage gap is widening; (2) Duality is endogenous. Such endogeneity is rooted from the institutional design before building of China's labor market and will have a long-term impact on the labor market; (3) The dual structure is indeed obstacle to the flow of labor, and its manifestations are: ① urban labor < rural labor; ② local non-rural labor < non-local non-rural labor < non-local rural labor < local rural labor; ③ labor of provincial capital ≈ labor of municipality directly under the central government < labor of prefecture-level city < labor of county\county-level city < labor of town/township.

5.3 Validating the Evolution of China's Labor Market from Double Duality to Integration (II): Segmentation Measurement

5.3.1 Methods for Measurement of the Labor Market Segmentation Based on Regression

In the literature review of Chapter 2, the methods for measuring labor market segmentation have been classified. In this part, domestic and overseas methods for measuring the labor market segmentation are used for reference to empirically study the level of segmentation of China's labor market on the basis of theoretical analyses of the dual structure.

Currently, there are few researches on this issue. Orr (1997) has constructed the labor market segmentation indexes based on the Mincer wage equation, measured the levels of segmentation of 59 American cities, respectively, and compared the segmentation strength of different cities. SLM theory believes that all factors including industrial structure, economic force, race, and gender play a role in creation and adjustment of the structure of the labor market, as well as the labor market segmentation. These characters are mixed together and the labor market varies greatly in different places, Orr (1997) believes that, if segmentation exists, the degree of labor market segmentation varies with the local labor market. By estimating the most parts in the labor market and comparing standard and segmented income function models, we can use the cross-regional change to distinguish truncation bias and explain the segmented labor market. Furthermore, Orr (1997) believes that if the institutional constraints have been correctly introduced in the model of segmented income function, the relatively simple human capital model can increase its true explanatory power. The provision of explanatory power relies on the degree of labor market segmentation existing everywhere and is positively correlated to industrial structural changes affecting the degree of segmentation. Hence, it is feasible to use the change of the explanatory power as the original index of the level of relative segmentation.

However, if the segmented income function is merely introductory truncation bias, all these changes of explanatory power are pseudo-structure of sample truncation. Hence, in different labor markets, the changes between explanatory power and industrial structures are seldom or barely related to each other. Therefore, Orr (1997) has established the segmentation index of the labor market on the basis of the Mincer wage equation. The steps are shown below:

Step 1. First, establish a traditional Mincer wage equation:

$$\log wage = a + b_1 educ + b_2 \exp + b_2 \exp^2 + b_2 voc + b_5 sex + b_6 race + e_\tau$$

Second, introduce dummy variables to distinguish the classification of workers (namely primary sector and secondary sector) to estimate the same equation:

$$\begin{aligned}\log wage = & a + b_1 educ + b_2 \exp + b_3 \exp^2 + b_4 voc + b_5 sex + b_6 race \\ & + b_7 \times S \times educ + b_8 \times S \times \exp + b_9 \times S \times \exp^2 \\ & + b_{10} \times S \times voc + e_u\end{aligned}$$

wherein, S is the individual variable given to distinguish the secondary labor market segmentation.

Step 2. Construct the segmentation index by using the formula below:

$$segndx = \frac{1}{N}\frac{1}{Y}\sum(|e_\tau| - |e_u|)$$

e_τ is the residual of the income function of human capital, e_u is the residual of the income function of the part taking segmented part into consideration. N is the estimated sample size of the income function; Υ is per capital income.

The index is used to measure sub-sectoral or local labor market segmentation, namely to what extent an individual has been misplaced or trapped in the secondary sector. If the human capital level of all employees of the sector is limited, it is out of question for the secondary sector to offer lots of jobs. On the one hand, under the new classics, if employees are effectively arranged, the sectors will not be important and the indexes will be very small. On the other hand, many employees in the secondary sector have a relatively high endowment level of human capital, but are trapped in the secondary sector due to the job allocation in the primary sector. As the scale of the secondary sector increases, the probability for an individual to fall into the secondary sector increases progressively, however, theoretically, the scale of a sector is not directly relevant to the segmentation index.

Zhang Zhaoshi (2009) considers that the segmentation of China's dual economic structure caused by registered permanent residence and corresponding systems is all-around, covering the differences of urban and rural laborers in securing job opportunities, differences in their pay level and the wage determination mechanism, and the differences in their social security and welfare access. On the basis of Orr (1997), we have established the urban–rural segmentation index in China's labor market by following the steps below: first, establish the basic Mincer wage equation of full samples. The estimated result is log $\widehat{wage}1$; and then, we introduce the variable of registered permanent residence to estimate the Mincer wage equation log $\widehat{wage}2$, and calculate $\hat{\varepsilon}^1 = \log wage1 - \log \widehat{wage}1$ and $\hat{\varepsilon}^2 = \log wage2 - \log \widehat{wage}2$ of the two equations. We believe that $\left|\left|\hat{\varepsilon}^1\right| - \left|\hat{\varepsilon}^2\right|\right|$ reflects the part in the wage gap that can be explained by the household registration system. By using the method of Orr (1997) for reference, we establish the following urban–rural segmentation index on the basis of the estimated results of the two wage equations: $SegIndex = \frac{1}{\overline{\log \widehat{wage}2}} \frac{1}{N} \sum\left(\left|\left|\hat{\varepsilon}^1\right| - \left|\hat{\varepsilon}^2\right|\right|\right) \times 100\%$, wherein, $\overline{\log \widehat{wage}2}$ is the estimated mean value of the wage logarithm, N is the number of samples. By verifying the survey data of urban and rural residents in Zhejiang Province in 2006, Zhang Zhaoshi (2009) measured that the overall level of urban–rural segmentation in the urban labor market of Zhejiang Province, which has a relatively high degree of marketization, is approximately 2.78 percent. Due to the limitations of data, we only discuss about the segmentation of the urban labor market in Zhejiang Province, and nest the household registration system in the "primary sector" and "secondary sector" on the basis of the theoretical assumption about the nested dual structure.

As shown in the discussions in Chapter 4 and Sect. 5.2 in this chapter, we believe that the household registration system and the ownership are the most fundamental cause for China's labor market segmentation. Lots of previous studies on urban–rural segmentation based on registered permanent residence caused by large-scale mobility of rural labor have indicated the existence of urban–rural segmentation. However, individuals' behaviors in the labor market show that registered permanent residents act on labor supply and classify laborers into two types, under the combined action of diversified labor demands and classification of laborers, the same laborers in different markets or different laborers in the same market may differ in pay level (the difference in pay level refers to the difference that still exists after individual characteristic factors have been controlled). Therefore, the double duality based on the household registration system and the ownership is the most fundamental segmentation status of China's labor market segmentation, and the differences in wage income and employment opportunities are the basic differences to be solved by means of policy or institution. Hence, by referring to the measurement method of Orr (1977) and Zhang Zhaoshi (2008), this paper uses CHIPS (2002) and CGSS (2006) data to contrast the level and changes of double duality caused by the household registration system and the ownership type at the two points of time.

However, if the labor market is segmented and we study the level of segmentation on the whole, we cannot judge which component makes the maximum or minimum contribution to the labor market segmentation, thus the meaning of our proposed policies will be vague. The researches in recent years indicate that China's income gap is widening, and so is the income gap between different regions, industries, sectors, and groups. Meanwhile, the database used in this study indicates that there are great differences in the distribution of wages at the two ends, as shown in Fig. 5.1. At both ends of CHIPS data, there are data points deviating from a normal distribution, while in CGSS, there are data deviating from normal distribution at the high quantiles. It is necessary to analyze the quantile segmentation at different pay levels, and we consider to subdivide the degree of labor market segmentation by means of quantile regression.

First, quantile regression is the extension of the least square method on the basis of mean value model under the classical conditions. The entire model is estimated by using multiple quantile functions. The model describes different quantiles of the research object, for example, it describes how some factors influence the median, 1/4 quantile, and 3/4 quantile of the research object, and these different quantiles represent research objects at different levels. Moreover, parameter estimators with different quantiles tend to be different, indicating that the functions of the same influencing factor are different for research object at different levels. Especially, when the distribution of research objects exhibits heterogeneity, such as asymmetry, fat tail, and truncation, this method tends to be resistant against outliers in data; second, from the perspective of assumed conditions that must be satisfied, general linear regression needs to meet a series of relatively strong assumed conditions, which is usually hard for economic variables. Comparatively, the assumed conditions of

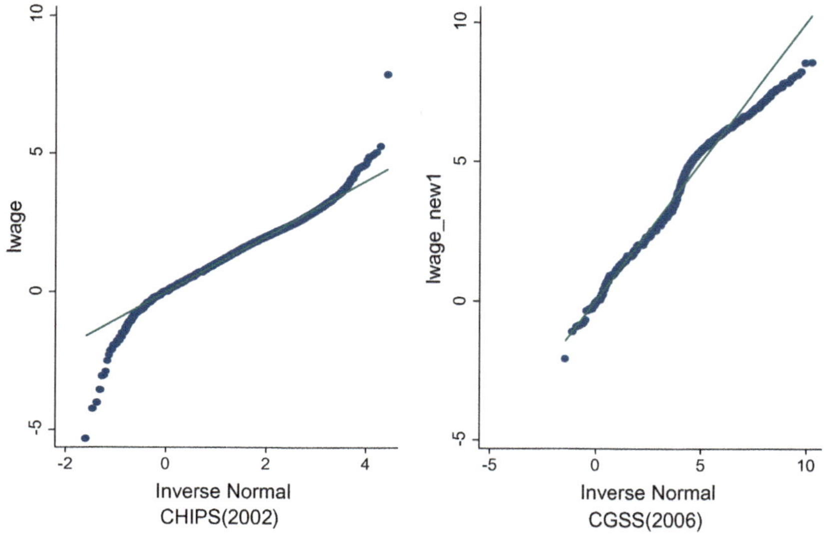

Fig. 5.1 The QQ diagram of CHIPS (2002) and CGSS (2006) hourly log pay level

quantile regression are much weaker and are closer to the actual situation. For example, it does not need to make any distribution assumptions for random disturbance terms in the model and makes the entire regression model have very strong robustness and stability, therefore, its parameter estimator is better than general linear regression in terms of effectiveness and other aspects. Especially, if there are some outliers in the economic issue (i.e., the value of a certain sample is suddenly and obviously higher or lower than other samples), the median regression method has more obvious advantages. All these make the relationship between economic variables obtained through quantile regression more real and accurate.

Therefore, the overall segmentation gives a general picture of the labor market, and the labor market segmentation discussed based on quantile further reveals the primary part and secondary part of the segment composition. For this, we will try to use the quantile regression method to study how different quantiles distributed under wage conditions vary with the independent variables. By using the regression results of multiple quantiles, we can describe in more detail, under the given conditions of other factors, how the level of segmentation of the labor market changes when the position and shape of wage income change.

We will make the following studies in Sect. 5.3.2: (1) the size of the urban labor market segmentation index and its test under the combined action of the household registration system and the ownership; (2) the level of double duality of laborers at the conditional income quantile (including urban labor and migrant labor force). For the above two issues, we use the method of OLS estimation for the former and quantile regression for the latter. We have made descriptive statistical analyses of CHIPS data and CGSS (2006) data and will not repeat them here.

5.3.2 Establishment of the Overall Segmentation Index and Judgment of Wage Convergence in the Dual Structure

By referring to the methods of Orr (1997) and Zhang Zhaoshi (2009), we first of all estimate three Mincer equations, it is necessary to note that in this part we use OLS and quantile regression to conduct contrastive analyses. To facilitate contrastive analyses, we simply process the model and introduce the factors of the household registration system and the ownership in it, namely introducing variables by using interaction terms. We aim to discuss about the level of segmentation under the combined action of the household registration system and the ownership. Hence, we set the model by using the stepwise regression method to finally introduce registered permanent residence and its interaction terms with the main variables, as well as the ownership and its interaction terms with registered permanent residence and other main variables. The results are shown in Table 5.10.

Table 5.10 indicates that with the combined action of the household registration system and ownership controlled, the impact of education on wage determination has changed. With Ramsy tested, the F value of CHIPS is 6.14, and that of CGSS is 10.86. The original hypothesis is rejected, showing that there is no omitted missing variable in the equation. Accordingly, we measure segmentation indexes by using uncontrolled OLS equation and OLS results with a controlled household registration system and the ownership, conduct 10 percent, 50 percent, and 90 percent quantile regression on the equations with controlled and uncontrolled household registration system and the ownership type, and measure the segmentation indexes of different parts.

Table 5.10 Estimated results of the Mincer equation of the dual structure

Variable	*CHIPS (2002)*				*CGSS (2006)*			
	(1)	*(2)*	*(3)*	*(4)*	*(5)*	*(6)*	*(7)*	*(8)*
Education	0.0956***	0.0499***	0.0691***	0.0472***	0.210***	0.128***	0.211***	0.127***
	(0.00179)	(0.00408)	(0.00328)	(0.00419)	(0.00693)	(0.0148)	(0.0109)	(0.0151)
Experience	0.0586***	0.0552***	0.0490***	0.0601***	0.113***	0.0645***	0.0914***	0.0570**
	(0.00616)	(0.0100)	(0.00874)	(0.0105)	(0.0179)	(0.0242)	(0.0234)	(0.0247)
Square of experience	−0.000488***	−0.000752***	−0.000510***	−0.000828***	−0.00141***	−0.00115***	−0.00111***	−0.000994***
	(7.59e–05)	(0.000136)	(0.000113)	(0.000142)	(0.000225)	(0.000317)	(0.000311)	(0.000323)
Gender	0.159***	0.261***	0.228***	0.270***	0.366***	0.242***	0.228***	0.208**
	(0.0124)	(0.0227)	(0.0191)	(0.0234)	(0.0473)	(0.0803)	(0.0693)	(0.0827)
Marital status	0.0620**	0.0454	0.102***	0.0351	−0.222***	−0.188**	−0.225***	−0.185**
	(0.0286)	(0.0303)	(0.0298)	(0.0304)	(0.0746)	(0.0734)	(0.0748)	(0.0735)
Registered permanent residence		−0.910***	0.147***	−0.801***		−0.721		−0.555
		(0.220)	(0.0193)	(0.242)		(0.595)		(0.667)
Ownership			−0.0972	0.236			−0.196	−0.201
			(0.203)	(0.221)			(0.637)	(0.674)
Interaction terms between registered permanent residence and main variables	Uncontrolled	Controlled	Uncontrolled	Controlled	Uncontrolled	Controlled	Uncontrolled	Controlled
Interaction terms between ownership and main variables	Uncontrolled	Uncontrolled	Controlled	Controlled	Uncontrolled	Uncontrolled	Controlled	Controlled
Region	Uncontrolled	Controlled	Controlled	Controlled	Uncontrolled	Controlled	Controlled	Controlled

Variable	*CHIPS (2002)*				*CGSS (2006)*			
	(1)	*(2)*	*(3)*	*(4)*	*(5)*	*(6)*	*(7)*	*(8)*
Constant term	−1.239***	−0.567***	−0.878***	−0.654***	0.150	1.707***	0.494	1.809***
	(0.109)	(0.178)	(0.158)	(0.185)	(0.313)	(0.446)	(0.416)	(0.458)
Observed value	13,546	13,546	13,148	13,148	4,098	4,098	4,090	4,090
R2	0.225	0.248	0.261	0.271	0.186	0.250	0.191	0.252
Log likelihood function	−14,367	−14,168	−13,444	−13,358	−7476	−7306	−7448	−7287

Note (1) The values in the parentheses are robust standard deviations. (2) The significance levels are *** $p < 0.01$, ** $p < 0.05$, * $p < 0.1$

Table 5.11 shows segmentation indexes measured on the basis of OLS and QRM (Quantile Regression Model). The main segmentation indexes listed in the table are higher than the segmentation indexes measured by Zhang Zhaoshi (2009) in the urban labor market of Zhejiang Province. On the basis of the overall market index measured based on the OLS, among the segmentation indexes in CHIPS (2002), the level of segmentation caused purely by the household registration system is 2.441 percent, the level of segmentation caused purely by ownership is 5.868, and the double duality caused by both the household registration system and ownership is 6.407 percent; correspondingly, among the segmentation indexes in CGSS (2006), the level of segmentation caused purely by the household registration system is 6.384 percent, the level of segmentation caused purely by ownership is 1.954, and the double duality caused by both the household registration system and ownership is 6.417 percent. Among the above two groups of data, the levels of segmentation caused purely by the household registration system and purely by ownership are different, and the segmentation indexes based on the household registration system in CHIP data are less than those in CGSS data, but those based on ownership are on the contrary. Moreover, the segmentation indexes of 2002 based on ownership nearly triple those of 2006, but the segmentation indexes of the dual structure of 2002 and 2006 are very close to each other, about 6.41 percent.

Based on the results of quantile regression, both the CHIPS database and the CGSS database reflect that a part with a lower quantile has higher level of segmentation, and the 10 quantile has the highest level of segmentation. The double duality of CHIPS is 23.47 percent, while that of CGSS is 9.751 percent. The segmentation indexes based on pure household registration system and ownership remain the highest at 10 quantile, but the segmentation index of CHIPS data is much higher than (twice or triple) that of CGSS data; among CHIPS data, what ranks second is the median, which has a level of segmentation of 7.03 percent, while CGSS data are different from CHIPS data as the double duality of medians is slightly higher than the level of segmentation of 10 quantile; 90 quantile has the lowest level of segmentation. Such contrast indicates that the segmentation index in low quartile regression is higher than that in high quartile regression.

The segmentation index measured through regression takes full advantage of the information on regression residual. We know that the residuals of the Mincer wage equation reflect the wage gap between laborers with

Table 5.11 Segmentation indexes calculated based on the estimated results of OLS and QRM

Model	*Segmentation index (SI) (percent)*	
	CHIPS (2002)	*CGSS (2006)*
OLS		
The household registration system	2.441	6.384
Ownership	5.868	1.954
The household registration system and ownership	6.407	6.417
Quantile regression		
10 quantile		
The household registration system	12.513	6.783
Ownership	21.724	6.429
The household registration system and ownership	23.467	9.751
50 quantile		
The household registration system	2.335	10.695
Ownership	6.679	3.568
The household registration system and ownership	7.031	10.823
90 quantile		
The household registration system	1.792	3.689
Ownership	1.656	1.271
The household registration system and ownership	2.57	3.608

identical individual characteristics. Therefore, the segmentation index reflects the wage gap to a certain extent, the changes in segmentation indexes at different time points represent the level of convergence or divergence of pay level of laborers with identical individual characteristics. The segmentation index changes of CHIPS (2002) and CGSS (2006) indicate to a certain extent that the difference in the dual wage did not change significantly at the above two points of time, but the double duality changed to some extent in 2002 and 2006. The factor of registered permanent residence was enhanced while that of ownership was weakened; the wage gap caused by registered permanent residence showed a tendency of expansion, while that caused by ownership showed a tendency of convergence; the part with lower conditional quantile decreased at the higher level of segmentation, while the part with higher conditional quantile increased at the lower level of segmentation. From this we can preliminarily judge that, in the two years, the pay level of the part with lower conditional quantile shows a tendency of convergence, while that with higher conditional quantile shows a tendency of divergence, on the whole, the wage gap did not become more divergent or convergent.

Of course, we should notice that the two databases differ significantly in the measurement of segmentation indexes, and there are likely the following two reasons for this: (1) Change of time. The years 2002 and 2006 were in different period of reform, respectively, the former is at the most difficult time of reform of state-owned enterprises, while the latter is the first year of the "11th Five-Year Plan" period and the year with the most active market-oriented development. The labor market will become more segmented or integrated over time, which is also an issue of concern in this paper; (2) Differences in the composition of samples. CHIPS data are from sampling surveys in 12 provinces. And its samples based on registered permanent residence and ownership are different from CGSS data from 30 provinces, municipalities, and autonomous regions excluding Tibet in their distribution, naturally leading to residual estimates. However, we have eliminated the differences in distribution by using the method of weighted sampling at the time of estimation. Hence, as shown in measurement of model setting and segmentation index, measuring error, especially that of wage income, has been controlled.

5.3.3 Measurement of Industrial Segmentation Index in the Case of Double Duality

Besides the household registration system and the ownership segmentation, the wage gap caused by industrial segmentation is one of the issues receiving high attention in recent years. One of the key reasons for this is the increasingly widening inter-industrial wage gap. In China, industrial segmentation does not merely mean industrial differences leading to different industrial pay levels, more importantly, industrial issues tend to intertwine with ownership. The monopoly position of state sectors in some industries has become the reason for intensified inter-industrial segmentation, that is, state-owned monopoly industries, by relying on their possession of resources and administrative privileges, use non-market approaches to gain excess profits and increase industrial wage and transfer the wage cost in the industry by monopolizing the market price (Zhang and Chen 2008). Hence, research on industrial differences is usually combined with ownership. According to the results of researches conducted by Ye Linxiang et al. (2011) on the data of industrial enterprises from China's first national economic census (2004), both ownership and industrial monopolization are factors influencing enterprises' wage income gap, but the impact of ownership is greater than the standard for industrial judgment. Specifically, the average pay level of state-owned enterprises is 30.5 percent–35.9 percent higher than that of private enterprises, the average pay level of foreign-invested enterprises is 19.8 percent–20.6 percent higher than that of private enterprises, the average pay level of collectively owned enterprises is 3.8 percent–6.0 percent lower than that of private enterprises, and the average pay level of monopoly industrial enterprises is merely 4.8 percent–13.0 percent higher than that of private enterprises. Many researchers have proposed that the monopoly of industrial ownership must be eliminated or restricted so as to narrow the inter-industrial wage gap (Chen and Chen 2002; Zhang et al. 2003; Xing 2006). Theoretically, we believe that the issue of wage gaps between different industries and enterprises can be fundamentally removed by removing barriers to industrial monopolization and creating a mechanism for fair industrial competition. However, as our analyses in Sect. 5.4 of this paper indicate, China's labor market is multi-tiered segmentation as a result of a number of factors on the basis of double duality. Specifically, industry is one of the most important factors for multi-tiered segmentation. Therefore, industrial segmentation is intertwined with ownership, the differentiation of laborers' identity is inevitably intertwined with the household registration system, and it is infeasible and unrealistic to solve the issue of industrial segmentation merely by getting rid of monopoly of industrial ownership. It is not difficult to see that industrial segmentation is directly intertwined with ownership segmentation, and the household registration system differentiates the identity of laborers rather than acting directly on industrial segmentation. The problem that must be solved first of all for segmentation measurement is how to integrate the function of the household registration system and industrial segmentation.

The household registration system cannot act directly on industrial segmentation, otherwise, it may cause the following problems if the household registration system is directly introduced into the OLS: (1) Sample selection bias. For example, at the time of regression of the primary industry, the wage equation about urban & state sectoral laborers relative to rural & non-state sectoral laborers is used. It means that those samples of urban non-state sectors and rural state sectors are not included in the estimation, thus producing sample selection bias; (2) It has changed the mechanism of action of the household registration system in the industrial wage gap and changed the indirect mechanism into the direct mechanism. A traditional and effective method for solving the problems at the abovementioned aspects is the Heckman two-stage estimation method or the switching regression method. The switching regression method is used to ensure consistency in this paper.

Through comparison of the two databases, it is found that the number of CGSS samples of segmented industries is relatively less, especially that of the agriculture, forestry, animal husbandry, and fishery. Therefore, for segmentation indexes of segmented industries, this paper only measures the level of industrial segmentation of CHIPS (2002) data.

First of all, as shown in Table 5.12, the overall industrial segmentation indexes are estimated by using the method in the previous part. The result shows that the segmentation level of the overall industrial double duality is 8.956 percent, 2.54 percentage points higher than 6.41 percent, which is the overall market segmentation index, the measurement result of quantile regression verifies the results of overall market measurement, the level of segmentation of low quantile makes the greatest contribution to the industrial double duality, and industries with higher quantile has lower level of double duality. Therefore, the level of segmentation increases under the influence of industrial monopolization factors, and the numerical value reflects the complexity and multiplicity of China's labor market segmentation.

Secondly, when measuring the segmentation index of segmented industries, only the double duality index can be measured as the switching regression model is used. The results are shown in Table 5.13.

Table 5.12 Segmentation indexes calculated based on estimated results of OLS and quantile (CHIPS), with industry controlled

Model	*Segmentation index (SI) (percent)*
OLS: registered permanent residence + ownership	8.956
Quantile regression: registered permanent residence + ownership	
10 quantile	27.408
50 quantile	9.674
90 quantile	4.412

Table 5.13 Measurement of double duality indexes of five industries

Segmentation index	*Industry*				
	1	*2*	*3*	*4*	*5*
$\frac{1}{n_j}\sum_{k=1}^{n_j}(\lvert\lvert\varepsilon_{jk}^1\rvert - \lvert\varepsilon_{jk}^2\rvert\rvert)$	27.394	574.959	192.771	623.942	809.431
$\frac{1}{n_j}\sum_{k=1}^{n_j}\log\widehat{wage}_{jk}^2$	1.670	1.540	1.184	1.9397	1.9397
SI (percent)	11.159	9.012	24.152	9.204	15.946
Number of samples	146	4143	673	3494	4701

Note 1 = primary industry (including agriculture, forestry, husbandry, and fishery); 2 = manufacturing industry (including the manufacturing industry and supplies of electric power, coal, and water); 3 = mining industry and construction industry; 4 = service industry I (including information transmission, computer services, geological survey, education, health, social security, social welfare, culture, sports and entertainment, public administration, social organization, and international organization.); 5 = service industry II (other service industries except for what is listed above); and 6 = other industries. This paper does not calculate the results of other industries

The results in the table show that the double duality of segmented industry is higher than the overall market segmentation, and the sequence of the levels of segmentation is 3 > 5 > 1 > 4 > 2 (in descending order). Among the industries, Category 4 and Category 2 have more good employers, while Category 1, Category 3, and Category 5 have more poor employers. In China, a good employer tends to be much more important than a good job, and a good employer means a good job. Before marketization, good employers were only in the state sectors. At present, with high degree of marketization, good employers concentrate in state-owned monopolized industries, as well as monopolized industries in the non-state sectors. The good occupations produced by these good employers have less urban–rural segmentation. However, it shall be noticed that there are competitive industries in Category 2, and there is a more significant difference between state sectors and non-state sectors in the competitive industries. Therefore, typical ownership segmentation is the main segmentation factor of these good employers and "good" professions. For this, the level of segmentation of Category 4 and Category 2 is the lowest in all professions. Comparatively, Category 1, Category 3, and Category 4 are characterized with features of poor units. Category 1 features the primary industry, and Category 3 is the service industry dominated by services aiming at urban residents and wholesale & retail services, the wage gap of which has both urban–rural segmentation and certain ownership segmentation, and the level of segmentation is in the middle of the five industries. Category 3 covers the mining industry and the construction industry, with the highest level of segmentation being 24.15 percent. The persons who work in the above three industries take more double duality.

When the double duality and industrial segmentation interact with each other, the level of segmentation will naturally rise. In addition, industries are generally divided into competitive industries and monopoly industries in the market. With enough data, we can further define the size of the part produced by monopolistic factors beyond the double duality.

5.3.4 Conclusions

Industrial difference is the common feature of the labor market. However, in China's labor market, this issue tends to be intertwined with ownership. To understand industrial segmentation, it is essential to connect it with ownership, which is in most cases intertwined with the household registration system. Therefore, we shall start from the household registration system, analyze how the household registration system exerts an impact on laborers working in ownership-based sectors, and discuss the inter-industrial income gap for analysis of industrial segmentation. In addition, under China's current household registration system and ownership type, it is not random to enter the state sectors or the non-state sectors. Hence, we continue to use the method of switching regression to measure industrial segmentation indexes, and its results evidently show that the level of industrial segmentation is much greater than the overall level of market segmentation, and the level of segmentation of the industry with more good employers is lower than the industry with more poor employers. There is a great difference in inter-industrial segmentation indexes and the industry with the highest segmentation index triples that with the lowest segmentation index. Also, it also indicates that the inter-industrial pay level widens due to the "dual" factor plus industrial segmentation. Since data at a single point of time are processed, it is very hard to judge whether the pay level of an industry is converged.

5.4 Summary

By using CHIPS (2002) and CGSS (2006) data, this chapter discusses the changes of the current segmentation state of China's labor market from the perspectives of flow of labor and pay level, respectively.

First, on the basis of the understanding of "duality," the switching regression model is used to judge the following three issues of labor market segmentation from the perspective of flow of labor. (1) Prove the existence of double duality in the labor market. Theoretically, if the labor market is uniform, only one pay level exists, otherwise, two wage equations are more applicable. For the testing results of likelihood statistics, two wage equations are more applicable, signifying the existence of the "duality"; (2) Prove that "duality" is a barrier to flow of labor. The results of the model indicate that "duality" is indeed a barrier to intersectoral labor mobility. By analyzing the impacts of different household registration systems on intersectoral mobility, we obtain a sequence of barriers to flow of labor, which is shown below in ascending order: ① urban labor < rural labor; ② local non-rural labor < non-local non-rural labor < non-local rural labor < local rural labor; ③ labor of provincial capital ≈ labor of municipality directly under the central government < labor of prefecture-level city < labor of county\county-level city < labor of town/township. (3) "Duality" features significant endogeneity, implying that it is difficult to change a certain aspect of double duality through policies.

Second, on the basis of the Mincer wage equation and by using the regression-based method for measuring segmentation index established by Orr (1997) and Zhang Zhaoshi (2009), we have, respectively, measured the segmentation indexes of the overall market and industries in the condition of double duality. It has again proved the existence of duality of China's labor market, and the level of segmentation is 6.41 percent. Generally, the level of segmentation did not change significantly in 2002 and 2006, and the differences in pay levels caused by duality did not diverge or converge at the above two time points. In the double duality, the factor of registered permanent residence was enhanced while the ownership factor was reduced. The wage differentials caused by registered permanent residence tend to expand, while the wage differentials caused by ownership tend to converge. The part with lower conditional quantile has been reduced at the higher level of segmentation, while the part with higher conditional quantile has been increased at the lower level of segmentation. Preliminary judges show that, in the above two years, the pay level of the part with lower conditional quantile showed a tendency of convergence, while that with higher conditional quantile showed a tendency of divergence. The level of industrial segmentation of the industry with more good employers is lower than that with more poor employers, there is great differences in inter-industrial segmentation indexes, and the highest segmentation index nearly triples the lowest segmentation index.

The analyses of the above two aspects reveal the existence of the double duality in China's labor market. Under the combined action of the complicated internal composition of the double duality and external factors including the industrial factors, multi-tiered segmentation has been derived in China's labor market. The discrimination between the concepts of equilibrium and integration in Chapter 2 indicates that convergence of pay level is the necessary condition of integration of the labor market, while free labor mobility between different markets is the sufficient condition of integration. The researches in this part have proved that China's current labor market has no law of one price, there are barriers to flow of labor, and the segmentation in China's labor market persists. However, the components of segmentation shift, showing a tendency of endogenous integration of the labor market.

In addition, on the basis of the theoretical analysis framework in Chapter 4, multi-tiered segmentation based on double duality, regional segmentation, and the sorting effect of social structure are important factors influencing segmentation. Due to data limitations, this paper will not discuss how the labor market segmentation changes under the action of the above two factors; since data processing involves a heavy workload, CHIPS (1989) and CHIPS (1995) data are not processed. If the data of the two years are integrated, the evolvement of labor market segmentation can be verified. Particularly, the changes around the starting period of marketization are more meaningful.

CHAPTER 6

Conclusions and Areas for Further Research

6.1 Summary and Conclusions

China is a major developing country. It means that China's development is faced with transition from a dual structure to a unitary structure and from the planned economy to the market economy. During the transitional period, the labor market, as an important market of factors allocation, has to trade-off between retaining the traditional system and transforming for system adaptation. In addition, the labor market involves the human itself and has a bearing on social equity and harmony, so there are great difficulties in the transition of the labor market. The starting point of the establishment of China's labor market is the strict urban–rural double duality and the planning system, therefore, the above two systems have been intertwined with the market system since the establishment of the labor market. It is such characteristics that cause the evolvement of China's labor market to integrate the most propulsive parts of the planning system and the market system and lead to the multi-tiered segmentation of China's labor market.

Firstly, this paper reviews the development of and verification methods for the theory of labor market segmentation. The debates between classical economics and institutional economics have run through the researches on labor economics. In accordance with the perfectly competitive labor market in classical economics, the neoclassical economics

Y. Chen, *China's Labor Market in the Transition*,
https://doi.org/10.1007/978-981-99-9160-0_6

considers non-market factors as key factors influencing the non-competitiveness of the labor market; based on institutional economics and development economics, economists represented by Lewis have proposed the dual structure of the labor market to analyze the non-competitiveness of the labor market. Due to the researches on the labor market starting from classical economics, the long-term issues of the labor market tend to be neglected. According to classical economics, unemployment only lasts for a short period of time rather than a long period of time. Therefore, the labor market is always balanced for classical economists. Nevertheless, as the starting point of economic research, classical economists' view of automatic market clearing occupied the principal position for a long time, and so have the researches on the issues of the labor market; the theory of labor market segmentation represented by the dual-structure theory and the development economics emphasize that the labor market is divided into two parts, which have a big wage gap, that is, one part believes that no labor flow exists between primary sectors and secondary sectors, while the other emphasizes free rural–urban mobility. However, the researches on the two theories on the labor market segmentation were in a state of segmentation for a long time in terms of research method and theoretical basis. Looking for a theoretical basis and an analytical framework for integrating the two theories represents the development trend of the labor market segmentation theory. Although the above two theoretical schools vary greatly in research method and theoretical basis, both of them regard the labor market as a "black box." Opening the "black box" and introducing the behavioral mechanism of enterprises and laborers in the labor market are the links between the two theories. The key to the "black box" is the job search-and-matching model proposed by Mortensen (1984). The job search theory assumes that workers search for the best opportunities provided by different employers, and based on this get different wage gaps in the labor market. After nearly three decades of development, the classical search-and-matching model proposed by Mortensen and Pissarides (1994) has been applied to double duality or multi-tiered segmentation in the labor market.

Looking back on the development course of the wage determination mechanism and the flow of labor since the founding of the People's Republic of China, we divide the establishment of China's labor market into four phases: phase 1 (1949–1978), the process of employment and wage determination before marketization, characterized by unified pricing, strict limitation of labor mobility and nearly "complete segmentation" under the condition of urban–rural dual structure; phase 2 (1978–1990), the labor market in the initial stage of marketization, during which marketization factors began to infiltrate into the planning system, the strictly uniform wage system still played a major role in the wage determination mechanism, but the pay level of some enterprises began to be linked with their economic efficiency; the restrictions on labor mobility between urban and rural areas were appropriately relaxed, but the policy constraints were still strong; the first stage of marketization of phase 3 (1990–2000): the keynote of market economy was established, and the labor market was formally established at the national level; under the influence of market factors, there are multiple wage determination mechanisms, and rural labor began to flow on a large scale, but the flow of labor between different cities and within a city was still limited, forming double duality; the second stage of marketization of phase 4, (2000–present): the degree of marketization became higher and higher; the proportion of market-allocated resources in the labor market exceeded the resources allocated through the planning system, the wage determination mechanism became diversified, labor flowed freely in space, and multi-tiered segmentation on the basis of double duality formed.

Secondly, starting with the issue of segmentation, this paper further reviews the researches and understanding of scholars at home and abroad regarding the issue of market segmentation of China's labor market and classifies the factors influencing the labor market segmentation into three types, endogenous factor, exogenous factor, and causative factor. The segmentation results caused by endogenous and exogenous factors are enhanced or reduced under the influence of causative factors, and for this the labor market is likely to become more segmented or integrated. Based on the understandings that in China a good job means a good employer, the function of the household registration system as a barrier to labor mobility reduces and its function of resource allocation persists, we analyze the functions of the three factors in China, propose that China's labor market shows a state of multi-tiered segmentation. Such multi-tiered segmentation is based on the double duality results of institutional factors and formed together with endogenous segmentation and spatial segmentation, and the choice of microscopic individual behavior will solidify or weaken such segmentation. The behaviors of laborers and enterprises are introduced into the labor market segmentation and the search-and-matching model including heterogeneity of enterprises and laborers is constructed on the basis of the search-and-matching theory by Mortensen and Pissarides (1994, 1999) and Pissarides (2000). The equilibrium outcomes of the model indicate that the double duality has resulted in multiple equilibria in China's labor market, as well as different wage determination mechanisms and labor demand conditions, causing differences in pay level. The mobility of labors, particularly rural labors, between state sectors and non-state sectors requires conversion cost and high cost of labor mobility, and the excessively high cost of labor mobility is the biggest constraint for rural labor to enter the urban state sectors. Dynamic analysis results indicate that double duality shows a tendency of integration, but the barriers to the flow of labor only reduce within a certain limit, implying that double duality will persist against China's current systems and background.

Thirdly, by using CHIPS (2002) and CGSS (2006) data, this chapter discusses the changes in the current segmentation state of China's labor market from the perspectives of the flow of labor and pay level, respectively. (1) On the basis of the understanding of "duality," the switching regression model is used to verify the existence and endogeneity of double duality of the labor market, but the segmentation is indeed a barrier to intersectoral labor mobility. According to the analyses of the impacts of different household registration systems on intersectoral labor mobility, the barriers to the flow of labor in ascending order are as follows: ① urban labor < rural labor; ② local non-rural labor < non-local non-rural labor < non-local rural labor < local rural labor; ③ labor of provincial capital ≈ labor of municipality directly under the central government < labor of prefecture-level city < labor of county\county-level city < labor of town/township. (2) On the basis of the Mincer wage equation and the regression-based method for measuring the segmentation index established by Orr (1997) and Zhang Zhaoshi (2009), we have, respectively, measured the segmentation indexes of the market and industries in the condition of double duality. It has again proved the existence of "duality" in China's labor market, and the level of segmentation is 6.41 percent. Generally, the level of segmentation did not change significantly in 2002 and 2006. The wage differentials caused by registered permanent residence tend to expand, while the wage differentials caused by ownership tend to converge. The part with lower conditional quantile has been reduced at the higher level of segmentation, while the part with higher conditional quantile has been increased at the lower level of segmentation. In the years 2002 and 2006, the pay level of the part with lower conditional quantile shows a tendency of convergence, while that with higher conditional quantile shows a tendency of divergence. The level of segmentation of the industry with more good employers is lower than the industry with more poor employers. There is a great difference in inter-industrial segmentation indexes and the industry with the highest segmentation index triples that with the lowest segmentation index. Relevant studies show that there is no law of one price in China's labor market, and certain barriers to flow of labor exist, indicating the existence of the segmentation of China's labor market. However, the wane and wax of the constituents of the segmentation indicate there is endogenous power driving the labor market to move toward integration.

6.1.1 Main Conclusions of This Paper

1. Integration of the labor market is, under the condition of search friction of the labor market, realization of the transfer of willingness of excess demands and excess supplies of labor between different markets. Pay level convergence is a necessary condition for the integration of the labor market, while the flow of labor between different markets is a necessary and sufficient condition for the integration of the labor market. When both the two conditions are satisfied, the labor market is completely integrated.
2. The evolution characteristics of China's labor market are manifested as with the household registration system and ownership as the main lines, under the impact of the process of marketization, China's labor market has gradually evolved from nearly complete segmentation before the adoption of the reform and opening up policy to multi-tiered segmentation on the basis of the household registration system and ownership and under the combined action of multiple factors.
3. There are three types of factors influencing the labor market, namely endogenous factor, exogenous factor, and causative factor. The segmentation generated by spatial factors in endogenous and exogenous factors has universal meaning. The labor market segmentation generated by institutional factors in exogenous factors is hard to relieve over a long period and even becomes more stable due to the institutional stability. The segmentation results of endogenous and exogenous factors are enhanced or reduced under the influence

of causative factors, and for this the labor market is likely to become more segmented or integrated.

4. China's labor market is in a state of multi-tiered segmentation, which is double duality based on the household registration system and ownership and formed together with endogenous segmentation and spatial segmentation, and the choice of microscopic individual behavior will solidify or weaken such segmentation.
5. The outcome of the classical MP model including bilateral heterogeneity of enterprises and laborers shows that double duality has resulted in multiple equilibria in China's labor market, as well as different wage determination mechanisms and labor demand conditions. The dynamic analyses of the model show that the double duality tends to be integrated in a certain range, but the feature of segmentation will continue to exist under China's current institutional conditions.
6. The empirical research results show that China's current labor market cannot meet the law of one price and barriers to the flow of labor still exist in a certain range, indicating the existence of segmentation of China's labor market.

6.2 Major Innovations of This Study

1. It tentatively analyzes and summarizes the concept of integration of the labor market, and discriminates the concepts of integration and equilibrium, helping to theoretically clarify the concept of integration of the labor market (segmentation).
2. It introduces the development history of China's labor market and summarizes the evolution characteristics of China's labor market based on changes in the household registration system and ownership.
3. It tentatively proposes the theoretical framework to analyze China's labor market segmentation, brings in the factors influencing market segmentation, including endogenous factors, exogenous factors, and causative factors, and analyzes the results of the labor market under the influence of the three factors. Based on such understandings, this paper theoretically analyzes and summarizes the characteristics of multi-tiered segmentation in China's labor market under the three factors above and the main influencing factors.

4. It has tentatively established the bilateral heterogeneity search-and matching-model based on the MP model and used the model to make preliminary discussions on double duality of the labor market. This is a meaningful exploration for theoretical analyses of China's labor market segmentation.
5. On the basis of early stage researches made by scholars at home and abroad, this paper makes further researches on the empirical work, makes further discussions on how to verify the labor market segmentation, and proposes to decompose the segmented part of the labor market by using quantile regression, making valuable attempts in detailing the composition of the labor market segmentation.

6.3 Deficiency and Areas for Further Research

This paper, based on the judgment of double duality, makes effort to establish a theoretical analysis framework and model related to the issue of segmentation, analyzes and examines the features of double duality in the evolution of China's labor market and the evolution trend. China's labor market itself is very complicated, which requires long-time researches. In the future, efforts should be made from the following aspects:

1. Further improve the bilateral heterogeneity search-and-matching model proposed in this paper. Due to the limited time, this paper does not complete the stability analysis of the equilibrium solution of the model, search for the saddle path, and analyses of derived policies. Further analyses in this regard are highly beneficial to theoretical discussions of double duality; in addition, the extension of the model in terms of spatial division and sorting effect will have more specific policy implications. Particularly, the introduction of the sorting effect makes it possible to analyze the issue of social stratification in the framework of economics.
2. This paper proposes that China's labor market is double duality based on the household registration system and ownership and multi-tiered segmentation formed under the combined action of endogenous segmentation, spatial segmentation, and sorting effect. This paper only discusses the existence, endogeneity, and possibility of future changes of double duality as well as the changes of double duality under the action of industrial segmentation. However, it is

necessary to make further discussions on the changes of the double duality when spatial segmentation and sorting effects exist from the aspects of theoretical and empirical analyses.

3. The empirical research data used in this paper are from different databases. Therefore, the consistency between different databases needs to be particularly considered in the process of research. Although the issue of endogeneity of model has been solved by measuring technologies, the external validity of model setting will also influence the conclusions of this paper to a certain extent due to the sampling principle of database and diversity of sources, and the analyses of data at different time points in the same database need to be further strengthened.
4. The labor market segmentation will affect the improvement of social welfare. This paper judges and evaluates the social welfare generated by the labor market segmentation, discusses about the issues of income equality and poverty, and seeks policies on improving social welfare. It points out that there are two kinds of externalities in the matching process of market allocation of labor resources, but makes neither theoretical analyses nor empirical analyses of social welfare of the two externalities. It is of theoretical significance and has policy implications to make detailed discussions about these issues.

The proposal of the analytical framework of double duality is merely a beginning as behind the complexity of the segmentation of China's labor market there are quite a few issues worthy of further study in the future.

Appendices

Appendix A

According to the remaining matching rule, the sum of Formulas (4.12) and (4.13):

$$
\begin{aligned}
& r(J_I + E_I) = y_I + \lambda[V_I - J_I - f + U - E_I) \Rightarrow \\
& r(J_I + E_I - V_I - U + f) = y - r(V_I + U - f) + \lambda(V_I - J_I - f + U - E_I) \\
& (J_I + E_I - V_I - U + f) = \frac{y - r(V_I + U - f)}{r + \lambda} \\
& \because J_I + E_I - V_I - U + f = S_I \\
& \therefore S_I = \frac{y - r(V_I + U - f)}{r + \lambda}
\end{aligned}
\tag{A.1}
$$

Then, by using Formula (4.7) and the rule of residual assignment:

$$(E_I - U_I) = \frac{w_I^P - rU_I}{r + \lambda}$$

$$(E_I - U_I) = \beta S_I = \frac{w_I^P - rU_I}{r + \lambda}$$

After the substitution of (A.1):

$$rU_I = \frac{b(1 + \eta)(r + \lambda) + \varphi\theta_I q(\theta_I)\beta(y - rk + rf)}{r + \lambda + \varphi\theta_I q(\theta_I)\beta} \tag{A.2}$$

Y. Chen, *China's Labor Market in the Transition*,
https://doi.org/10.1007/978-981-99-9160-0

In accordance with the wage equation:

$$W_I^P = \beta^* P + (1-\beta) r U_I$$
$$= \beta^* P + (1-\beta)\frac{b(1+\eta)(r+\lambda) + \varphi\theta_I q(\theta_I)\beta(y - rk + rf)}{r+\lambda+\varphi\theta_I q(\theta_I)\beta}$$

Make
$\Gamma(\theta_I) = \frac{r+\lambda+\varphi\theta_I q(\theta_I)}{r+\lambda+\varphi\theta_I q(\theta_I)\beta}\beta$,
then,

$$w_I^P = \beta P + [1-\Gamma(\theta_I)]b(1+\eta) + [\Gamma(\theta_I)-\beta]y + [\Gamma(\theta_I)-\beta]r(f-k) \tag{A.3}$$

Likewise, the wage determination equation of non-state sectors is:

$$w_O^B = \alpha y_o + (1-\alpha) r U(j = O)$$

After the substitution of rU:

$$\Gamma(\theta_0) = \frac{r+\lambda+\gamma+(1-\varphi)\theta_0 q(\theta_0)}{r+\lambda+\gamma+(1-\varphi)\theta_0 q(\theta_0)\alpha}\alpha$$

$$W_I^P = b + \Gamma(\theta_0)(y_0 - b) \tag{A.4}$$

Appendix B

$$U(j = I) - Z = J^O \tag{B.1}$$

$$\because rU(j = I) = b(1+\eta) + \varphi\theta_I q(\theta_I)(E_I - U - z) \tag{B.2}$$

In accordance with Formula (4.7): $E_I - U + z = \frac{w_I^P - rU + (r+\lambda)z}{r+\lambda}$
After the substitution of the formula above:

$$rU(j = I) = \frac{b(1+\eta)(r+\lambda) + w_I^P(r+\lambda)z}{r+\lambda+\varphi\theta_I q(\theta_I)} \tag{B.3}$$

In accordance with Formula (4.4),

$$J_O = \frac{y_O - w_O^B}{r+\lambda+\gamma} \tag{B.4}$$

Substitute (B.3) and (B.4) into (B.5):

$$Z = \frac{T_3 - (y_O - W_O^B)T_1 + \varphi\theta_I q(\theta_I) W_I^P T_2}{[rT1 - (r + \lambda)\varphi\theta_I q(\theta_I)]T_2} \quad \text{(B.5)}$$

Appendix C

China's minimum wages in 2011

Province and city	*Practicable date*	*Minimum wage standard*	*Province and city*	*Practicable date*	*Minimum wage standard*
Beijing	2011/1/1	1160 yuan/ month	Qingyuan	2011/3/1	850 yuan/ month
Chongqing	2011/1/1	870 yuan/ month–710 yuan/month	Dongguan	2011/3/1	1100 yuan/ month
Guangzhou	2011/3/1	1300 yuan/ month	Zhongshan	2011/3/1	1100 yuan/ month
Shenzhen	2011/4/1	1320 yuan/ month	Chaozhou	2011/3/1	850 yuan/ month
Zhuhai	2011/3/1	1100 yuan/ month	Jieyang	2011/3/1	850 yuan/ month
Foshan	2011/3/1	1100 yuan/ month	Yunfu	2011/3/1	850 yuan/ month
Shaoguan	2011/3/1	850 yuan/ month	Wuhai	2011/1/1	900 yuan/ month
Shantou	2011/3/1	950 yuan/ month	Jiangsu	2011/2/1	800–1140 yuan/month
Jiangmen	2011/3/1	950 yuan/ month	Nanjing	2011/2/1	1140 yuan/ month–930 yuan/month
Zhanjiang	2011/3/1	850 yuan/ month	Changzhou	2011/2/1	1140 yuan/ month–930 yuan/month
Maoming	2011/3/1	850 yuan/ month	Suzhou	2011/2/1	1140 yuan/ month
Zhaoqing	2011/3/1	850 yuan/ month	Nantong	2011/2/1	1140 yuan/ month–930 yuan/month
Huizhou	2011/3/1	950 yuan/ month	Taizhou	2011/2/1	930 yuan/ month
Meizhou	2011/3/1	850 yuan/ month	Shandong	2011/3/1	1100 yuan/ month–800 yuan/month

(continued)

(continued)

Province and city	*Practicable date*	*Minimum wage standard*	*Province and city*	*Practicable date*	*Minimum wage standard*
Shanwei	2011/3/1	850 yuan/month	Qingdao	2011/3/1	1100 yuan/month–950 yuan/month
Heyuan	2011/3/1	850 yuan/month	Yantai	2011/3/1	1100 yuan/month–950 yuan/month
Yangjiang	2011/3/1	850 yuan/month			

References

Acemoglu, D. (1999). Changes in Unemployment and Wage Inequality: An Alternative Theory and Some Evidence. *American Economic Review, 89*(5), 1259–1278.

Acemoglu, D. (2001). Good Jobs versus Bad Jobs. *Journal of Labor Economics, 19*(1), 1–21.

Akerlof, G., & Yellen, J. (Eds.). (1986). *Efficiency Wage Models of the Labor Market*. Cambridge University Press.

Alan, M. (2011). Chapter 11: Imperfect Competition in the Labor Market. In *Handbook of Labor Economics* (Vol. 4b, pp. 976–1041).

Albrecht, J., & Vroman, S. U. S. A. N. (2002). A Matching Model with Endogenous Skill Requirements. *International Economic Review, 43*(1), 283–305.

Albrecht, J., Lang, H., & Vroman, S. (2002). The Effect of Information on the Well-Being of the Uninformed: What's the Chance of Getting a Decent Meal in an Unfamiliar City? *International Journal of Industrial Organization, 20*(2), 139–162.

Anderson, K. H., Butler, J. S., & Sloan, F. A. (1987, January). Labor Market Segmentation: A Cluster Analysis of Job Grouping and Barriers to Entry. *Southern Economic Journal, 53*(3), 571–590.

Arnott, R. (1998). Economic Theory and the Spatial Mismatch Hypothesis. *Urban Studies, 35*(7), 1171–1185.

Ashenfelter, O., & Card, D. (Eds.). (1999). *Handbook of Labor Economics* (pp. 2567–2628). Elsevier.

Äunther, I. G., & Launov, A. (2006). *Competitive and Segmented Informal Labor Markets* (IZA Working Paper).

Y. Chen, *China's Labor Market in the Transition*,
https://doi.org/10.1007/978-981-99-9160-0

Baffoe-Bonnie, J. (2003). Distributional Assumptions and a Test of the Dual Labor Market Hypothesis. *Empirical Economics, 28*, 461–478.

Bardhan, P. K., & Rudra, A. (1981). Terms and Conditions of Labour Contracts in Agriculture: Results of a Survey in West Bengal 1979. *Oxford Bulletin of Economics and Statistics, 43*(1), 89–111.

Baumol, W., & Gomory, R. E. (1992). *Toward a Theory of Industrial Policy-Retainable Industries*. CV Starr Center for Applied Economics, New York University.

Becker, G. S. (1962). Investment in Human Capital: A Theoretical Analysis. *Journal of Political Eocnomy, 70*(supplement), 9–49.

Becker, G. S. (1964). *Human Capital, a Theoretical and Empirical Analysis, with Special Reference to Education* (1st ed.). Columbia University Press.

Becker, G. S., & Chiswick, B. R. (1966). Education and the Distribution of Earnings. *American Economic Review, 56*, 358–369.

Berardi, M. (2009). Expectations, Learning and Policy Rule. *Centre for Growth and Business Cycle Research Discussion Paper Series, 4*, 561–562.

Bian, Y., et al. (2008). *Overseas Scholars' Advanced Research on China: Social Stratification and Mobility*. China Renmin University Press.

Blanchard, O. J., & Diamond, P. A. (1989). *The Aggregate Matching Function*.

Blauner, R. (1964). *Alienation and Freedom: The Factory Worker and His Industry*. The University of Chicago Press.

Boeri, T. (2009). Institutional Reforms and Dualism in European Labor Markets. In *The Handbook of Labor Economics* (Vol. 4B). Elsevier.

Bosworth, D., et al. (2003). *The Economics of Labour Market*. China Economic Press.

Boyer, G. R., & Hatton, T. J. (1994). Regional Labor Market Integration in England and Wales (1850–1913). In M. Mackinnon & G. Grantham (Eds.), *Labor Market Evolution: The Economic History of Market Integration, Wage Flexibility and the Employment Relation*. Routledge.

Brandt, L., & Rawski, T. G. (2008). China's Great Economic Transformation. In L. Brandt & T. G. Rawski (Eds.), *China's Great Economic Transformation*. Cambridge University Press.

Brandt, L., & Rawski, T. G. (2009, October). *China's Great Economic Transformation*. Truth & Wisdom Press and Shanghai People's Publishing House.

Brueckner, J. K., & Martin, R. W. (1997). Spatial Mismatch: An Equilibrium Analysis. *Regional Science and Urban Economics, 27*(6), 693–714.

Cahuc, P., & Postal-Vinay, F. (2002). Temporary Jobs, Employment Protection, and Labor Market Performance. *Labor Economics, 9*, 63–91.

Cahuc, P., & Zylberberg, A. (2007). *Labor Economics*. Shanghai University of Finance & Economics Press.

Cai, F. (1998). The Segmentation of Urban Labor Market and Difficulties in the Transformation of the Employment System. *Review of Economic Research, 45*, 39–40. https://doi.org/10.16110/j.cnki.issn2095-3151.1998.45.044

Cai, F. (2002). *Reports on China's Population and Labor: Urban and Rural Employment Issues and Countermeasures*. Social Sciences Academic Press.

Cai, F. (2007, May). *Reports on China's Population and Labor, No. 8, The Coming Lewisian Turning Point and Its Policy Implications*. Social Sciences Academic Press.

Cai, F. (2008, October). *Lewis Turning Point: A Coming New Stage of China's Economic Development*. Social Sciences Academic Press.

Cai, F. (2008, October). *Reports on China's Population and Labor, No. 9, Linking Up Lewis and Kuznets Turning Points*. Social Sciences Academic Press.

Cai, F. (2008, November). *Research on the 30 Years of China's Labor and Social Security System Reform*. Economy & Management Publishing House.

Cai, F. (2010, July). *Reports on China's Population and Labor, No. 11, The Challenges in the Labor Market in the Post-Financial Crisis Era*. Social Sciences Academic Press.

Cai, F. (2011, August). *Reports on China's Population and Labor, No. 12, Challenges during the "12th Five-Year Plan" Period: Population, Employment and Income Distribution*. Social Sciences Academic Press.

Cai, F., & Bai, N. (2006, June). *China's Labor Movement in Transition*. Social Sciences Academic Press.

Caliendo, M., Schmidl, R., & Uhlendorff, A. (2010). *Social Networks, Job Search Methods and Reservation Wages: Evidence for Germany* (IZA DP No. 5165).

Chakravarty, S. R., & Silber, J. (2007). A Generalized Index of Employment Segregation. *Mathematical Social Science, 53*(2007), 185–195.

Chen, J. (2008). Duan Jinghui. An Analysis of the Quantile Regression of the Gender-Based Wage Gap in China. *The Journal of Quantitative & Technical Economics, 10*.

Chen, X., Xizhe, P., Li, Z., & Kailai, W. (2011). Regional Differences of Requirements on Urban Residency: An Analysis of the 46 Sample Cities in China. *Population and Development, 4*.

Chen, Y., & Chen, S. (2002). An Analysis of Employees' Income Level at State-Owned Monopoly Industries. *Statistical Research, 8*, 76–77. https://doi.org/10.19343/j.cnki.11-1302/c.2002.08.021

Cheng, G., & Ma, B. (2003). Changes and Causes of Institutional Segmentation of China's Labor Market Since Reform and Opening-Up. *Journal of Socialist Theory Guide, 7*, 21–23.

Cheng, G. (2005). A Literature Review of Labor Market Segmentation. *Journal of Xihua University* (Philosophy and Social Sciences Edition), 3.

Clark, J. B. (1899). *The Distribution of Wealth: A Theory of Wages, Interest and Profits*. MacMillan.

Cortez, W. W., & Islas-Camargo, A. (2004). *Regional Labor Market Integration: Northern Mexico and Southern USA*. Urban/Regional.

Costain, J. S., & Reiter, M. (2008). Business Cycles, Unemployment Insurance, and the Calibration of Matching Models. *Journal of Economic Dynamics and Control, 32*(4), 1120–1155.

Costain, J., & Nakov, A. (2011). Distributional Dynamics Under Smoothly State-Dependent Pricing. *Journal of Monetary Economics, 58*(6–8), 646–665.

Costain, J., et al. (2011, February). *Employment Fluctuations in a Dual Labor Market* (Working Paper).

Coulson, E., Laing, D., & Wang, P. (2001). Spatial Mismatch in Search Equilibrium. *Journal of Labor Economics, 19*, 949–972.

David, P. A., & Rosenbloom, J. L. (1990). Marshallian Factor Market Externalities and the Dynamics of Industrial Localization. *Journal of Urban Economics, 28*(3), 349–370.

Démurger, S., Fournier, M., Shi, L., & Zhong, W. (2009). The Issue of Urban Labor Market Segmentation in China's Economic Transition: An Analysis on the Wage Income Gap of Those Working in Different Sectors. *Journal of Management World, 3*, 55–62+71.

Department of Population and Employment Statistics of the National Bureau of Statistics, Department of Planning and Finance of the Ministry of Human Resources and Social Security. (2009). *China Labor Statistical Yearbook 2009*. China Statistics Press.

Dessy, S., & Pallage, S. (2003). Taxes, Inequality and the Size of the Informal Sector. *Journal of Development Economics, 70*(1), 225–233.

Diamond, P. A. (1982a). Wage Determination and Efficiency in Search Equilibrium. *Review of Economic Studies, 49*(2), 217–227.

Diamond, P. A. (1982b). Aggregate Demand Management in Search Equilibrium. *Journal of Political Economy, 90*(5), 881–894.

Dickens, W. T., & Lang, K. (1985a). *Testing Dual Labor Market Theory: A Reconsideration of the Evidence* (NBER Working Papers).

Dickens, W. T., & Lang, K. (1985b). A Test of Dual Labor Market Theory. *The American Economic Review, 75*(4), 792–805.

Doeringer, P., & Piore, M. J. (1971). *Internal Labor Markets and Manpower Analysis*. Heath.

Dong, X., Bowles, P., & Ho, S. (2002). The Determinants of Employee Ownership in China's Privatized Rural Industry: Evidence from Jiangsu and Shandong. *Journal of Comparative Economics, 30*(2), 415–437.

Douglas, V. O. (1997). An Index of Segmentation in Local Labor Markets. *International Review of Applied Economics, 11*(2).

Drèze, J., & Mukherjee, A. (1989). Labour Contracts in Rural India: Theories and Evidence. In S. Chakravarty (Ed.), *The Balance Between Industry and Agriculture in Economic Development*. Macmillan.

Du, Y., & Fang, C. (2004). Regional Convergence of Wages in China's Manufacturing Industry and the Integration of the Labor Market. *The Journal of World Economy, 8*, 42–49.

Easterlin, R. (1960). Interregional Differences in per Capita Income, Population, and Total Income, 1840–1950. In *Trends in the American Economy in the Nineteenth Century* (pp. 73–140). Princeton University Press.

Feng, J. (2009). *Economic Development and Spatial Layout: Urbanization, Economic Agglomeration, and Regional Disparities* [Doctoral Dissertation at Tsinghua University].

Fields, G. S. (1999). Employment Generation and Poverty Alleviation in Developing Economies. In U. Hiemenz (Ed.), *Growth and Competition in the New Global Economy*. OECD Development Centre.

Fields, G. S. (2009, September 2). Segmented Labor Market Models in Developing Countries. In D. Ross & H. Kincaid (Eds.), *The Oxford Handbook of Philosophy of Economics* (Online Edn.). Oxford Academic. https://doi.org/10.1093/oxfordhb/9780195189254.003.0018

Fields, G. S., & Wan, H., Jr. (1989). Wage-Setting Institutions and Economic Growth. *World Development, 17*, 1471–1483.

Flatau, P. R., & Lewis, P. E. (1993). Segmented Labor Markets in Australia. *Applied Economics, 25*(3), 285–294.

Fu, W. (2007). Structural Barriers to Population Mobility: An Empirical Analysis Based on Competitions in Public Spending. *The Journal of World Economy, 12*, 32–40.

Fugazza, M., & Jacques, J.-F. (2004). Labor Market Institutions, Taxation and the Underground Economy. *Journal of Public Economics, 88*, 395–418.

Gan, C., & Bingshen, Z. (2007). China's Labor Relations Adjustment in the Era of Economic Globalization. *Review of Economic Research, 36*, 37. https://doi.org/10.16110/j.cnki.issn2095-3151.2007.36.034

Ge, Y. (2007). Gender Differences in Wage Distribution: A Method for Quantile Decomposition. *Shanghai Journal of Economics, 4*.

Giles, J., Park, A., & Cai, F. (2006). How Has Economic Restructuring Affected China's Urban Workers? *The China Quarterly, 177*, 61–95.

Gobillon, L., Selod, H., & Zenou, Y. (2007). The Mechanisms of Spatial Mismatch. *Urban Studies, 44*(12), 2401–2427.

Goldberger, A. S. (1983). Abnormal Selection Bias. In *Studies in Econometrics, Time Series, and Multivariate Statistics* (pp. 67–84). Academic Press.

Guo, C. (2004). The Validation of the Theory of Dual Labor Market Segmentation in China. *Education & Economy, 3*, 7–11.

Hall, F. S., & Wanous, J. P. (1981). Organizational Entry: Recruitment, Selection, and Socialization of Newcomers. *Academy of Management Review, 6*(3), 513.

Hall, R. E., & Milgrom, P. R. (2008). The Limited Influence of Unemployment on the Wage Bargain. *American Economic Review, 98*(4), 1653–1674.

Heckman, J. J., & Hotz, V. J. (1986). An Investigation of the Labor Market Earnings of Panamanian Males Evaluating the Sources of Inequality. *Journal of Human Resources, 21*(4), 507–542.

Holzer, H. J. (1991). The Spatial Mismatch Hypothesis: What Has the Evidence Shown? *Urban Studies, 28*(1), 105–122.

Holzer, H. J. (1988). Search Method Use by Unemployed Youth. *Journal of Labor Economics, 6*(1), 1–2.

Hoisos, A. J. (1990). On the Efficiency of Matching and Related Models of Search and Unemployment. *The Review of Economic Studies, 57*(2), 279–298.

Hou, L. (2007, November). *A Study on the Wage Formation Mechanism of Chinese Enterprises from the Perspective of Economic Globalization*. Central China Normal University Press.

Hu, F. (2005, May). *On the Pay Level at the Stage of China's Economic Take-Off*. Economic Press China.

Hunt, E. H. (1973). *Regional Wage Variations in Britain, 1850–1914*. Oxford University Press.

Hunt, E. H. (1986). Industrialization and Regional Inequality: Wages in Britain, 1760–1914. *The Journal of Economic History, 46*(4), 935–966.

Ihlanfeldt, K. R. (1992). Intraurban Wage Gradients: Evidence by Race, Gender, Occupational Class, and Sector. *Journal of Urban Economics, 32*(1), 70–91.

Jin, L. (2008). A Study on Institutional Changes of the Labor Market Segmentation Since the Adoption of the Policy on Reform and Opening Up. *Research on Economics and Management, 8*.

Jin, L. (2009). The Validation of Industrial Segmentation of the Labor Market in China. *Population & Economics, 5*.

Johnson, R. C. (2006). Landing a Job in Urban Space: The Extent and Effect of Spatial Mismatch. *Regional Science and Urban Economics, 36*(2006), 331–372.

Kain, J. F. (1968). Housing Segregation, Negro Employment, and Metropolitan Decentralization. *The Quarterly Journal of Economics, 82*(2), 175–197.

Kerr, C. (1954). The Balkanization of Labor Markets. In E. W. Bakke et al. (Eds.), *Labor Mobility and Economic Opportunity*. Technology Press of MIT.

Kuznets, S. (1955). Economic Growth and Income Inequality. *American Economic Review, 45*, 1–28.

Lai, D. (1996). On the Institutional Segmentation of the Labor Market. *Economic Science, 6*.

Lai, D. (2001). The Labor Market Segmentation in the Process of EU Integration. *The Journal of World Economy, 4*.

Laing, D., Park, C., & Wang, P. (2005). A Modified Harris-Todaro Model of Rural-Urban Migration for China. In F. Kwan & E. Yu (Eds.), *Critical Issues in China's Growth and Development* (pp. 245–264). Ashgate.

Lang, K., & Dickens, W. (1992). Labor Market Segmentation. In *Wage Dispersion and Unemployment*.

Launov, A. (2004). *An Alternative Approach to Testing Dual Labor Market Theory* (IZA Working Paper).

Lebergott, S. (1964). *Manpower in Economic Growth: The American Record Since 1800* (p. 125). McGraw-Hill.

Leibenstein, H. (1957). Underemployment in Backward Economies. *Journal of Political Economy, 65*(2), 91–103.

Leontaridi, M. R. (1998). Segmented Labor Markets: Theory and Evidence. *Journal of Economic Survey, 12*(1), 103–109.

Lewis, A. (1954). Economic Development with Unlimited Supplies of Labor. *The Manchester School, 22*(2), 139–191.

Li, J. R., & Barrett, C. B. (1999). Distinguishing Between Equilibrium and Integration in Market Analysis. *SSRN Electronic Journal, 81*(5), 1286–1286.

Li, J. R., & Barrett, C. B. (1999). *Distinguishing Between Equilibrium and Integration in Market Analysis* (International Agriculture Trade Research Consortium, Working Paper, 99–98).

Li, S. (1997). The Model of Labor Mobility in China's Economic Transition. *Economic Research Journal, 1*, 23–30.

Li, Q. (2008). *Ten Lectures on Social Stratification.* Social Sciences Academic Press.

Li, J. (2002). Multi-segregation of China's Labor Market and Its Impact on Labor Supply and Demand. *Chinese Journal of Population Science, 2*, 1–7.

Li, J., & Yanfeng, G. (2011). The Hierarchy of Registered Permanent Residence in China's Urban Labor Market. *Sociological Study, 2.*

Li, P., & Can, L. (1999). On the Institutional Segmentation of China's Labor Market. *Economist, 6*, 18–22.

Loayza, N. V. (1996). The Economics of Informal Sector: A Simple Model and Some Empirical Evidence from Latin America. *Carnegie-Rochester Conference Series on Public Policy, 45*, 129–162.

Lokshin, M., & Sajaia, Z. (2004). Maximum Likelihood Estimation of Endogenous Switching Regression Models. *The Stata Journal, 4*(3), 282–289.

Lu, M. (2004). *The Bargaining Theory of Wages and Employment—An Empirical Study on China's Dual Employment System.* Shanghai People's Publishing House.

Lu, Y. (2008). Does the Registered Permanent Residence Work? The Household Registration System and Social Stratification and Mobility. *Social Sciences in China, 1.*

Lu, M., & Zhao, C. (2009). *Moving Towards Balance in Agglomeration: An Empirical Study on the Coordinated Development of China's Urban and Rural Economy and Regional Economy*. Peking University Press.

Lu, M. (2010, January). *China's Economy at the Crossroads—What Decides the Future of the Chinese Economy*. China CITIC Press.

Lu, M. (2011). Labor Migration Facing a Glass Wall: Institutional Constraint, Social Interaction and Lagged Urbanization. *South China Journal of Economics, 6*, 23–37.

Luo, C., & Shi, L. (2007). Human Capital, Industry Characteristics and Income Gap: An Empirical Study Based on Data from the First National Economic Census. *Management World, 10*, 19–30+171. https://doi.org/10.19744/j.cnki.11-1235/f.2007.10.003

Luo, W. (1998). Abnormal Dual Economic Structure and China's Employment Issue. *Journal of Zhejiang University (Social Science Edition), 2*, 84–90.

Maloney, W. F. (2004). Informality Revisited. *World Development, 32*(7), 1159–1178.

Mao, X., & Jing, L. (2010). Has the Lewisian Turning Point Really Come? *Journal of Financial Research, 8*.

Marcouiller, D., & Young, L. (1995, June). The Black Hole of Graft: The Predatory State and the Informal Economy. *American Economic Review, American Economic Association, 85*(3), 630–646.

Marshall, A. (1890). *Principles of Economics (Great Minds Series)*.

McNabb, R. (1987). Testing for Labor Market Segmentation in Britain. *The Manchester School of Economic & Social Studies, 55*(3), 257–273.

Merlino, L. P. (2009). *Segmentation in a Labor Market with Two-Sided Heterogeneity: Directed versus Undirected Search* (Working Paper).

Mill, J. S. (1885). *Principles of Political Economy*. Appleton.

Mincer, J. (1974). *Schooling, Experience and Earnings*. Columbia University Press for NBER.

Montgomery, J. D. (1991, December). Social Networks and Labor-Market Outcomes: Toward an Economic Analysis. *The American Economic Review, 81*(5), 1408–1418.

Mortensen, D. (1984). Job Search and Labor Market Analysis. *Discussion Papers, 2*, 849–919.

Mortensen, D. T., & Pissarides, C. A. (1994). Job Creation and Job Destruction in the Theory of Unemployment. *Review of Economic Studies, 61*, 397–415.

Mortensen, D. T., & Pissarides, C. A. (1999). New Development in Models of Search in the Labor Market. In *Handbook of Labor Economics*. Elsevier.

Mortensen, D. T., & Nagypal, E. (2007, March). Labor-Market Volatility in Matching Models with Endogenous Separations. *Scandinavian Journal of Economics, 109*(4), 645–665.

Mortensen, D., & Nagypál, É. (2007). Macroeconomic Fluctuations and the Labor Market || Labor-Market Volatility in Matching Models with Endogenous Separations. *The Scandinavian Journal of Economics, 109*(4), 645–665.

MyCOS Institute. (2010, June). *Chinese College Graduates' Employment Annual Report*. Social Sciences Academic Press.

Nie, S. (2004). Labor Market Segmentation in Economic Transition Period: From Ownership Segmentation to Industry Segmentation. *Modern Economic Science, 6*.

Orr, D. V. (1997b). An Index of Segmentation in Local Labor Markets. *International Review of Applied Economics, 11*(2), 229–247.

Ortega, J. (2000). Pareto-Improving Immigration in an Economy with Equilibrium Unemployment. *Economic Journal, 110*, 92–112.

Osmani, S. R. (1991). Wage Determination in Rural Labour Markets: The Theory of Implicit Co-Operation. *Journal of Development Economics, 34*, 3–23.

Osterman, P. (1975). An Empirical Study of Labor Market Segmentation. *ILR Review, 28*(4), 508–523.

Petrongolo, B., & Pissarides, C. A. (2001). Looking into the Black Box: A Survey of the Matching Function. *Journal of Economic Literature, 39*(2), 390–431.

Pissarides, C. A. (1985). Short-Run Equilibrium Dynamics of Unemployment, Vacancies, and Real Wages. *The American Economic Review, 75*(4), 676–690.

Pissarides, C. A. (1989). Unemployment and Macroeconomics. *Economics, 56*(221), 1–14.

Pissarides. (2000). *Equilibrium Unemployment Theory*. Cambridge Publisher.

Pissarides, C. A. (2011). Equilibrium in the Labor Market with Search Frictions. *American Economic Review, 101*(4), 1092–1105.

Psacharopoulos, G. (1978). Educational Planning: Past and Present. *Prospects, 8*(2), 135–142.

Psacharopoulos, G. (1981). Returns to Education: An Updated International Comparison. *Comparative Education, 17*(3), 321–341.

Psacharopoulos, G., & Tinbergen, J. (1978). On the Explanation of Schooling, Occupation and Earnings: Some Alternative Path Analyses. *De Economist, 126*(4), 505–520.

Postel-Vinay, G. (1994). The Disintegration of Traditional Labor Markets in France: From Agriculture and Industry to Agriculture or Industry. In M. Mackinnon & G. Grantham (Eds.), *Labor Market Evolution: The Economic History of Market Integration, Wage Flexibility and the Employment Relation*. Routledge.

Qi, L. (2005). The Impact of the Wage System Reform in State-owned Departments on the Return of Education—An Empirical Study on the Return of Education in Urban China from 1988 to 1999. *Education & Economy, 4*, 19–25.

Qiao, M., Qian, X., & Yao, X. (2009). Labor Market Segmentation, Registered Permanent Residence and Differences in Urban-Rural Employments. *Chinese Journal of Population Science, 1.*

Rauch, J. (1991). Modelling the Informal Sector Formally. *Journal of Development Economics, 35*(1), 33–47.

Rees, A. (1966). Information Networks in Labor Markets. *American Economic Review, 56*(2), 559–566.

Reich, M. (1984). Segmented Labour: Time Series Hypothesis and Evidence. *Cambridge Journal of Economics, 8*(1), 63–81.

Reich, M., Gordon, D. M., & Edwards, R. C. (1973). A Theory of Labor Market Segmentation. *The American Economic Review, 63*(2), 359–365.

Robertson, R. (2000). Trade Liberalization and Wage Inequality: Lessons from the Mexican Experience. *The World Economy, 23*(6), 827–849.

Rodrik, D. (2009, September). *In Search of Prosperity: Analytic Narratives on Economic Growth* (p. 242). CITIC Press.

Rosenberg, R. D., & Rosenstein, E. (1980). Participation and Productivity: An Empirical Study. *ILR Review, 33*(3), 355–367.

Ryan, P. (1984). Segmentation, Duality and Internal Labor Market. In F. Wilkinson (Ed.), *The Dynamics of Labor Market Segmentation*. Academic Press.

Sakamoto, A., & Chen, M. D. (1991). Sample Selection Bias and Dual Labor Market. *Research in Social Stratification and Mobility, 10*, 171–198.

Sala, H., & Silva, J. I. (2009a). Flexibility at the Margin and Labor Market Volatility: The Case of Spain. *Investgaciones Económicas, XXXIII*(2), 145–178.

Sala, H., & Silva, J. I. (2009b). *Flexibility at the Margin and Labor Market Volatility in OECD Countries*. Mimeo.

Sampsford, D. (2000). *Border Issues in Labor Economics*. China Tax Press.

Sapsford, D., & Tzannatos, Z. (1998). *Current Issues in Labour Economics*. China Taxation Publishing House.

Sato, Y. (2004). City Structure, Search, and Workers' Job Acceptance Behavior. *Journal of Urban Economics, 55*(2), 350–370.

Schultz, T. W. (1961). Investment in Human Capital. *American Economic Review, 51*, 1–17.

Schultz, T. W. (1962). *Reflections on Investment in Man* (NBER Chapters).

Sheng, L. (2008). *Flow or Migration—An Economic Analysis of Flow of Labor in the Rural Areas of China*. Shanghai Far East Publishers.

Shimer, R. (2005a). The Assignment of Workers to Jobs in an Economy with Coordination Frictions. *Journal of Political Economy, 113*, 996–1024.

Shimer, R. (2005b). Cyclical Behavior of Equilibrium Unemployment and Vacancies. *The American Economic Review, 95*, 25–49.

Shimer, R., & Smith, L. (2000). Assortative Matching and Search. *Econometrica, 68*(2), 343–369.

Bao, S., Bodvarsson, Ö. B., Hou, J. W., & Zhao, Y. (2009, October). *The Regulation of Migration in a Transition Economy: China's Hukou System* (IZA, Discussion Paper No. 4493).

Smith, A. (1981). *An Inquiry into the Nature and Causes of the Wealth of Nations* (W. Yanan, Trans.). The Commercial Press.

Smith, T. E., & Zenou, Y. (1997). Dual Labor Markets, Urban Unemployment, and Multicentric Cities. *Journal of Economic Theory, 76*(1), 185–214.

Smith, T. E., & Zenou, Y. (2003). Spatial Mismatch, Search Effort and Urban Spatial Structure. *Journal of Urban Economics, 54*(1), 129–156.

Solow, R. (1990). *The Labour Market as a Social Institution.* Blackwell.

Tumen, S. (2011). *Social Interactions and Labor Market Search* (Working Paper of University of Chicago).

Turner, M. A., Fix, M., & Struyk, R. J. (1991). *Opportunities Denied, Opportunities Diminished: Racial Discrimination in Hiring.* The Urban Institute.

Wahba, J., & Zenou, Y. (2005). Density, Social Networks and Job Search Methods: Theory and Application to Egypt. *Journal of Development Economics, 78*(2), 443–473.

Wang, M. (2005). Differences in Employment Opportunities and Wage Gap in the Urban Labor Market: A Study on Employment and Returns of Migrant Labor. *Social Sciences in China, 5.*

Wang, S. (2008). Opportunity Set, Relationship Choice and Structural Effects. In L. Lulu & B. Yanjie (Eds.), *The Institutional Transition and Social Stratification—Based on the 2003 China National General Social Survey.* China Renmin University Press.

Wasmer, E., & Zenou, Y. (2002). Does City Structure Affect Job Search and Welfare? *Journal of Urban Economics, 51*, 515–541.

Wauthy, X., & Zenou, Y. (2010). How Does Imperfect Competition in the Labor Market Affect Unemployment Policies? *Journal of Public Economic Theory, 4*(3), 417–436.

Wilson, W. J. (1996). *When Work Disappears: The World of the New Urban Poor.* Alfred A. Knopf.

Wooldridge, J. M. (2005, December). *Introductory Econometrics: A Modern Approach.* China Renmin University Press.

Xin, M. (2001). The Two-Tier Labor Market in Urban China: Occupational Segregation and Wage Differentials Between Urban Residents and Rural Migrants in Shanghai. *Journal of Comparative Economics, 29*, 485–504.

Xing, C. (2005). A Survey on the Wage Determination Mechanism with Different Ownership Types. *Economic Research Journal, 6.*

Xing, C. (2008). Quantile Regression, Return to Education and Income Gap. *Statistical Research, 5.*

Xing, F. (2006). Income Gap Across Industries in Current China from the Economic Perspective. *Enterprise Economy, 8*, 13–15.

Xu, L. (2002). Impact of China's Labor Market Segmentation on Rural Human Capital Accumulation. *Lingnan Journal, 4*, 59–62.

Xue, X. (2008). An Empirical Study on the Differences of the Wage Determination Mechanism Between the State Sectors and the Non-state Sectors. *Review of Industrial Economics, 7*(1).

Xue, X. (2010). An Analysis of the Industrial Distribution Features of Wage Gap Between Sectors with Different Ownership Types. *Review of Industrial Economics, 1.*

Yan, S. (2006). Personnel Mobility in the Urban Labor Market and its Determination Mechanism: An Analysis of the New Dual Structure of Large Cities. *Journal of Management World, 8.*

Yan, S. (2007). Human Capital, Institution and Wage Gap: An Empirical Analysis of the Dual Labor Market in Large Cities. *Journal of Management World, 6.*

Yang, Y., & Jinyong, C. (2000). The Stratification and Competitions in the Labor Market in Transition: An Empirical Analysis of Wuhan. *Social Sciences in China, 5.*

Yao, X., & Xu, L. (2005). Labor Market Segmentation: A Literature Review. *Journal of Bohai University (Philosophy and Social Sciences Edition), 27*(1).

Yao, X., et al. (2007). The Rise of Wage Inequality: Structural and Price Effects. *Chinese Journal of Population Science, 1.*

Yao, X. (2010, February). *A Study on Investments in China's Human Capital and Management of the Labor Market*. China Labor and Social Security Press.

Yao, Y. (2010). The Global Significance of the Chinese Path. *International Economic Review, 1*, 7–18.

Yao, Y. (2011, January). *Global Implications of Chinese Development Path*. Peking University Press.

Yao, Y. (2004). *Land, Institution and Agricultural Development*. Peking University Press.

Ye, L., Li, S., & Luo, C. (2011). Industrial Monopolization, Ownership and Enterprise Income Gap: An Empirical Study Based on Enterprise Data of China's First National Economic Census. *Management World, 4*, 26–36+187. https://doi.org/10.19744/j.cnki.11-1235/f.2011.04.005

Ye, L., Li, S., & Luo, C. (2011). Industrial Monopolization, Ownership and Enterprise Income Gap: An Empirical Study Based on Enterprise Data from China's First National Economic Census. *Management World, 4.*

Yi, J. (2006). Flow and Employment of China's Rural Labor: An Empirical Study Based on the Job Search Theory. *New Political Economics, 1.*

Zax, J. S., & Kain, J. F. (1996). Moving to the Suburbs: Do Relocating Companies Leave Their Black Employees Behind? *Journal of Labor Economics, 14*(3), 472–504.

Zenou, Y. (2009). Endogenous Job Destruction and Job Matching in Cities. *Journal of Urban Economics, 65*(3), 323–336.

Zhang, M. (2000). The Past and Future of the Reform of the Wage System. *WEISHI, 5.*

Zhang, B., & Weiping, Z. (2000). The Dual Structure of China's Urban Labor and Its Transformation. *Journal of Jinan University (Philosophy and Social Sciences Edition), 22*(2).

Zhang, Y., Tian, Y., & Li, X. (2003). Analysis of the Income Gap and Control Measures Across Industries. *Modernization of Management, 1*, 7–10.

Zhang, Z. (2004). Industrial Segmentation of the Labor Market and Mobility of Working Population. *Chinese Journal of Population Science, 2.*

Zhang, L., & Lunqu, Y. (2007). Causes Leading to the Formation of Chinese Civil Servants' Revenue Decision Mechanism: An Explanation Based on Labor Market Segmentation Theory. *Journal of Beijing Jiaotong University (Social Sciences Edition).*

Zhang, Y., & Jianqi, C. (2008). Human Capital or Industry Characteristics: An Analysis of the Cause of Intersectoral Differences of Wages and Rewards in China. *The Journal of World Economy, 5.*

Zhang, Z. (2009a). *Urban-Rural Segmentation of China's Labor Market.* Zhejiang University.

Zhang, D. (2009b). *Report on China's Household Income Distribution (2009).* Economic Science Press.

Zhang, Z., & Qian, X. (2009). Double Duality of China's Labor Market: Theory and Reality. *Xueshu Yuekan, 8.*

Zhang, Z., & Xueya, Q. (2009). The Labor Market Segmentation Theory: Theoretical Background and Its Evolution. *Journal of Chongqing University (Social Science Edition), 6*, 57–62.

Zhang, J. (2011). Problems of Difficult Employments and the Transformation of the Economic Development Pattern During the 12th Five-Year Plan Period. *China Employment, 1.*

Zhang, J., Ke, L., & Zhibiao, L. (2011). Market Transformation and Enterprise Productivity: A Study of the Chinese Economy. *China Economic Quarterly, 10*(2).

Zhang, Y., & Gao, H. (2011). Impact of Urban Dual Labor Market on the Registration of Migrant Workers and Regional Discrimination—Taking Shanghai as an Example. *Chinese Journal of Population Science, 5*, 67–74+112.

Zhang, Y., & Wang, H. (2011). Household Registration Discrimination and Geographic Discrimination in Urban Labor Markets: A Study Based on Census Data. *Journal of Management World, 7.*

Zhong, J. (1990). Wages of State-owned Industrial Enterprises: 1980–1987. *Tianjin Social Sciences, 3.*

Zhu, J. (1999). The Two-stage Urban-Rural Migration Theory in the Context of China's Ternary Labor Market. *Chinese Journal of Population Science, 1.*

Zhu, N. (2001). Population Migration in China's Quadruple Economy—Theoretical, Current, and Empirical Analysis. *Population & Economics, 1*, 44–45.

Batch number: 10725993

Printed by Printforce, the Netherlands